SEEKING CHICAGO

SEEKING CHICAGO

THE STORIES BEHIND THE ARCHITECTURE OF THE WINDY CITY—ONE BUILDING AT A TIME

TOM MILLER

PIMPERNEL
PRESS LTD
www.pimpernelpress.com

For my Mother, Jeanne Eloise Miller 1927–2017

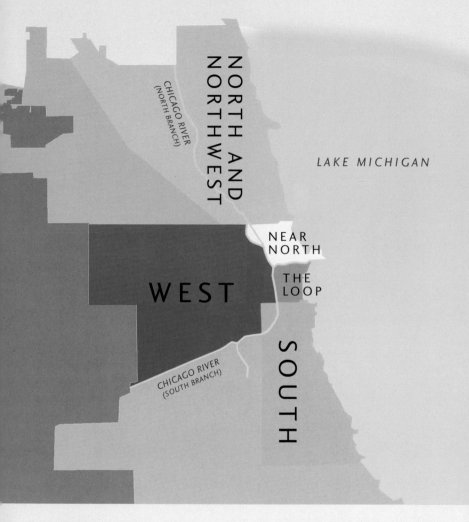

CHICAGO RIVER
(NORTH BRANCH)

NORTH AND
NORTHWEST

LAKE MICHIGAN

NEAR
NORTH

THE
LOOP

WEST

SOUTH

CHICAGO RIVER
(SOUTH BRANCH)

Seeking Chicago
Copyright © Pimpernel Press Limited 2019
Text copyright © Tom Miller 2019
Photographs copyright © Tom Miller, except as listed
on page 256
First Pimpernel Press edition 2019
www.pimpernelpress.com

Designed by Becky Clarke

A catalogue record for this book is available from the
British Library.

ISBN 978-1-910258-72-9

Typeset in Perpetua and Charlotte Sans
Printed in China

9 8 7 6 5 4 3 2 1

CONTENTS

THE LOOP

A MIDWESTERN PALACE OF ART: ART INSTITUTE OF CHICAGO

111 SOUTH MICHIGAN AVENUE

For decades American art was scoffed at not only by Europeans, but by collectors in the major cities of the United States. Wealthy citizens of Boston, Philadelphia, Chicago, and New York scoured the galleries of London, Rome, and Paris for paintings and sculptures for their mansions back home.

Although the stigma would last in degrees throughout the 19th century, by the mid-1860s American artists were flexing their skills and individuality. In 1866, 35 Chicago artists organized the Chicago Academy of Design. The proposed free art school would include an art gallery, the first museum of art in the burgeoning city.

The concept of a free school proved infeasible, and when the Academy of Design opened in 1868 the cost of daily classes was $10 a month—in the neighborhood of $7.50 daily by current calculations. Within only two years, the school had outgrown its Dearborn Street studio and a new, five-story structure at 66 West Adams Street opened on November 22, 1870.

Less than a year later, the Great Chicago Fire obliterated the school and gallery. Several attempts to resuscitate the Academy of Design were unsuccessful, resulting in the organization of the Chicago Academy of Fine Arts in 1879, which also failed before the year was out.

Refusing to give up on the concept of a Chicago academy and gallery, wealthy art patrons and philanthropists tried once more. In 1882, the Art Institute of Chicago was formed from what had been the Chicago Academy. This time it was a success—in no small part because banker Charles L. Hutchinson was elected its president. The financier not only had great financial acumen, but a keen artistic eye. Almost single-handedly, he would eventually bring the fledgling institution into the first rank of art museums worldwide.

Shortly after the institute's founding, its trustees purchased a lot on the southeast corner of South Michigan Avenue and Van Buren Street for $45,000. The existing building on the site was enlarged and improved. Within three years more space was necessary and, in January 1885, an adjoining lot to

Motorcars in variety line the curb on South Michigan Avenue in the years just after World War I.

the north was purchased, the old structure demolished, and architect John Wellborn Root hired to design a structure of "impressive presence."

On November 22, 1887, the oddly named Missouri paper the *Sedalia Weekly Bazoo* reported, "The new buildings of the Chicago art institute for the permanent art museum are completed, and will be formally opened this evening. A superb collection of pictures is displayed. The programme to-night will include an exhibit of the art treasures so far collected and belonging to the institute." The article mentioned that four rooms of art, valued at $10,000, had been presented by Mrs. Hall Ellis; and that J. W. Ellsworth provided a trust from which "$250 will be annually given as a prize for the best picture by an American painter."

Three months later, an article in the *New-York Tribune* encouraged New York artists to participate in the first contest, the deadline for which was May 22, 1888. The writer admitted on February 26 that Chicago had beaten New York to the punch: "Experience has not demonstrated the wisdom of prize giving in New-York, but these offers and the other generous inducements will no doubt draw plenty of pictures from New-York to Chicago."

This first all-American art competition opened at the Art Institute on May 27, 1888 with over 300 paintings. Between 400 and 500 canvases had been rejected. Among the artists represented were Winslow Homer, Frederic Edwin Church, George Inness, John Ferguson Weir, and George de Forest Brush.

The long-existing feeling of superiority on the part of some New Yorkers, however, was reflected in the *Sun*'s fun-poking review of the exhibition in what it considered a cow town. On Wednesday, May 30, 1888, it reported, "The Chicago Art Institute is holding its first exhibition, and the glittering gin galleries of that proud hyopolis, or Porktown, have contributed their choicest paintings…. The most admired of the sculptures is a group of heroic size called 'Joseph Medill hurling Defiance at Murat Halstead and William Penn Nixon.' A frieze representing the Genius of Chicago driving a street car drawn by four Texan steers is also well spoken of."

Despite the newspaper's aspersions, the permanent collection was highly impressive. It boasted casts of the Parthenon and the Phigalian friezes, along with 340 other casts of ancient works. In 1890, the ancient artifacts included Greek vases, marble Hellenic busts and statues, Roman terra-cotta lamps, and marble sculptures. The collection of European paintings embraced Old Masters and modern works.

Discussions had already taken place between the Art Institute and the organizers of the 1893 Chicago Columbian Exposition (later popularly known as the "Chicago World's Fair"). A fine arts building had been proposed to exhibit paintings and sculpture. However, the proximity of the fairgrounds and the institute building prompted concerns. Two fine arts venues in the same area would battle for attention and might negatively affect the number of visitors to both.

On May 6, 1891, Charles Hutchinson presented his solution to the Exposition's Committee on Fine Arts. The committee had budgeted $200,000 for a temporary "palace of art" at the exposition. But if that money were turned over to the Art Institute of Chicago, it would add its own funds to create a replacement structure at a cost of between $600,000 and $700,000. By Hutchinson's plan, the exposition would have its art palace and afterward, rather than having spent funds on an expensive and transitory building, the city would have a magnificent, permanent palace of art.

The city agreed, and in 1892 construction began on Michigan Avenue, opposite Adams Street. The Boston architectural firm of Shepley, Rutan & Coolidge had designed a dignified palace of Bedford limestone splashed with Beaux Arts decoration. Completed before May 1893, the building came in on budget at $600,000. Two massive bronze lions, commissioned and donated by Florence Field, sister-in-law of Marshall Field, and executed by famed New York animal sculptor Edward Kemeys, flanked the broad entrance plaza.

A more social and political aspect of the exposition was the World's Congress Auxiliary, a week-long convention of 150,000 people, mostly women, who voiced concerns about issues pertinent to women. The 81 meetings were held in 33 halls and six committee rooms of the completed building, earning it the temporary name of the World's Congress Building.

The *Wichita Daily Eagle* explained, on April 2, 1893, that in these halls more than 100 congresses of mostly females would discuss "education, industry, art and literature, philanthropy and charity, moral and social reform, religion, science and philosophy, civil law and government." The discussions, said the article, were not about the issues in general, but specifically focused on "the relation of the woman of the world to the subject."

On May 22, 1893, the *Rock Island Daily Argus* reported that the first week of women's meetings was over. "For a week the many halls of the Art Institute have been packed each day with the fair sex, the audiences being composed mostly of women of middle age or beyond, but there being quite a sprinkling of fresh young faces. These women have talked and been talked to by the most noted of their sisters in this time of noted women."

The crush of attendees was not without mishap, however. A day earlier, a wire described how "A hundred or so ladies, crowded on the floor of the lobby of Washington hall in the Art Institute, were precipitated to the basement, a distance of 12 feet, by the floor giving way. The scene for a

The front of the Art Institute, still guarded by Edward Kemeys' lions

few minutes was one of great excitement, and it was a miracle that no one was killed."

When the Columbian Exposition was over, the Art Institute of Chicago settled into its new palace. Additions followed. Among them was a lecture room (included in the original plans), added in 1897; and in 1900-01 the Ryerson Library was built, opening with about 3,500 volumes on art and named for trustee and major book donor Martin A. Ryerson. (His father, also Martin Ryerson, was an early Chicago settler and the donor of *The Alarm* statue in Lincoln Park.) In 1903, Blackstone Hall was constructed to display Classical sculpture; and the Burnham Library of Architecture opened in 1912, named after renowned Chicago architect Daniel Burnham (who, incidentally, had been Director of Works for the Columbian Exposition). Other additions would follow throughout the decades.

On October 10, 1904, the *Chicago Tribune* deemed the Art Institute "If not the richest... one of the most comprehensive exhibits of paintings and sculptures in the world." And by that year the art school had grown to the largest in the United States with an enrollment that year of about 2,500, including the "Juvenile Saturday School."

During the Chicago Exposition, Jules Breton's *Song of the Lark* had been voted the most popular painting in America. It hung for decades in the galleries here, delighting generations of school children. When an art teacher sought it out in 1936, an attendant insisted that the Art Institute did not have it.

The institute's director, Robert B. Harshe, soon had a miffed school teacher standing before his desk. His brusque explanation shocked her.

"It's not good enough for us. That's why it isn't hanging.... It's just a picture of great popular interest which is not a good painting." And he added that the voting during the World's Fair "just shows the low taste of America." Modern art, he thought, was "more important." To emphasize his point, as the teacher moved to leave, Harshe added, "As for Jules Breton, he wasn't even a good painter."

The school teacher was not beaten yet. She went to Mrs. Frank G. Logan, a wealthy patron of the institute whose husband was honorary president. The benefactress was aghast at hearing the beloved painting was in storage, while "all those modernistic distortions are hanging there."

Newspaper coverage resulted in a public uproar and indignation. *The Song of the Lark* was soon back on the institute's walls, no doubt to the significant disgruntlement of Robert B. Harshe.

The floor-to-ceiling windows of Renzo Piano's 2009 light-filled Modern Wing overlook Millennium Park, separating fine arts from garden arts.

In April 1941, the *Chicago Tribune* reported on the "Janitor Show" at the Art Institute. For years a select group of students worked 12 to 30 hours a week, cleaning the building in exchange for tuition. "In their spare time they ply brush or rag to canvas or paper. The results of their leisure time activity may be seen in the seventh annual janitors' art show, which, with its emblem of two brooms crossed over a mop, will be on display two weeks."

Another interesting show was held two years later, when America entered World War II and art students were drafted. On Thursday, September 2, 1943, an exhibition opened "of paintings and sketches by former students now in service. Drawings and paintings already have been received from camps in this country and Hawaii, and pictures are expected from former students serving overseas."

The Art Institute of Chicago hit a low point in the 1970s, when attendance dropped and deficits forced a cut in hours. Then, in 1978, three masterworks by Paul Cézanne, worth $4 million, were stolen. It was the largest art theft in American museum history at the time. Fortunately, they were recovered five months later.

A further blow came in December 1980, when Muriel Newman, who had promised the Art Institute her $12 million art collection upon her death, decided to bequeath it to the Metropolitan Museum of Art in New York instead. According to institute director James Wood, who had taken the position only in April, "It was a meaningfully symbolic tip of the iceberg." That financial "iceberg" threatened the future of the Art Institute.

But the institute turned things around, with the significant help of a $10 million grant from the Rice Foundation in 1988.

That was, incidentally, the same year that the institute became embroiled in an international tug-of-war. An elaborate 2½-by-3-foot sculpture of the Hindu god Vishnu from the 12th century sat crated in a storeroom in the building. It had disappeared from the Khmer temple of Phanom Rung in the Thai town of Buriram in 1960. Now the community wanted its "stolen" statue back.

The Art Institute would only return the relic if the government of Thailand agreed to a continuous loan of comparable works. Both factions dug in. Things escalated to the point that Prince Subhadradis Diskul came to Chicago to obtain the release of the hostage deity. When the institute held firm, the *Chicago Tribune* reported, "Now the angry prince says he wouldn't be at all surprised if his government decided to put a big poster over the temple gateway that states: 'This piece has been stolen. We tried to get it back, but they wouldn't give it back.'"

An agreement was finally reached when the officials of the Art Institute conceded returning the 878-year-old relic, "as long as the Thais replace it with a comparable work of art." Because such a trade was illegal in Thailand, Thai politicians arranged a gift as a "good-will gesture."

The Art Institute of Chicago continues as one of the world's foremost repositories of fine art. In 2009, award-winning architect Renzo Piano's Modern Wing opened, expanding the museum's square footage by one third and making it second in size in the nation only to the Metropolitan Museum of Art in New York. The $300 million light-flooded structure is as much art as the works it houses.

In 2015, the Art Institute received a gift from local philanthropists Stefan Edlis and Gael Neeson of 42 works by contemporary masters like Andy Warhol and Jasper Johns. The collection was valued at $400 million, and deemed the largest gift of art in the institute's history. Because of gifts like this and other support, the magnificent palace of art stands today as nobly as (and perhaps more soundly than) it did in 1893, when 100 unwitting women fell through the lobby floor.

AUDITORIUM BUILDING

50 EAST CONGRESS PARKWAY

A single sentence appeared in *Farm, Field and Stockman* on February 5, 1887: "Ground is broken for the Chicago Auditorium Building, to be eleven stories high, have a seating capacity of 5,000 to 8,000, and cost $1,500,000." The brevity of the announcement understated the importance of the building, and drastically underestimated the price—the completed structure would top $3 million, $77 million today.

Some Chicagoans grappled at the time with a sort of inferiority complex. The East Coast cities of New York, Boston, and Philadelphia boasted opera houses, museums, and world-class theaters. Among the wealthy citizens who wanted to see Chicago on a cultural par with its eastern counterparts was businessman Ferdinand Peck. He also had altruistic ideas about the fine arts, believing that the arts could uplift and unite all classes of people.

In the early 1880s, Peck first envisioned an opulent performance space that could accommodate grand opera, symphony concerts, music festivals, and dance. Like the opera houses of New York City, he imagined it being used for society balls (the auditorium of Manhattan's famous Academy of Music, for instance, could be floored over at a level with the stage), mass meetings, and conventions.

As he bounced the idea around among his moneyed friends, however, the stark realization arose that such a massive facility would not be able to support itself simply through the arts. Ferdinand Peck's solution was innovative and brilliant—what today is called a "mixed-use" structure. By the time the concept was presented to the Commercial Club on May 29, 1886, it included not only the theater, but a hotel and an office building as well.

Three hundred supporters purchased stock in the Chicago Auditorium Association and the project went forward. Normally a competition among architects would be initiated for a venture of this scale; but Peck insisted that the firm of Adler & Sullivan receive the commission. He was familiar and impressed with Dankmar Adler's 1879 design of the Central Music Hall, the acoustics of which were deemed "unmatched."

Louis Sullivan, just 30 years old, and Adler (he was 42) accepted a job that would bring tremendous headaches. Among them was the mere nature of the site at the northwest corner of South Michigan Avenue and Congress Street (later renamed Congress Parkway). The soft clay near the lake's edge was more than 100 feet deep, which made it unable to uphold a heavy structure. Adler, working with engineer Paul Mueller, devised a "raft foundation"—a floating mat of interconnecting railroad ties topped with steel rails encased in concrete. The men carefully calculated the weight of the projected building and engineered the raft to distribute it.

When construction began, however, the project changed—and grew. The Auditorium Association continually expanded and improved the design. Floors were added, amenities like a banquet hall in the hotel had to be worked into the plans, and the lightweight terra-cotta cladding Sullivan had designed was scrapped for granite and limestone. (Incidentally, this heavy stone facing was not calculated into Adler and Mueller's design for the raft foundation, resulting in the warped flooring visible today.) As the structure rose, Adler and Sullivan scrambled to keep up with the changes, drawing and redrawing their plans until they had spent more than $60,000 in reworks.

A year after the cornerstone was laid, the auditorium space was sufficiently complete to house the Republican National Convention of 1888. Here, Benjamin Harrison was nominated for president and Levi Morton as his running mate.

In October 1889, the Auditorium Building was nearly finished. The *Real Estate Record & Builders' Guide* pointed out an innovative element. "Venetian blinds are fast becoming a prominent feature in our building," it noted, saying they had been selected "for the new Auditorium building, in Chicago (in which there are 1,500 windows)."

A month later, on November 23, the *True Republican* reported, "Fifteen hundred workmen are now busily engaged in getting the interior of the great Auditorium building into shape for the formal dedication two weeks hence." The article advised that invitees included President Harrison and several members of his cabinet, the Canadian Minister of War, the Speaker of the Canadian House of Parliament, Wisconsin Governor William D. Hoard, Illinois Governor Joseph Fifer, Chicago Mayor DeWitt Clinton Cregier, and other dignitaries.

The *Chicago Journal* announced, "Adelina Patti, who sails from London in a few days, cables that she will sing 'Home, Sweet Home,' on the dedication

From the 'remarkable' auditorium, a grand view of the stage, where Adelina Patti sang gratis for the opening.

night, although her contract does not call for her participation in these exercises." The internationally renowned opera star did, indeed, sing. And both the president and the vice-president attended the ceremonies on December 10, 1889. It was a shocking first in United States history, for never before had the two highest-ranking political figures been away from Washington, D.C. at the same time while Congress was in session.

The auditorium was filled with 4,000 people. *American Architect and Building News* called the affair "certainly the most gorgeous spectacle of its kind ever beheld in the West." The journal lamented, however, that "Messrs. Adler and Sullivan, the architects to whose thought, study, and conscientious work the whole magnificent pile was due, were not even mentioned by name in the exercises, and received no public recognition whatsoever."

The exterior of the building, generally Romanesque Revival in style, featured an orderly repetition of arched openings and minimal ornamentation. *American Architect and Building News* was confused as to why the architects made the central tower, "the great exterior feature of the building," in the shape of a chimney—being twice as wide as it was deep. The journal felt the shape was "rather disappointing," but admitted it grew on the viewer after a while.

An entire page of the journal was spent in describing Sullivan's interior decorations. "In the interior of the great hall itself, the sight is one of the most remarkable of its kind in the world," it said. "As for the hotel portion, that has not yet been formally opened, and all that one may say about it is that it is expected to be like the auditorium itself—without any equal in the United States."

LEFT Lush decoration of the auditorium included murals, an open-work metal fan with Roman medallions in the spandrels, and colorful mosaics.

RIGHT Hotel diners were dazzled by the innovative electric lights that lined the arches overhead.

FAR RIGHT A staircase with signature Louis Sullivan railings spills through a mawlike arch in the hotel lobby.

Within three months the *True Republican* predicted that the hotel and office spaces would easily support the Auditorium financially. The hotel, like all upscale hotels of the period, offered both transient and permanent accommodations. On March 22, 1890, the newspaper opined, "When the Auditorium building in Chicago was projected, it was prophesied that it would be for its projectors a financial failure. The present returns do not indicate it; in fact its success is already demonstrated. The room rent of the hotel alone amounts to $3,000 per day."

The article pointed out that one long-term renter with his wife, two children, and one servant, was paying $18,000 per year for a suite of five rooms. (That astonishing rate would equal about $40,000 a month now.) The writer went on, "Another gentleman, with a wife and one child, pays $12,000 per year for three rooms and is so well pleased that he intends to pass the remainder of his life there. There are many other families among the permanent guests who pay nearly or quite as high rates."

The Auditorium Theatre was not performing too badly financially, either. On January 11, 1890, four weeks of Italian opera came to a close, grossing $232,954. On October 16, 1891, nationally celebrated conductor Theodore Thomas debuted his newly formed Chicago Orchestra here. By the time of Thomas's death in 1905, it had attained world-class status.

In the meantime, the offices in the commercial section were leased to various-sized concerns. The R. T. Booth Company occupied Suite 20-21 in 1898, selling Hyomei, an inhaled medicine. An advertisement in the *Rock*

Island Argus promised, "It is nature's own remedy carried to all parts of the head, throat and lungs by the air you breathe. It can be taken at all times and in any place. There is no danger, no risk." The Hyomei Inhaler outfit retailed for $1; and extra bottles of the medicine cost 50 cents. The firm also marketed Hyomei Balm, "a wonderful healer," for 25 cents.

Other tenants included artist May Armstrong, whose studio was in Room 106. A china painter, she exhibited vases and portrait plaques in the Chicago Ceramic Art Association show in December 1900. Professional pianist George G. Lewis also had a studio in the building, where he taught music students; and Suite 27 was the headquarters of the Goat Lymph Sanitarium Association. Supporters of goat lymph treatments insisted, according to one physician, "There is no longer any doubt but that goat lymph when properly administered will effect cures in locomotor ataxia, paralysis, primary dementia, chronic articular rheumatism and some forms of tuberculosis."

On January 4, 1905, Theodore Thomas died in his home on Bellevue Place. His passing was somewhat symbolic, for at the time the offices of the Chicago Orchestra were piled with packing boxes as the organization relocated to the new Orchestra Hall, nearby on Michigan Avenue. In fact, Thomas had never truly felt at home in the Auditorium Theatre, calling it "too cavernous." He conducted the dedicatory concert of Orchestra Hall on December 14, 1904, and then led two weeks of subscription concerts before falling ill with influenza, which resulted in his death.

By 1906, the second floor of the Auditorium Building was home to the Chicago Conservatory of Music and Dramatic Art. It boasted, "For more than a quarter of a century [it] has stood in the front rank of educational institutions in its special field of instruction."

Despite the income from the commercial sections of the building and its occasionally successful productions, the Auditorium Theatre had never operated in the black. The end seemed near in 1908. On February 14 that year, the *Chicago Tribune* reported, "It is reasonably certain that the Auditorium theater, which Heinrich Conried once observed was the finest on the American continent, will pass into history after next year."

The directors of the Chicago Auditorium Association pointed out that not even vaudeville and musical comedies had turned a profit. "Tentative plans have been prepared, it became known yesterday," said the *Tribune*, "for a remodeled hotel, twenty-two stories high, with the most magnificent rotunda of any hotel in the world, at an expense of $3,000,000." The existing hotel would be reconfigured into offices and the Michigan Avenue entrances blocked up.

A bizarre incident happened a month later, when George B. McGuire, from Jacksonville, Florida, entered the Auditorium Building and went to the seventh floor. Forcing an elevator door open, he flung himself down the shaft in a suicide attempt. Unfortunately for him, his plan failed. He landed on top of the ascending elevator cab, resulting in a thud but no injuries. He explained to authorities that his drinking had resulted in his losing his job, and that he had been drunk for the two weeks he had been in Chicago.

In the meantime, the grandiose plans of the Chicago Auditorium Association had run into a roadblock by the name of Ferdinand Peck. The man who was almost single-handedly responsible for the building had no intentions of seeing it torn down. He took the syndicate to court, resulting in a bitter battle that seemed to have no end.

Nearly two decades later, Peck and the association were still at a stalemate. The *Tribune* reported on June 14, 1923, that Peck's attorneys were poised to "carry the legal fight to the United States Supreme Court." The newspaper wrote, "Mr. Peck denied allegations that the Auditorium was obsolete, or a losing venture financially, and asserted its prestige and the affection in which it is held by Chicagoans was a considerable asset."

The fight to save the Auditorium Building was no doubt helped along by the Great Depression, which made the then $15 million price tag for the

The Auditorium Building's Romanesque Revival exterior, with its "rather disappointing" chimneylike tower

replacement building out of reach. But the poor economy took its toll as well. The last long-term tenant of the Auditorium Theatre moved to the Civic Opera House in 1929 and the theater was closed.

After a decade of disuse, it seemed certain that the Auditorium Building would be lost. The date of July 31, 1941, was announced for demolition "because of the heavy tax burden," according to the *Daily Illini.* But suddenly newspapers and city officials were inundated by torrents of letters of protest from Chicagoans.

Among the staunchest advocates for preservation was Mrs. Julius Weil, Dankmar Adler's daughter. She professed her goal to "save it from oblivion." Among those she reached out to was Frank Lloyd Wright, who had worked in her father's office at the time of the Auditorium Building's construction. He responded with a letter outlining inside information about the building, the architects, and the process. "The Auditorium was entirely

Adler's commission," he noted, "and more largely Adler's own building than Sullivan's—where its constitution and plan were concerned." He explained that Adler ruled the construction site with an iron fist, "but a good one." He wrote, "Those who knew him feared him and respected him mightily."

"The dramatic expression of the interior was Sullivan's," he said, but that "even the interiors were not solely the work of Sullivan.... The receding elliptical arches spanning the great room were the best feature of the interior and they were a development by Sullivan of Adler's invention of the sounding board or sloping ceiling above the proscenium that had marked all Adler auditoriums before he took the genius Sullivan in on 'the ground floor.'

"And now I think no great room for opera in the world has ever excelled or even equaled for that purpose that same Chicago Auditorium Building."

In 1942, the building was acquired by the city, which reopened it in September that year as a servicemen's center. The *Daily Illini* reported, "Members of the armed forces marched through a foyer still dotted with potted palms, and formed a chow line into the once ivory and gold dining room. The sound of bowling balls echoed through the corridors, and the ballroom quivered under the pounding of jitterbug feet."

The newspaper recalled, "There Fiodor [*sic*] Chaliapin sang his Mephistopheles, Enrico Caruso his Pagliacci, Lotte Lehmann her Isolde, and Geraldine Farrar her Tosca. Sarah Bernhardt, Ellen Terry, Galli-Curci, Paderewski, John Philip Sousa, and Lillian Russell performed there to capacity audiences."

In 1945, Roosevelt College was founded by Edward J. Sparling. An accredited school of liberal arts, science, commerce, and music, it permanently saved the Auditorium Building by purchasing it the following year. During the next half century, restoration brought Sullivan's brilliant performance space back to its glory. Instead of Caruso and Bernhardt, the audiences applauded artists like Aretha Franklin, Stevie Wonder, The Doors, and Elton John.

The theater continues to host performing arts, including American Ballet Theatre and The Royal Ballet. And the often-threatened, innovative complex survives as Adler & Sullivan's masterpiece.

WATER AND LIGHT:
CLARENCE BUCKINGHAM MEMORIAL FOUNTAIN
GRANT PARK AT 301 SOUTH COLUMBUS DRIVE

Kate Sturges Buckingham was 15 years old in 1873. A child of privilege herself (her father amassed a fortune building grain elevators, banks and, later, Chicago's elevated train), she turned her attention to the children in the county hospital as Christmas neared that year. Unusually compassionate, she devised a plan to single-handedly raise funds for Christmas gifts for the young patients.

With her father's permission, she set out to collect donations from her wealthy neighbors. Her endeavor was viewed as somewhat surprising by the well-heeled Victorians; yet their contributions enabled her to arrive at the hospital on Christmas Eve laden with gifts.

Disaster waited. The burning candles on the Christmas tree set it ablaze and all Kate's prettily wrapped presents were destroyed. The *Chicago Tribune* later wrote, "But young Miss Buckingham, nothing deterred, set forth to raise anew money enough for gifts for each child. And did." It was a hint to Chicagoans of the caring heart of Kate Sturges Buckingham.

Her father, Ebenezer Buckingham, died in the family mansion at 2036 Prairie Avenue in 1912. His several-million-dollar estate was divided among his three children, Kate, Clarence, and Lucy Maude. The following year, Clarence, a financier and broker, died a bachelor. His $1.5 million estate went to his sisters, who lived on in the Buckingham mansion. Lucy Maude, an invalid, died in 1920. She left her entire $2.5 million estate to Kate, making her one of Chicago's wealthiest women.

Fabulously rich, she could have taken her place at the uppermost levels of society. Instead, she ordered her name removed from the Social Register, and limited her friends to a few trusted and cherished old acquaintances, while continuing her generous philanthropy.

She spent her money freely, but wisely, to improve Chicago. She gave valuable gifts to the Art Institute, always insisting that her name not appear as benefactor, but that the donations be listed as memorials to her brother or sister. She supported the Chicago opera, was patron to more than 200 music and art students, and heavily contributed to the Field Museum.

Other than regularly attending the opera, most often on the arm of a young protégé, Kate Buckingham rarely appeared outside her Prairie Avenue mansion. On those nights out, the tall, imperial woman came handsomely dressed, with her white hair worn in a "Queen Mary pompadour"—the high hairstyle made fashionable by the wife of George V.

Because she stayed mostly at home, a visit to the Continental Illinois National Bank & Trust Company, in which she owned much stock, resulted in a teller failing to recognize her. She tried to withdraw cash, but had no identification on her. The teller asked her if there were anyone in the bank who could identify her. Kate glanced around the room and replied, "They're all dead."

Three years after her sister's death, Kate completed construction of a cooperative apartment house on Lake View Avenue. She had rooms removed from the family mansion and installed in her apartment there. After she moved into her new home, she had the old Prairie Avenue house demolished.

In 1925, Kate began her most ambitious project to date. On June 13, the *Chicago Tribune* reported, "Work on an elaborate fountain, the gift of Miss Kate Buckingham, art patron, in memory of her brother, Clarence Buckingham, will begin shortly in Grant park." The announcement had been made by the architects, Bennett, Parsons & Frost.

They took their inspiration from the Bassin de Latone at Versailles. But the Buckingham Fountain would far surpass that of Louis XIV. The architects promised, "it will be twice as large and the flow of water three to four times as great."

Although the *Tribune* predicted, "It is to be in a garden 600 feet square. Four smaller pools will surround the main pool, which is to be 300 feet across," those smaller pools never came to pass. Instead, the three tiers, which rose 25 feet, would spill into a single 280-foot-wide pool. The main fountain was to be composed of 72 jets, which would discharge 1,600 gallons of water per minute for "everyday displays," 5,500 gallons on holidays, and 7,000 gallons for special occasions.

French sculptor Marcel F. Loyau executed the four pairs of bronze seahorses, which appear to rise from the main pool—each an allegory of a state bordering Lake Michigan: Michigan, Indiana, Wisconsin, and Illinois. Prior to their being shipped to Chicago, they were awarded the Prix National in Paris.

A vintage postcard captures Buckingham Fountain with its jets at everyday level.

The ambitious engineering by Edward H. Bennett took months to perfect and included experimenting with the water jets and colored lighting for nighttime. Closely monitoring the project was Kate Buckingham, whose goal was to ensure the lighting resembled "moonlight."

Kate's addition to Grant Park was meant not only to be a memorial to her brother, but to beautify Chicago and its waterfront. A year later, on August 28, 1926, the *True Republican* opined, "Grant park, Chicago's front yard, once a desolate dumping ground, today is blossoming into one of the most beautiful park developments in America." It attributed this in part to the rising "$600,000 fountain of pink marble, a gift to the city."

By the evening of Friday, August 26, 1927, when the Buckingham Fountain was dedicated, the number of jets had increased to 134. And the cost of the entire project had reached $700,000—in the neighborhood of $9.5 million today.

John Philip Sousa conducted his band that night, playing his own "Stars and Stripes Forever" before a crowd of 50,000. The assemblage was treated to a 30-minute water and light show, accompanied by Sousa's music. Although Kate Buckingham was in the grandstand, she characteristically did not address the crowd.

The *Tribune* was quick to praise Kate's dazzling addition to Grant Park. "Here is a gift that puts beauty where it is altogether well that it should be…. Thugs and gunmen Chicago has in plenty; from her city hall come rude and raucous words; her politics are less mannerly than those of other pools of politics…. The thugs will go their way all the quicker for this fountain, for such things are educators that do their work well; the young folk who make audiences for Chicago's great fountain will carry away a vision that does not set well with thuggery. Water and light are two of the cleanest partners in beauty making."

The new fountain played for an hour at noon every day; and every evening during the summer. On certain nights, musical accompaniment added to the colorful water display.

Kate Buckingham made sure that her magnificent monument to her brother would not fall into disrepair. She provided enough for the Buckingham Fountain Endowment Fund to maintain the fountain in perpetuity.

The fountain was the scene of a "dance drama" in the summer of 1936. For three nights, nearly 300 dancers performed on special platforms constructed on and around the fountain. "Spraying water and colored lights will be turned on the dancers who are to wear water-proof costumes," advised the *Chicago Tribune*.

When word arrived in Chicago on August 15, 1945, that World War II had ended, Chicago—like every other American city—erupted in unbridled celebration. Scores of happy people jumped into Buckingham Fountain and displayed their joy with splashing water.

Visitors to Grant Park were enchanted in the early 1950s, when a mother mallard duck decided that the fountain would be a good place to raise a family. She made a nest in the shrubbery nearby and when the ducklings hatched, taught them to swim in the fountain, rather than the nearby lake. On July 25, 1953, the *Tribune* announced that she was back again "for the third successive year." The newspaper explained how the tiny waterfowl were able to get into the basin. "Several times a day she leads her family to the edge of the fountain basin and Frank Daly, park engineer, lifts them into the water. The park district is supplying grain for the duck and bread and lettuce for the ducklings."

Quite appropriately, when Queen Elizabeth's royal yacht, *Britannia*, arrived in Chicago in July 1959, it landed near Buckingham Fountain. The area around the fountain swarmed with 2,000 policemen for the occasion.

Marcel Loyau's four pairs of bronze seahorses represented the states of Wisconsin, Illinois, Indiana, and Michigan

The fountain often served as a venue for social and political demonstrations. On July 10, 1965, for instance, Reverend A. D. King, brother of Martin Luther King, spoke at the fountain, and then led a group of 200 protestors from the fountain to City Hall to oppose the ousting of school superintendent Benjamin J. Willis. Two months later the fountain served as the background for an anti-Vietnam rally and a speech by Steve Carey, assistant secretary of the American Friends Service Committee.

Most importantly, through it all, Buckingham Fountain remained a place of beauty and calm. When journalist Thomas Fitzpatrick paused by the fountain in September 1964, an old man with a trimmed beard struck up a conversation. He had been coming here to sit and watch the water and the people for decades.

"You see, this fountain means so much to so many people. There are so many who are given a mental lift just by coming to look at it for a few minutes whenever they get a chance. There's something about all that water shooting so freely in the air that takes your mind off everything else for just an instant. I know several men, and there must be many more, who make it a practice to come here and visit the fountain whenever they feel depressed."

It is still that calming beauty that is Kate Buckingham's legacy.

CHICAGO BUILDING

7 WEST MADISON STREET

Business could not have been better for the Chicago Savings Bank in the first years of the 20th century. In fact, although the institution had already broken ground on a new headquarters at 7 West Madison Street, it could not wait for that building's completion.

On December 5, 1903, the *Chicago Tribune* remarked on its extraordinary success: "The growth of the business of the Chicago Savings bank, State and Washington streets, has compelled it to seek more commodious quarters during the construction of the new Chicago Savings bank building." The directors had taken over the old Merchants' Loan & Trust Building, despite optimistic construction projections. "The bank will be located in its permanent quarters, State and Madison streets, within a year," promised the newspaper. The prediction proved to be only slightly overconfident. Designed by the architectural firm of Holabird & Roche, the 15-story structure was completed in 1905.

While the basics of the building's design were Renaissance Revival, William Holabird and Martin Roche liberally splashed it with elements that place it squarely within the style of the Chicago School. These include the Chicago windows (three-part geometric openings, compatible with the Arts and Crafts movement), along with the 12-story angular bays. The handsome bays not only provided dimension and movement to the facade, they captured passing breezes in the sultry days before air conditioning.

Originally known as the Savings Bank Building, the Chicago Building sat on what was considered "the World's busiest corner." At the third floor, a stone marked the 0-0 degree axis of the city and became the point from which all Chicago addresses begin.

While the Chicago Savings Bank took the lower floors, the majority of the upper stories were filled with medical offices. In 1913, the same year that the bank left the building, there were no fewer than a dozen dentists and 30 physicians here. One of them, Dr. E. C. Martin, suffered the embarrassment of being arrested in his office here in April that year.

Martin had concocted a scheme to bilk farmers in the rural areas outside of Chicago of thousands of dollars. The *True Republican*, on April 16, explained, "His methods were original. His advance agent, named Phillips, would make a canvass of the farmers, and glibly tell how a great Chicago specialist was being employed on a local case, and if anyone in the family were ill, he, Phillips, would put them in touch with the eminent specialist who would cure them at very little expense."

Within a day or two, Phillips would reappear, accompanied by Dr. Martin. The doctor would convince the country folk that they were sick, and then charge various amounts to treat them. One farmer, Otis Richmond, complained, "This man came out to Woodstock one day and hired an automobile. He started out to visit every farmer in the county.... Grabbing the head of the household by the coat lapel he would say: 'My dear sir, I am Dr. Martin, the famous physician from Chicago. I understand you are a victim of heart disease. I have just discovered a sure cure for the malady. I have dashed out here in a hurry in order to save your life. I am working for humanity."

Richmond told a grand jury that most farmers were "scared to death by this. If they didn't think they had heart disease the doctor examined them and invented the symptoms." Martin signed contracts with 203 "patients" for six months of treatment. The fee of $212 he received from William Senns would be in the neighborhood of $5,230 today. Richmond presumed, "He must have cleaned up a fortune."

Dr. Martin was charged with "swindling." In default of his $2,000 bail, the disgraced doctor was sent to jail.

After the departure of the Chicago Savings Bank, a portion of the ground floor of 7 West Madison was taken by the Richelieu Wine Company for its saloon. Following a meeting of the Painters and Decorators Union at 20 West Randolph Street on the night of August 18, 1914, at least one of its members dropped into the bar. Around 10:30 that night, the central police office received a telephone call, advising of a shooting at the Richelieu bar. When Lieutenant James McMahon and four detective sergeants arrived, no one in the saloon knew of any shooting. Bloodstains trailing out of the bar and down the sidewalk suggested otherwise.

According to the *Chicago Tribune* the following day, "They traced these stains to Madison and Dearborn streets. They arrested two men and learned the injured man had been carried aboard Madison street car No. 151." As if in a scene from a black-and-white movie, the cops commandeered a taxicab and

The building, completed in 1905, sits on the axis of State and Madison
streets, where all Chicago addresses begin.

ordered it to follow the streetcar. When they overtook the car, its conductor said three men had carried the wounded man off the car at Peoria Street. From there the police followed the trail of blood to a physician's office on Madison Street. The office was closed and the blood trail continued to Madison and Morgan Streets, where it abruptly disappeared.

In the meantime, the two men arrested earlier were questioned, and one, William Flynn, admitted shooting the unnamed man. The victim was the business agent for the Painters and Decorators Union. "Flynn denied knowledge of the shooting at first. In his pocket, however, was the pistol with five empty chambers. The weapon had been fired recently," reported the *Tribune*.

Police told reporters, "It was the same old story of a labor dispute 'arbitrated' with a gun."

Back at the Richelieu saloon, bartender Thomas Murphy wanted no part of the investigation. The *Chicago Tribune* noted that he not only witnessed the shooting, "in fact he was pretty close to it. Two bullets were found lodged in the bar." Despite the evidence, Murphy insisted that the shooting took place in the alley.

Architects and jewelers soon joined the medical practitioners on the floors above the bar. As early as 1913, the architectural firm of Lebenbaum & Marx was here, as were several jewelry firms. In the building that year were Rittig, Hess & Madsen Company, manufacturers of wholesale watches; and Edward B. Voynow, diamond importer. Over the next decades other architects—like Allen E. Erickson and A. B. Jensen—would move in, as would additional jewelry concerns.

One jeweler, J. E. Harrison, endured a harrowing ordeal when he was bound and gagged by thugs on December 13, 1922. The robbers made off with $102,000 in jewels. In reporting on the theft, the *Chicago Tribune* still referred to 7 West Madison as the "Chicago Savings Bank Building."

A long-time tenant was manufacturing jeweler Leo Feldstein & Sons in Room 1001 on the 10th Floor. Feldstein had operated his business for 40 years until his death, when his two sons, Milton and Lester, took over. In October 1929, the month of the Stock Market Crash, 33-year-old Milton Feldstein found himself in serious financial trouble. Using promissory notes from the family firm, he obtained $15,000 in diamonds on credit from various merchants, and then pawned them to pay his debts.

It did not take police long to catch on and he was arrested on November 29. At the police station, he asked permission to telephone his brother. Lester

Feldstein was in the shop in the Savings Bank Building when he received the call. Milton explained his circumstances, then told his 28-year-old brother, "You tell mother about it." Lester refused. According to newspapers the following day, "Sergt. Knowles then took the telephone and advised Lester to call his mother, pointing out that she must learn of her son's arrest eventually." "I can't tell mother," Lester said.

Five minutes after Knowles hung up the phone, a report came into the detective bureau that there had been a shooting at 7 West Madison Street, in Room 1001. A squad rushed to the scene, where they found Lester Feldstein lying on the floor of the workroom with a bullet wound in his right temple. A revolver lay by his side. Police told reporters they believed that the young jeweler had chosen death "in preference of the task of telling his mother... of the plight of his brother...which involved the name of her dead husband's jewelry company."

The building continued to house medical, architectural, and jewelry concerns for the next few decades. By the 1950s, various other businesses had moved in, like the newly formed vending machine firm, Lunch Box, Inc. *Billboard* magazine explained on July 15, 1950, that it "uses an eight-column machine to sell five or six food items, selected so that two or three purchases will make a complete small meal."

By the time the Chicago Board of Education took over the property, it was being called the Chicago Building. Rather startlingly, when the building was considered for Landmark status in June 1987, it was rejected by a resounding 9 to 2 vote. The *Chicago Tribune* was puzzled, saying that the decision put the structure's "future in doubt" and added that it "is regarded as one of the purest examples of the Chicago School of design."

Almost a decade later, on March 26, 1996, the Chicago Landmarks Commission rethought its decision and designated the Chicago Building a city landmark. The following year it was converted to a dormitory for the School of the Art Institute of Chicago. Except for alterations at street level to accommodate a long series of retail tenants, Holabird & Roche's striking Chicago School design survives wonderfully intact.

CHICAGO CULTURAL CENTER

(FORMER PUBLIC LIBRARY)

78 EAST WASHINGTON STREET

Along with houses and commercial buildings, the Great Chicago Fire of 1871 destroyed thousands of books. That tremendous loss was not completely overshadowed by the general devastation. One reaction to the calamity was the movement to establish a free library. As the city took the first steps in the arduous process of rebuilding, several leading citizens, besides the mayor, proposed the Chicago Free Library. Before long, other cities and nations began shipping volumes to stock the library. On New Year's Day 1873, it opened in an old iron water tank at LaSalle and Adams Streets.

The outpouring of donations was staggering. In June, the trustees presented their first report since the fire. *The New York Times* remarked, "It is a document of considerable interest, particularly in so far as it is a record of large-hearted generosity."

England had already donated 3,530 volumes and promised 1,200 more. Queen Victoria named the drive the "English book donation." Germany was the second largest contributor. The report projected, "When the contributions from each have been completed, the whole number of volumes will be increased to 10,752." At the time of the report, an average of 331 Chicagoans were visiting the library each day.

Less than a year later, on May 1, 1874, the number of books had risen to 17,355. Yet the trustees were troubled. "With no competing library in the city, and with a population of 500,000 looking to it for reading, it seems now impossible to fix any limit to the use which will be made of its books when the shelves are fully supplied," reported *The New York Times* on July 12. "What is needed is more books."

With more books and more users came the need for more space. In 1893, the Chicago Library was the sixth largest in the country. Continually moving to larger accommodations, it was now temporarily housed on the top floor of City Hall. Since 1881, city officials had been eyeing Dearborn Park, a half block of land on Michigan Avenue between Randolph and Washington streets, for a new structure. The problem was a clash of interests among the three property owners—the federal government, the state government, and the city.

A compromise was achieved when the Grand Army of the Republic, the organization of Civil War Union Army veterans that held a 50-year lease on a quarter of the property, agreed to share a new building with the library. A competition among 13 architects was held in 1893, with the Boston firm of Shepley, Rutan & Coolidge winning the commission. (Anticipating the expense, the state legislature had imposed a small tax levy in 1881 to help pay for the structure.)

By the end of the year, the cornerstone was laid and construction well under way. On December 10, the *New York Times* published a sketch of the coming edifice with the headline, "A Palace for Its Books." The newspaper said, "The architectural style is Roman classic. The idea has been to make the structure substantial, plain, and easy of access, with an abundance of light and ventilation."

The projected completion date of 1894 came and went; but finally, on September 11, 1897, four years after groundbreaking, the *Chicago Tribune* ran the headline "Chicago Library Soon to Open." Dedication ceremonies of the $2 million structure were scheduled for October 9.

The city expressed its apologies to Chicagoans for the long construction process of their first permanent Public Library building. Reporters were told one cause was "the use of only the finest materials, interior and exterior, and the lasting nature of the place and of all its appointments. No cheap imitation or sham material of any sort has been employed and while in some instances it has been deemed better economy to use other than the highest priced woods, in these places the solid American oak shows out in its native colors."

The technologically up-to-the-minute structure contained its own complete telephone exchange; plants below ground supplied its own light, heat, power, and ventilation; and 400 tons of coal could be stored in its vaults. An ingenious system tied the 30 electric clocks throughout the building to one master clock; and pneumatic tubes connected the various departments.

The dignified structure was clad in blue Indiana limestone, known as Bedford stone. Basically Neoclassical in style, the architects had splashed it with Italian Renaissance Revival elements. Regimented, arched windows at the second floor lined up below grouped openings embellished with engaged Ionic columns on the third. The result was an imposing, stately design.

Bronze lampposts with milk-glass globes line up along the sidewalk around the palatial library at the turn of the 20th century.

The interiors were lushly decorated. Carrara marble for the lobby was imported from the same quarries chosen by Michelangelo. The white Italian marble staircase in the book delivery room was inlaid with glass mosaic and green Irish marble and pearl. J. A. Holzer of New York designed the glass mosaics, which were executed in Favrile glass by Tiffany Glass & Decorating. The stairway of the Randolph Street entrance was faced with pink marble and the entry hall clad in green-veined Vermont marble. Each of the wings had a 38-foot glass dome. The southern dome for the library portion of the building was designed by Holzer and executed by Tiffany Glass & Decorating. It is the largest Tiffany dome in the world. The northern example was created by the Chicago firm Healy & Millet.

While *American Architect and Architecture* praised the decorative work of Tiffany & Company, it noted, "one would question how wise it was to put such a large sum into mosaics and stained-glass." In fact, there was an astonishing 10,000 square feet of glass mosaic in the new building.

The walls of the vast reading room, or "Renaissance Room," were a rich, dark red above a wainscot of green marble. Capable of seating 340 readers, the room stretched 140 feet long and 55 feet wide, with the ceiling 33 feet above the floor. The *Chicago Tribune* reported, "The tables are liberally supplied with gas and electric lamps. At one end of the room are the newspaper files, so many that seventy-five persons may stand at them, each one reading a different paper."

The Reference Room was "Greek" in decor. The walls were clad in Siena marble. A clock at the end of the room was flanked by bas-reliefs of nude boys, representing day and night.

The 17,000-square-foot section used by the Grand Army of the Republic was accessed on Randolph Street. Lavish materials and decorations included East Indian mahogany, old English oak, limestone, and marble. "Rich rugs adorn the rooms," said the *Tribune*. Of note were the Memorial Hall, "a reception-room of mighty proportions," and the Assembly Hall.

Only a month after the library opened, controversy erupted. Methodist ministers passed a resolution at a meeting in October condemning the library being opened on Sundays. The sharp back-and-forth between the clergy and the library board reached the East Coast. On October 26, 1897, *The New York Times* quoted an irate Board President Azel F. Hatch, who said, "If they close the library they should close the Sunday schools. Those persons who wish to close the circulating department of the library on Sunday are to be classed with those who want to stop the publication of Sunday newspapers."

The library remained open on the Sabbath.

The use of "only the finest materials" presented a problem in 1899. Newspapers reported that on a Sunday night, January 8, crooks "carried away three valuable bronze plates ornamenting the fancy lampposts" outside the library. Police Captain Colleran initially thought it was malicious defacing by vandals. However, he later told reporters, "I concluded that it was the work of thieves, who stole the bronze to sell to junk dealers or pawnbrokers."

Frederick H. Hild, head librarian since the building opened, made a serious decision in 1906 concerning Upton Sinclair's newest novel, *The Jungle*, which portrayed the harsh conditions and exploited lives of immigrants in Chicago. In June, a concerned citizen pointed out "certain passages" in the book, particularly in one chapter. Hild removed the book from the shelves, feeling that "Mr. Sinclair's work was a trifle too strong for general reading." Dr. Cigrarud, a member of the library board, supported Hild's decision, saying, "Whatever truth there may be in the novel, it is hardly the matter that we can allow to go out to young people. If read at all it should be by persons of mature minds."

Intricate stone inlay, a magnificent coffered ceiling, and the stained-glass light fixtures combine in a near visual overload on the marble staircase.

The board's support of Frederick Hild's restrictive perspective soon eroded, however. In 1909, he was ousted because of his refusal to accept updated ideas. Board members accused him of being "headstrong," and Library Director Julius Stern explained, "He has shown a lack of the progressive spirit which would make the library most effective."

The handsome library building was threatened in 1927 when Mayor William Hale Thompson proposed replacing it with a 22- to 25-story structure to house both the library and the Board of Education. Offices on lower floors would be leased to independent firms. He also wanted all the books about England and by British authors burned. According to the *Chicago Tribune*, he felt doing so would "cleanse the shelves of King George III." (He apparently still held a grudge against the long-dead sovereign over the American Revolution.) Thompson's projects were derailed by the Great Depression, which saved not only British books but the building itself.

In 1939, another proposal surfaced. Two professors from the University of Chicago Library School suggested remodeling the old structure and erecting an addition within the courtyard. That plan was bounced around until World War II put it on the shelf.

The library's progressive thinking displayed itself when, on September 29, 1950, the board chose Gertrude E. Gescheidle as head librarian—the first female in the position since the library's founding in 1873. The native

Chicagoan stepped into what the *Tribune* called "one of the top library jobs in the nation." She earned $11,700 a year with her promotion from branch librarian—a comfortable salary of about $115,000 in today's dollars.

The Chicago Library building was threatened again in February 1969, when a survey team, headed by Dr. Lowell A. Martin of Columbia University, recommended demolition. In its place would be, as Mayor Thompson wanted four decades earlier, a multi-use office and library building.

Mayor Richard J. Daley once said of his wife, Eleanor (known popularly as "Sis"), "She is able to speak for herself very well, whatever she has on her mind." When a *Chicago Tribune* reporter asked her opinion of the proposed demolition of the library building, she replied, "I don't think that would be nice." She later added that what *would* be nice was "restoring and keeping all the beautiful buildings in Chicago."

Sis Daley's polite but firm response fostered a grass roots movement, as well as her husband's support. Shortly after the interview, the City Commission voted down the project. Once again the library hung on to its old home.

Then, in 1987, Harold Washington, Chicago's first African-American mayor, proposed the construction of a new central library, to be built in the South Loop. Known as the Harold Washington Library Center, it opened in 1991. With the library now gone, the future of the Washington Street building was once again in question.

The new first lady, Maggie Daley, wife of Richard M. Daley, followed closely in the footsteps of her mother-in-law by volunteering to raise funds for the renovation and repurposing of the structure. She worked closely with Lois Weisberg, commissioner of cultural affairs, and in 1991 the nation's first free municipal cultural center opened to the public.

Much of the sumptuous interior detail was preserved; and outwardly Shepley, Rutan & Coolidge's impressive Neoclassical structure is essentially unchanged since 1897.

Hundreds of events are held here each year—including concerts, dance performances, literary presentations, and visual arts. The handsome building also provides opulent surroundings as the official reception space of the Mayor of Chicago.

"WONDER THEATRE OF THE WORLD": CHICAGO THEATRE

175 NORTH STATE STREET

By 1920 motion pictures had progressed from short vignettes seen in nickelodeons to full-length "picture plays." Instead of the renovated playhouses where they had been shown, more and more elaborate theaters were being erected specifically to screen silent movies. Their zenith would be achieved in the 1920s, when lavish movie houses deservedly earned the name "palaces."

In Chicago, two sets of brothers—Abe and Barney Balaban (former nickelodeon owners) and Sam and Morris Katz—had teamed up in 1916 to form the Balaban & Katz theater chain. That year they turned to another set of brothers, Cornelius W. and George L. Rapp, to design their first luxury movie theater.

George Rapp had begun his career designing vaudeville theaters, which resulted in his knowing the Balabans. Rapp and his brother would devote their careers primarily to designing sumptuous movie houses, several of them for Balaban & Katz. In 1919, the six men would work together again, creating what was their mutual masterpiece.

An enormous plot of land was acquired at Lake and State Streets, and construction started on what was to be the Capitol Theatre. On June 22, 1921, the *New York Clipper* reported a surprising announcement. "Balaban & Katz' newest theatre, now in course of construction at Lake and State streets, will not be named The Capitol, as first announced. It will be known as the Chicago Theatre."

The name change was unexpected, since it risked being confusing. Until only recently a legitimate theater named The Chicago had operated at Wabash Avenue and 8th Street, and in August 1921, the *New York Clipper* pointed out that no fewer than six other theaters had carried the name The Chicago.

The newspaper remarked that "building troubles have continually delayed the opening of the theatre" but the contractor promised it would be ready on October 1. Reporting that it would be the largest motion picture theater in the world, the *Clipper* noted, "It will have a seating capacity of 5,500 seats."

October 1 came and went, but finally, on October 26, 1921, the elaborate venue opened. Patrons in evening clothes lined the sidewalk, much less interested in the film than in the theater. Rapp & Rapp had produced a brick, stone, and terra-cotta French Neoclassical behemoth. The facade was dominated by a massive arched opening above the marquee. Elaborate terra-cotta bands, panels, and spandrels contained festoons, flowers, and faces.

The architects had reserved the real spectacle for inside. Patrons entered a cavernous French-style lobby clad in marble and dripping with crystal chandeliers. Lounges were furnished in Louis XIV reproductions, and paintings and statuary lined the walls. A majestic sweeping staircase rose two stories before splitting and turning back on itself. The auditorium, embellished with frescoes by local muralist Louis Grell, was worthy of a French court. Altogether, the sumptuous surroundings made the $4 million price tag and the long delays worth waiting for.

Silent movies required accompaniment. It was provided on opening night by organist Jesse Crawford on the enormous Wurlitzer organ and a 50-piece orchestra. That evening, the feature film was *The Sign on the Door*, starring Norma Talmadge. Patrons were also treated to a live stage show and "a spectacular pageant of Chicago's progress."

The *New York Clipper* (slightly adjusting its earlier seating estimate) mentioned, "The theatre, which seats 5,000 people, is advertised as the wonder theatre of the world... The Chicago has one of the largest stages in the world—175 feet wide, 35 feet deep and eight stories high." Even by today's terms, admission was affordable. Morning moviegoers paid 25 cents; tickets for the afternoon showing cost 35 cents; and after 6 p.m. admission was 50 cents—around $6.75 now.

That vast stage caught the eye of New York producers the Shubert Brothers. Only two months after the theater opened, the *New York Clipper* reported, "It is rumored that the local office of the Shubert Circuit has approached Balaban & Katz in an effort to induce them to play Shubert vaudeville in their Chicago Theatre."

Balaban and Katz apparently liked the idea—except for the Shuberts' involvement. On February 1, 1922, the *Clipper* announced, "The Chicago Theatre, which opened as a strictly movie house, is offering one or two

The exterior of the Chicago Theatre.

acts of vaudeville weekly. Balaban & Katz are reported to be endeavoring to secure the services of well known standard vaudeville acts, to play the house weekly." The newspaper added, "They are said to be offering prominent artists enormous salaries."

Not every vaudeville act was a rousing success. Bird Millman opened her *An Oriental Flower* in November 1923, at "the leading picture theatre of the entire world." It was deemed by one critic as "only moderately successful." A newspaper advised of the motley lineup, "It consists of Miss Millman, wire walker; Bernard Ferguson, baritone; and a Japanese boy, who assists Miss Millman."

The most stellar evening ever presented at the Chicago Theatre began at midnight on Tuesday, May 7, 1929. A benefit performance for the National Vaudeville Artists' Sick and Benefit Fund featured more than 100 notable stage and screen stars. The *Vaudeville News* boasted, "The bankroll of no producing manager that ever lived could stand the combined salaries of all these stars in one show—but they all gave their services free."

Stage actor Otis Skinner hosted the evening. Among the renowned performers were Guy Lombardo and His Royal Canadians, Mae West, Ray "Rubberlegs" Bolger, Helen Lowell, Frances Williams, and scores of others. The *Vaudeville News* reported that patrons lined the sidewalk until morning, hoping to get in.

Other artists appearing on stage here over the decades were Duke Ellington, Benny Goodman, Frank Sinatra, and Jack Benny.

As the Century of Progress Exposition was being planned for 1933, the interior of the theater was slightly updated. New carpeting, upholstery, and draperies were installed; and a new proscenium mural was executed. Sixteen years later, Rapp & Rapp were recalled to institute more substantial renovations. In a press release, the firm referred to the project as "Streamlining for a Palace of the 20's."

The Louis XIV-style furniture, the bronze and crystal lighting fixtures, the paintings and statuary were all hauled away. The gilded and brightly colored lobby, staircase and auditorium areas were painted over in muted gray and beige colors. A false ceiling was installed over the lobby ceiling and the plaster pilasters hidden behind flat surfaces.

With television came a noticeable decrease in motion picture attendance. Across the country the grand movie palaces, once crowded every night, closed down one by one. Finally, on September 19, 1985, the Chicago Theatre shut its doors, supposedly for the last time.

One of a pair of statues in alcoves on opposite sides of the stage at the theater. The statues were executed by Michelangelo Studios of Chicago, which had supplied all the statues at the 1893 Chicago World's Exposition.

However, the Chicago Theatre Restoration Associates was formed to save the structure. A relatively early preservationist group, it purchased the building and launched a nine-month restoration led by Chicago architectural firm Daniel P. Coffey & Associates. The $1 million project ended when Frank Sinatra headlined the gala reopening on September 10, 1986.

Within its rejuvenated Versailles-like atmosphere, the "Wonder Theatre of the World" once again presented live shows. What was formerly a dusty relic was now, as it had been in the 1920s, an entertainment destination. Patrons have since seen artists like Aretha Franklin, Diana Ross, Dolly Parton, Alicia Keys, and Harry Connick Jr. on the Chicago Theatre stage.

DEARBORN STREET STATION

47 WEST POLK STREET

As Chicago got back on its feet in the decade following the Great Fire of 1871, its growing system of railroads demanded substantial depots. New York City architect Cyrus L. W. Eidlitz was commissioned in 1883 to design a station at the corner of Dearborn and Polk streets. From here passengers would board trains headed to Southern California and the Southwest on the Santa Fe Railway; or to New York City, St. Louis, and Toronto on various lines like the Erie Railroad; or southbound to Alabama.

Eidlitz had been on his own for only five years, having previously worked for his architect father, Leopold Eidlitz. Completed in 1885, his Dearborn Street Station (also known as the Polk Street Station) was an imposing red-brick and pink granite Romanesque Revival structure. Its soaring four-faced clock tower wore a four-story Flemish Revival cap from which breathtaking views could be had.

Decorative dormers punched through the main peaked roof and the hip roofs of the corner pavilions. Eidlitz ornamented the station with the arched openings and medieval touches expected of the style. Passengers arriving at or departing from the station were protected from the elements by a broad canopy on ornate cast-iron supports.

The station had been open for business only a few months before its first major incident took place. On May 31, 1885, Chicago police received a message from the conductor of a train inbound from Kansas City. "I have an insane man on my train who has possession of one car," William Putnam telegraphed. "Policemen at Kansas City, Jacksonville, and Peoria all afraid to take him. Please send ten or twelve policemen out on No. 1 to take him when we arrive in Chicago. They had better come in citizens' clothes, and will have to look sharp or some will get hurt."

The train was due to arrive at 2:30 that afternoon. Police Lieutenant Laughlin, with a dozen detectives and patrolmen, arrived in the station at 2:15. Laughlin had not heeded the conductor's warning and all the policemen were in uniform. A reporter in the station noted that the officers did not

Dearborn Street Railroad Station, Chicago.

A late-19th-century postcard shows the soaring tower of Chicago's rail gateway to the rest of America.

consider the matter much of a threat. One suggested that they throw a blanket over the man's head; another thought that Buffalo Bill should be found so he could lasso him. "And so, chatting and laughing, they passed the time."

Word spread through the terminal that the police were waiting in ambush to arrest a maniac. A crowd began to gather in the vicinity of the inbound track. As the train approached the station, the engineer saw the large crowd. He blew a series of short warning whistles, and passengers and train employees waved frantically from the windows that the people needed to get out of the way. Even before the train had come to a full stop, passengers jumped from the train and fled in every direction. Suddenly the throng realized the danger of the situation and ran in what the *Chicago Tribune* called "a veritable stampede."

The officers slunk carefully along the sides of the train. There was the loud report of a gunshot, and 34-year-old Patrolman "Connie" Barrett grasped his chest, gasping, "I'm shot!" They were his dying words. A bullet had entered his heart and exited through his back.

Pistols were being fired from every direction. Throughout the station men and women cowered behind columns and doorways, afraid to move. The *Tribune* reported, "Lieut. Laughlin, who had gone to the rear of the train, followed by Detective Terry, was making his way, hatless, toward the chair-car on the west side when he caught sight of the murderer through the car window. Leveling his revolver he fired." Two officers, Ryan and Keenan, managed to sneak in to the chair-car through the smoking car. Every shot they fired at the gunman was met with return fire. Then they raised the alert: "The man's leaving the train!"

The *Tribune* reporter described what happened next: "A young man of medium stature, with a slight, sandy mustache, dressed in a worn suit of light brown and wearing a broad-brimmed white felt hat of the pattern affected by cowboys, leaped off the cat-steps on to the east side of the platform. He started north, brandishing, as he ran, a large revolver. The weapon was a Colt's six-shooter, 44-calibre, the make used by the army and cowboys and frontiersmen. It was a murderous weapon."

The deranged gunman ran through the station, causing would-be passengers to scatter, with Lieutenant Laughlin on his heels. At one point, he stopped, turned and fired directly at the policeman, who did not pause, but rushed his prey.

There was almost a disaster when a station employee, mistaking Laughlin for the maniac, hollered, "Kill the bastard!" and brought a heavy brick down on the detective's head. When order was finally restored, the perpetrator, 33-year-old Lewis Beaume and the "overzealous" employee were both arrested. They were temporarily jailed in the same station house where the body of Officer Barrett lay. The *Tribune* noted that "hundreds came to see the victim of demoniac insanity."

Beaume, a fresco artist by trade, was riddled with bullets. He was taken to the county hospital, where doctors said it was impossible for him to survive. The young man said that he had a wife and two children in Detroit. He seemed to be suffering from delusions, explaining, "I am being pursued by a large body of armed men…. They are armed to the teeth and want to hang me."

When he asked a policeman what would be done with his remains, the officer replied coldly, "You ought to be burned."

While extraordinary, the Beaume incident was merely the first in a string of unpleasant situations. Train terminals often attracted loiterers, thieves, and ne'er-do-wells. It was a lesson that Mrs. Frances Fernandez learned all too well on December 4, 1897.

She had spent the day shopping on the South Side and was heading back to her Lake Street home. It was rush hour, around 6:30, and the station was packed with commuters. While pushing through the crowd, she suddenly felt someone grab her arm. Surprised, she looked into the face of a heavily built man. He held her arm tighter and growled, "You utter a scream and I will put an end to your yelling, right in this crowd."

He grabbed her pocketbook, but when Frances refused to yield, a struggle ensued. Now people in the crowd took notice. Seeing this, and before anyone could come to her aid, he roughly twisted her arm, snapping it. He ran through the mass of people and escaped. Bystanders helped Mrs. Fernandez to a drugstore. She had suffered a broken wrist and arm. Her stolen purse had contained a total of $4.

In 1912 Peter Gigas worked in a silk sweatshop in Passaic, New Jersey. Among the many factory "girls" there was one named Mary. According to the *Day Book*, "She had amassed a fortune of $500 and other workers considered her wealthy."

Despite a considerable difference in age—Peter was just 21 and Mary was 38—the two were married. When he soon told her that he was suffering from tuberculosis and doctors advised a milder climate, she agreed that they would go to California. They had a stopover in Chicago on January 28, 1913, and got a hotel room. The next morning Peter left to get a shave. Mary waited. And waited. When police picked her up in the Dearborn Street Station, she was frantically looking for her missing husband—and her missing money. She told authorities that she was firmly convinced "that Peter must have been murdered and robbed."

Albert Tardy drove a mail wagon at the Dearborn Street Station. On November 10, 1913, the new Mrs. Tardy opened her door to find postal inspectors on her doorstep. Albert had not come home yet, and the men asked a few questions about a mysterious $10,000 mail robbery that had happened that afternoon. The missing mail, it seems, had been in a pouch on Albert's wagon.

Postal inspectors found themselves talking to Mrs. Tardy again the following morning. She appeared at their office saying, "After the post office inspectors went away yesterday Al came home. I hardly knew him. He was all dressed up and wore diamonds. 'What happened to you?' I asked. 'Did you make a haul?' 'I certainly have,' was all he'd say then. I became suspicious."

She told investigators that her husband finally confessed that he had cut open one of the registered mail pouches and taken out "a lot of letters." He told her not to be afraid, "but that he'd get away until the thing blew over." As soon as he left the house, she went to the postal police. The Tardy marriage did not make it to their first anniversary.

A disturbing trend appeared at the terminal in 1914. Five years earlier, prosecutor Clifford G. Roe called Chicago "the center of white slavery in the United States" and pledged war against "its social cancer." Now the vice had spread into Dearborn Street Station. As prostitutes began working the crowds of rushing businessmen, police soon tied them to a "white slavery" ring.

Dearborn Street Station lost the top of its tower in a 1922 fire.

On the afternoon of March 20, a 16-year-old girl was picked up and identified as Florence Grey, who had disappeared from a fashionable boarding house in New Rochelle, New York. According to the *Day Book,* she told Detective Sergeant Edward Birmingham "that she had been lured from surroundings of wealth and fashion by a man named Sidney Hargreave, whom she met through the medium of a matrimonial bureau ad. The detective believes there may be a white slave connection."

Four months later, undercover police watched a girl, "with her hair in braids, wandering around the railroad station July 6." She was approached by a man; they talked, and started out of the station together. Policewoman Mary Crot stopped them and pulled the girl aside. She explained that her name was Mrs. Lucy Rappetti and the man was her husband. They had married in Canada. Officer Crot then questioned the "husband." He gave his name as Charles Smitteri and explained that he and his extraordinarily young wife had been married in Pittsburgh. "After hearing these two stories the policewoman brought the couple to the station," reported the

Day Book. The newspaper's headline read, "Policewoman Arrests Pair—Suspects White Slavery."

Increased police presence was most likely responsible for the dwindling reports of "white slavery" and prostitution incidents within the next few years.

Albert Tardy's mail robbery was nothing compared to the $500,000 job committed on April 6, 1921. Five gangsters pulled up to the Dearborn Street Station in an automobile at dusk, then waited until an accomplice gave a signal—lifting his hat—that a government truck had pulled up. The men piled out of the car with revolvers drawn. The heist took only two minutes.

On April 23, Chicagoans were shocked to read that Ruel H. Grunewald, a prominent attorney, was being held in connection with the robbery. Grunewald and one of the other crooks, Edward S. Stevenson, were arrested after they entered a downtown bank with $20,000 in $1 bills. They wanted to exchange them for tens and twenties. They carried with them registered mail sacks.

The clumsy act was surprising, considering the high-level mobsters involved in the job. Before long, "Big Tim" Murphy was arrested (he was later murdered in a gang hit), as were Pete Gusenberg (killed in the St. Valentine's Day Massacre), Vincenzo Cosmano, Jack Berry, Eddie Guerin, and Paul Volanti.

The police had only one more accomplice to apprehend—Harold "Fat" Watkins. All eight arrested gangsters had served their terms before Watkins was finally nabbed on September 8, 1932. The 45-year-old claimed he never knew the police were looking for him, and lamented, "It will be tough on the kids to learn that their father was wanted for robbery." He added, "The Government sure sticks on the job until they get their man."

In the meantime, the Dearborn Street Station had suffered significant damage. In 1922, a devastating fire tore through the upper floors, destroying parts of the structure. The four-story cap of the clock tower was removed and the wonderful roofs and dormers were not replaced. The repaired terminal emerged with a slightly more industrial appearance.

Train travel continued to be both faster and more luxurious. On May 17, 1937, the Santa Fe Railway proudly clocked the arrival of its new Super Chief as it pulled into the station at 11:48 a.m. The railroad announced that the train "broke the record for the 2,228 mile run from Los Angeles to Chicago with an elapsed time for the trip of 36 hours and 49 minutes." It had broken the previous record by two hours.

Byron C. Hanna, president of the Los Angeles Chamber of Commerce, was on board. He told reporters, "It is a long step from the covered wagon to the modern railroad train as we have recently known it and certainly it is a long step from that train to the Super Chief."

But it would not be very long before trains would be competing with, and losing to, air travel. On December 30, 1961, the *Chicago Tribune* noted that of the five railroads that used the Dearborn Street Station, "only the Atchison, Topeka and Santa Fe and the Wabash railroads have any substantial passenger operations." Discussions were already under way to "eliminate" the station, a term that avoided the word "demolish."

The station limped along; but more bad news came on August 2, 1965, when the Dixie Flyer left the Dearborn Street Station on her final trip between Chicago and Florida. There was no longer a demand for the train that had once offered 24-hour service to Miami and operated over as many as five railroads. The *Tribune* reminisced, "Noted as much for its speed and wild revelries as for its most famous dish, hog jowls and turnip greens, the Dixie Flyer carried the cream of Chicago's society to Florida during the heydays of the 1920s."

Six years later, the Dearborn Street Station lost its battle and was boarded up. The tracks were pulled up and the train shed behind demolished, but local citizens and preservationists intervened in time to save the main building. In 1985, the architectural firms Kaplan McLaughlin Diaz and Hasbrouck Hunderman were commissioned to convert the century-old structure to office and retail space. The renovated station, where mail robberies, broken hearts, and luxurious train accommodations all came together, is an admirable example of urban recycling of vintage structures.

JEWELERS' BUILDING
15–17 SOUTH WABASH AVENUE

In 1881, 25-year-old Martin Antoine Ryerson was already making waves in Chicago. The son of lumber magnate and early settler to the area, Martin Ryerson, he grew up in Chicago, was educated in Europe and graduated from Harvard Law School in 1878. Two years later he joined his father's business, Williams, Ryerson & Company, the sole surviving lumberyard in Chicago after the 1871 fire.

With his personal fortune burgeoning, young Ryerson, like his father, invested in downtown Chicago real estate. In 1880, construction began on his cast-iron-clad Rothschild Building, designed by Adler & Sullivan. Dankmar Adler had hired Louis Sullivan, then 23 years old, in 1879 as a draftsman and designer. Only a year later, the two were partners.

In 1881, Ryerson hired the fledgling firm again. It would be the second of four projects on which the men would collaborate. This time Ryerson set them to work designing a five-story structure at 15-17 Wabash Avenue for paper-goods dealer S. A. Maxwell & Company. That firm, located in Lacon, Illinois since its founding in 1855, was now looking to make its move into Chicago. Ryerson acted as developer and landlord in the project.

The brick and stone structure was completed in 1882 at a cost of $90,260, or just over $2 million today. The architects created an unusual and eye-catching design, using cast iron for the openings, which provided not only expanses of glass, but exciting contrast to the vibrant red-brick and white stone facade. By chamfering the corner at the alley, they provided not only additional light, but visual interest. Adler & Sullivan forewent a cornice in favor of a chunky parapet, decorated in up-to-the-minute style.

Some of the ornamentation—stylized sunflowers and incised plants, influenced by the intensely popular Aesthetic Movement—was perhaps expected, but most was pure Louis Sullivan. Lush floriform panels were stacked above the uppermost windows, executed in his signature style.

Three years after S. A. Maxwell & Company moved into the newly completed building, the book *Origin, Growth, and Usefulness of the Chicago Board*

S. A. Maxwell's paper goods emporium filled the entire building in 1882.

of Trade described it: "The premises occupied are very extensive and commodious, all comprise a splendid five-story building with basement, which is handsomely fitted up with every convenience and facility for the accommodation and display of the large and valuable stock."

Maxwell was by then the largest wallpaper dealer in the United States and had branched into "books, blank books and stationery." Soon the firm would diversify even more broadly. The company had a substantial crew of salesmen who traveled the country, selling wholesale to book and department stores. *Origin, Growth, and Usefulness* commented that the "booksellers and stationers" had "obtained a liberal and influential patronage from all classes of society."

By January 1891, Maxwell had overestimated the number of items it could carry. The *Bookseller and Newsman* explained, "The business of S. A. Maxwell & Company, which consists of four special departments—wall paper, books, stationery, fancy goods and druggists' sundries—has for some time past been growing and developing at such an enormous rate as to be a serious tax on the head of the house." Therefore, management decided to drop the least profitable department—books. S. A. Maxwell himself supported this decision by saying, "Where is the book and stationery house that has ever retired a rich partner?"

In place of the book business, Maxwell announced the retail wallpaper department would be expanded—to the point of altering the main floor of the building. "We propose to turn the first floor of our establishment on Wabash avenue into a retail wall paper showroom, and to this end we intend to take out the present front, building in the corner with solid glass and change the entrance nearer to that corner so as to give an unbroken sweep of display windows fronting on the avenue. This front will extend 14 inches beyond its present position."

Alterations were not sufficient for the exploding business. S. A. Maxwell & Company expanded into the entire five-story building next door and then, at around the turn of the century, moved to larger quarters.

From at least 1914 through 1919, the building was home to Cross-Wells, a restaurant and hospital supplier. The *Modern Hospital Year Book* listed the firm's astoundingly vast offerings, including curtains and materials, draperies, general dry goods, clothing (chef and waiters), general kitchen equipment, motors, buffers and polishers, general utensils, cutlery, dishwashing apparatus, refrigerators, china and glassware, and table linens.

At the beginning of the 1920s a variety of tenants moved into the upper floors, including Superior Optical and the Chicago headquarters of the Royal Typewriter Company, which would remain until 1933.

In the meantime, the ground floor, once bustling with wallpaper buyers, became two businesses. The Harmony Café operated in one half, and in March 1928 the Fannie May Candy Shop moved into the other. H. Teller Archibald, president of Fannie May, moved his "sweet shop" from 22 South Wabash across the street after signing a 10-year lease.

Later that year, early on the morning of September 16, an employee opened the Harmony Café to discover a safecracker had been at work. The *Chicago Tribune* reported that the "thief had entered during the night and worked the combination," and $1,600 was missing.

Six months later, the Fannie May Candy Shop would be the victim of a robbery. This one, however, would be far more terrifying. Mary Rheinhart was standing behind the candy counter when a man brandishing a gun entered the store and demanded the cash. Mary gave the robber the $30 in the register. It was one of 12 robberies committed on the West Side and the South Side within two hours on the evening of March 21, 1929.

To help keep its patrons during the Great Depression, the Harmony Café chain lowered its prices. Its employees were seemingly happy as well; so when three of the restaurants, including the Wabash Avenue café, were targeted by "stench bombers" on Thursday night, January 7, 1932, management was puzzled.

Putrid-smelling bombs were a somewhat common form of union retaliation against management, but the Harmony Café had no labor problems. The 400 patrons inside did not wait for an explanation. The *Tribune* reported the customers "were driven out when the bomb was broken near a ventilating shaft." General Manager S. J. Kaplan told police, "We have received no threats of any kind." The intention behind the attack remained a mystery.

Signature floriform patterns by Louis Sullivan flow around the chamfered corner.

The stink bomb was nothing when compared to the attack on the John P. Harding restaurant across the street at 21 South Wabash Avenue three years later. By now Fannie May Candy had moved to 12 South Wabash and the Imperial Watch Repair Shop had taken its place.

At around 3:00 on the morning of November 3, 1935, a "dynamite bomb" exploded in the doorway of the Harding restaurant. The plate-glass windows along the block, including those of the watch repair shop, shattered and the elevated railway station shook. The eight employees of the restaurant—cooks and scrubwomen—were in the back and were unhurt. But the damage to business was estimated to be about $2,500. As with the Harmony attack, the restaurant's vice president said he knew "of no reason for the bombing."

As the area became the unofficial center of Chicago's jewelry district, Litt & Meyers Jewelry Company moved into 15-17 South Wabash by the late 1930s. At some point the building became popularly known as the Jewelers' Building (this despite the structure at 35 East Wacker Drive having already been given the same nickname). When Iwan Ries Company took it over in the 1970s, it was sometimes referred to by that firm's name.

The ground floor received a regrettable makeover in the late 20th century, but the upper floors—comprising a stunning and rare example of Adler & Sullivan's earliest works—remain remarkably intact.

WORTH WAITING FOR:
JAY PRITZKER PAVILION
201 EAST RANDOLPH STREET IN MILLENNIUM PARK

In 1997, the James C. Petrillo Music Shell on Butler Field in Grant Park was in sad shape. Constructed during the Great Depression, it was named in 1975 in honor of Petrillo, the president of the Chicago Federation of Musicians from 1922 to 1962, and president of the American Federation of Musicians from 1940 to 1958. Concerts began in the band shell in 1931 and for the next six decades it was the scene of free concerts, music festivals, and other events. But as the century drew to a close, according to the *Chicago Tribune*, "That structure had become so ramshackle and unsafe that the Grant Park Orchestra and Chorus threatened to discontinue its summer concerts there."

In January 1977, the Chicago Park District proposed replacing the band shell. But George Ranney, president of the Metropolitan Housing and Planning Council and his wife, Vicky, president of the relatively new group Friends of the Parks, had a different idea. At the edge of Grant Park, between Randolph and Monroe Drives, were the unsightly Illinois Central Gulf Railroad yards.

Ranney, who was aware that the Illinois Central rarely used the facility, met with its executives and predicted that if the railroad tried to develop the Grant Park land, it would face years of litigation. Instead he proposed it donate the land for park use and enjoy the resulting tax breaks and positive public relations.

The Ranneys envisioned transforming the rail yards into a 20-acre park, Lakefront Gardens, which would include a new band shell. The project forged ahead and, on October 6, 1977, Ranney unveiled the plans for the $20 million venture. They included designs by the architectural firm of Skidmore, Owings & Merrill for an "outdoor music bowl." Reaction was positive overall, including firm support from Mayor Richard J. Daley.

But the Ranneys would soon discover what poet Robert Burns had known two centuries earlier. The best laid—and noblest—plans often go awry. George Ranney later explained, "The Park District was absolutely dug in. They wanted their plan." Negotiations finally resulted in a "demountable" band shell in Butler Field in 1978 and the plans for Lakefront Gardens moved forward again.

A giant stainless-steel web spreading over the lawn carries the speakers for the Pritzker Pavilion.

Without the Park District behind the project, however, fundraising was a challenge. Also, a reassessment of the costs of relocating the railroad's tracks and acquiring its air rights brought the total cost to nearly $50 million. The project stalled again as city administrations came and went.

While Mayor Michael Bilandic had been enthusiastic, his successor, Jane Byrne, was iffy. And Mayor Harold Washington disliked the idea entirely. Finally, in 1996, the Illinois Central took the reins. It retrieved the two-decades-old files from Ranney and met with city officials. The talks eventually resulted in a grand reworking of Lakefront Gardens into Millennium Park, with the staggering price tag of $230 million.

As plans evolved, the Petrillo family was concerned that James Caesar Petrillo's name would be forgotten. His granddaughter, Donna De Rosa, initiated a lobbying effort in November 1999 to keep his name on the proposed new band shell. Letters went out to Italian-American organizations and the mayor himself. She was already too late. The park's planners were focused on something more important than legacy: cost.

In exchange for paying for major elements of the park—like the band shell—donors' names would be attached to them. The billionaire Pritzker family was approached to pay for the $15 million band shell. They agreed "only if a world-class architect were involved," said the *Chicago Tribune* later. Frank Gehry certainly fell into that category. And Cindy Pritzker knew him personally.

Pritzker proposed that Gehry design the band shell. She told the *Chicago Tribune*, "Once you've made a suggestion, you have to be willing to put your money behind it." She convinced the architect to take on the project, but not before serious negotiations. He took on the commission in April 1999, but he already had a backlog of projects. Everyone involved accepted the fact that there would be "a delay."

Gehry presented preliminary plans in November. The *Tribune* called the design "a highly sculptural form topped by ribbons of stainless steel that suggest the petals of a flower, curling whips of chocolate atop a cake, or Betty Boop's eyelashes." The article added that it had "his characteristic explosive shapes. Yet it contains a new wrinkle for him—the giant trellis, which would be 600 feet long and as wide as a football field." The "ribbons" concerned architect Adrian Smith of Skidmore, Owings & Merrill, who suggested "Gehry ought to shrink his oversized curls of stainless steel, given the havoc that the stiff breezes blowing off Lake Michigan are known to wreak."

They also concerned those who pointed out that they well exceeded the city's zoning law, which placed the legal ceiling for a Grant Park structure at 75 feet. The law was cagily sidestepped. City planning commissioner Christopher Hill told reporters it would not be a problem "because city officials are looking at the ribbons as sculpture, not as a building."

Cities across the planet were simultaneously preparing for the turn of the century. London, for instance, was constructing the Millennium Bridge and the Millennium Dome. As 1999 rolled over to 2000, those venues were the scenes of enormous worldwide celebrations. Millennium Park's Jay Pritzker Pavilion would be a bit late to the party.

Four years after the millennium, construction was still under way. Workers ran into problems trying to piece together the countless parts of Gehry's complex structure. Long after the pavilion was scheduled to be completed workers were still at work high above the ground. The long delays translated into additional costs in salaries and overtime for construction companies, which resulted in their filing lawsuits for more than $16 million.

The patience of Chicago music lovers may have been growing thin in June 2004, when it was announced that the free concerts of the Grant Park Orchestra and Chorus would have to be held indoors at the Harris Theater for Music and Dance. *Tribune* music critic John von Rhein grumbled on June 25, "The new Jay Pritzker Pavilion at Millennium Park is a bit like a pampered diva

The stage nestles in the shining metal curls of the shelter.

taking her sweet time getting ready for a first date while her companion waits impatiently in the car."

The park officially opened in July 2004 but, as reported in the *Tribune* on July 18, "lawsuits over the construction of its elaborate Gehry-designed music pavilion provided a reminder of the numerous difficulties that have plagued the park project."

In anticipation, *The New York Times* had remarked on July 12, "Even in a city with a worldwide reputation for innovative urban design, the opening this month of a spectacular new park and performance center near Lake Michigan promises to be a huge event. The site, Millennium Park, is opening four years late and at three times the original budget, but few here are complaining."

A week later, the newspaper's Christopher Hall added, "The centerpiece of the 24-and-a-half acre park is the Pritzker Pavilion, a 120-foot-high outdoor music stage framed with a signature Gehry flourish—a billowing jumble of colossal stainless steel ribbons. Arcing over the 4,000 fixed seats and a lawn with space for 7,000 more people is an open-air acoustic canopy fashioned from crisscrossing steel pipes hung with speakers."

Architecture critics were wowed. Blair Kamin called it "powerful and eloquent" and said, "Frank Gehry has proved himself a worthy match for the city of Louis Sullivan, Frank Lloyd Wright and Ludwig Mies van der Rohe." *The New York Times*'s Anne Raver wrote that she "stood agog at the Gehry pavilion. Its maw of curling steel looks like a celestial gateway to another universe."

While the sculptural band shell (and the park in general) was in the minds of many Chicagoans inexcusably over budget and its many construction delays unpardonable at the time, those issues are largely forgotten. Today park-goers agree with the fundraising consultant James Feldstein, who remarked on July 15, 2004, "We were all so disappointed with what happened in the 1970s, but maybe it was for the best. No one at the time could contemplate what we have now. Millennium Park was worth waiting for."

THE ROOKERY

209 SOUTH LASALLE STREET

Following the devastation of the 1871 Great Fire, City Hall operated out of a decrepit structure at the corner of LaSalle Street and Adams Street. The annoying flocks of pigeons that roosted along its eaves prompted citizens to nickname the building "The Rookery." In New York City at the same time, the term was used derogatorily to describe low-class saloons and tenements, often with a racist slant. But in Chicago the term was less vitriolic, although it did put the character of the politicians in City Hall into question.

By 1884 the city looked toward moving out of the makeshift structure. Because the land was city-owned it could not be sold, merely leased. On April 6 that year, the *Chicago Tribune* cautioned the city fathers against acting hastily, saying "there is no reason for making a hurried transfer of the leasehold, and especially on terms which may prove to be too low."

Technically, the land was restricted to school purposes, but Edward Waller, a real estate lawyer and speculator, had been boyhood friends with Mayor Carter Harrison Sr. and could be persuasive. He and four other investors—Peter Brooks, a real estate developer from Boston and the largest investor; Owen F. Aldis, another developer; elevator mogul William Hale; and architect Daniel Burnham—had formed a consortium to erect a money-making structure on the site. When Waller conferred with the mayor on May 13, 1885, the *Chicago Tribune* noted, "Mr. Waller said he was not prepared at present to say who his backers were."

What he did tell reporters was they had agreed to pay $2,500 for the old Rookery building and were prepared to remove it "inside of thirty days." Waller was confident enough that the city would accept their offer that the architects (of course Daniel Burnham and his partner John Wellborn Root) were already at work on the plans.

Waller told reporters, "Our plans and specifications are still in the hands of the architects and are not complete, but it is our intention to erect a building which shall be first-class in all particulars, to cost $1,000,000, and come up

LEFT The cast-iron newel posts of the interior staircase sprouted fantastic electric lights in 1892. Note the spittoons placed on either side to capture the saliva spat by men chewing tobacco. **RIGHT** Even without its exuberant Victorian lighting fixtures, the main staircase commands attention.

to the contract in every detail. It will be an office-building, of course, and we expect to make it ten stories high."

Construction began in 1885 and continued for three years. The resultant Romanesque Revival structure of brick, terra-cotta, and stone was monumental. Although the masonry walls were load bearing, as in past construction, Burnham & Root added a steel skeleton for further stability. The *Engineering and Building Record* explained that it all had to do with Chicago's soil—a "black miry clay, which at the surface is fairly firm in its nature but which becomes soft a few feet below grade." The journal noted that steel beams were "a new feature in Chicago construction" and "such a construction would hardly be called for anywhere except in Chicago. The soil is so weak, as previously explained, that it is not considered safe to load it very heavily, and any other construction would imply so much heavy masonry as to be bulky and clumsy in the extreme."

The investors had grappled with a fitting name for their new building and, despite fervent opposition by Peter Brooks, "The Rookery" stuck. As a matter of fact, John Wellborn Root, who was responsible for the elaborate carvings on the facade, incorporated crows, or rooks, into some of the designs.

Despite today's overwhelming approval of the architecture (it is often cited as one of Burnham & Root's masterworks), it got mixed reviews. *American Architect & Architecture* commented, "The Rookery Building is, all things considered, the most satisfactory of the Chicago office-buildings. A great deal can be said against it, but there is so much that is good in detail, that it easily holds its place as the best designed structure of its kind."

Among its most innovative features was the central light court within. In 1891, *Industrial Chicago: The Building Interests* pointed out, "There it stands, the [most] admired of all office buildings. Lighted on four sides from streets and alleys and in the center from a great court, it is a thing of light." Burnham & Root foreshadowed the late 20th-century "atrium" architecture of food courts and vertical shopping malls with its expansive glass-and-iron skylight, which still impresses.

Other than Burnham & Root, which moved its offices into Room 1142, the tenant list was heavily industrial. Early renters included the Calumet Iron & Steel Company, the Illinois Steel Company, the American Steel & Wire Company, the Lassig Bridge & Iron Works, Universal Construction Company, Chicago Ship Building Company, the Fort Wayne Foundry & Machine Company, and the Burton Stock Car Company.

Early skyscrapers presented the dilemma of keeping the windows of the upper floors clean. It was a problem that cost A. Lindahl his life on July 29, 1892. The *True Republican* reported that the window washer "fell from an eighth-story window and was dashed to death on the stone pavement below."

One tenant not engaged in the construction business was the National Capital Savings Building & Loan Association of North America. Operating out of Room 35, its representatives marketed a get-rich-quick scheme to farmers and rubes in small towns.

The conditions for a $1,000 loan seemed exemplary. For monthly payments of $11.05, it would be paid off in 96 months, after incurring only $60.80 interest. But the *Rock Island Argus* explained on August 11, 1891, "Then there was a membership fee of $30, an appraisement fee of $20, and $45 for three months' payment in advance, thus making $95. The concern made one $500 loan that was genuine, and this was just enough bait to lead others to invest."

Hundreds of investors sent their money to the Rookery building office. They contracted for new homes and stores, and construction was started. But the money never came. A raid on the office of the National Capital Savings Building & Loan Association of North America on August 10 resulted in

The exterior of the building.

several arrests. Federal marshals estimated that the bogus firm had "taken in from $200,000 to $350,000, and given not one penny in return."

A more upstanding banking firm was John H. Wrenn & Company. Among its employees in 1897 was James M. Treadway. Many Chicagoans in the 19th century carried handguns and Treadway was no exception. On August 27, the 35-year-old went to the fairgrounds a mile south of town to do target practice. Treadway was either a decidedly bad shot, or he was murdered. His body was found with a bullet in his heart, and his revolver was near his side. Officials declared that he accidentally shot himself.

When Prince Henry of Prussia visited Chicago in 1902, the Rookery was on his list of sights. On the morning of March 5, Mayor Carter Harrison Jr. (whose father, also the city's mayor, had been assassinated in 1893) acted as his tour guide, and after visiting the Art Institute and the Illinois Trust & Savings Bank building, they went to the Rookery. Here the prince gazed at the vast skylight and then, wrote one reporter, "he passed through the barber shop in the basement, while those being shaved sat up in amazement."

Three years after Prince Henry viewed the magnificent light court of the Rookery, Frank Lloyd Wright was commissioned to update the heavily Victorian interior. During the two-year project, Wright scaled down much of Burnham & Root's overblown ornamentation, replacing it with Prairie School elements and signature Wright details, like his geometric copper lighting figures, a masterful blend of art and architecture.

Wright's former assistant, William Drummond, did more modernization in 1931. Updated elevators were installed and Art Deco touches were added to the accumulation of styles. Throughout the rest of the century, rather astonishingly, the Rookery survived with little change. Today, the exterior of Burnham & Root's masterful office building that took on the logistical challenges of Chicago soil looks essentially as it did on opening day, 1888.

ROSENBERG FOUNTAIN

GRANT PARK AT SOUTH MICHIGAN AVENUE AND 11ᵀᴴ STREET

On November 29, 1892, the *Chicago Tribune* reported on the bequests laid out in the will of Joseph Rosenberg. Among the generous amounts left to family members and to charities, like the Michael Reese Hospital, was $10,000 "to the City of Chicago for a drinking fountain on some prominent corner on the South Side of the City."

Although he was born in Chicago, Rosenberg had for years operated a high-end clothing store on Market Street in San Francisco until his death in 1891. Chicago city lore would attribute the gift to his youthful days as an impoverished newspaper vendor to whom South Side merchants refused to give a drink of water. In 1976, the *Tribune* explained, "He vowed that when he became a rich and powerful industrialist he would return and erect a drinking fountain there in memory of many dry afternoons and as a savior to those following his footsteps."

As quaint as the poor newsboy story is, it most likely does not hold water. In reporting on Rosenberg's death on July 30, 1891, the Sacramento *Record-Union* noted, "He was the only son of Jacob Rosenberg, head of the oldest and one of the wealthiest Hebrew families of Chicago."

A more plausible explanation behind the magnanimous gift was the Temperance Movement. It started around the time of the Civil War and it blamed alcohol for a raft of social ills, including domestic violence, poverty, and immorality. Around the nation, groups like the American Temperance Society and the Women's Christian Temperance Union cropped up to stamp out the evils of liquor. Among their favorite weapons was the temperance fountain. It was believed that by making available an abundant supply of healthful, clean water to the working classes, the temptations of alcohol could be thwarted.

It was an idea that another San Francisco resident, Henry Cogswell, grasped on to. In 1878, he donated the first of 50 temperance fountains across the country. The one he donated to the City of New York in 1891 was typical—a Grecian-inspired canopy, supported by four 10-foot columns, sheltered the

A vintage postcard depicts the fountain in the center of a pathway, easily accessible to thirsty park-goers.

Chicago, Jll.

The Rosenberg Fountain in Michigan Ave

fountain. Atop it was a statue of the goddess Hebe. In Greek myth, she was the daughter of Zeus and Hera and fulfilled the role of cup bearer to the gods. Temperance reformers preferred to ignore the fact that the cup was normally filled with ambrosia or nectar; instead they concentrated on her duties as water bearer (much more in line with their anti-alcohol stance).

Whether Rosenberg and Cogswell ever met is unclear; however, the Rosenberg Fountain, completed in 1893, bore striking similarities to those of Henry Cogswell. The appearance of the fountain was clearly laid out in Rosenberg's will, as was the name of the sculptor: Franz Machtl of Munich.

There was some backlash following the *Chicago Tribune*'s publication of Machtl's sketch of the statue on December 29, 1892. Although the *Tribune* felt that the figure of Hebe would "quicken, possibly, the love of the beautiful, which is too often forgotten in sordid pursuits," and promised that "The whole will be a rare combination of beauty and utility," certain women's groups were offended by the goddess's unclothed torso. It was, however, a traditional depiction—in the myth, Hebe lost her position as cup bearer when her garment became caught and fell open. A compromise was achieved for the statue, which resulted in only one exposed breast.

The architectural firm of Bauer & Hill designed the Greek pavilion that covers the fountain. Above, Machtl's 11-foot bronze statue of Hebe holds a water pitcher at her side and offers a shallow cup in her outstretched hand. The simple inscription, "Presented by Joseph Rosenberg, San Francisco, Cal." runs along the entablature. The fountain was finished just in time to be admired by visitors arriving for the Columbian Exposition.

Those who picked up *Rand, McNally & Co.'s Guide to Chicago* were treated to a gushing description: "This beautiful work of art, the gift of Joseph Rosenberg of San Francisco, stands at the southwest corner of Lake Front Park, near the

Franz Machtl's original concept for the statue was a nearly nude Hebe. The finished product was markedly more modest.

junction of Lake Park Place and Michigan Avenue.... The work consists of an elaborate granite pedestal composed of an ample base supporting a basin, from the rim of which rises a low yet stately Doric peristyle, surmounted by a simple entablature. From the center of the basin the fountain ascends, illuminated by a candelabrum shedding electric light, the water falling within access of the visitor."

The *Guide* called the Hebe statue "the crowning figure" and said, "The pose of the head as well as that of the figure suggests something of the refinement visible of Canova's masterpiece, the sensuous contours of the countenance softened by an expression of winning loveliness."

The Rosenberg Fountain survived the 20th century mostly unharmed by vandals and weather. It was restored in 2004. Although at some point it lost its electric "candelabrum", its water (while no longer drinkable) still plays within its Doric columns. And Hebe still looks down, a reminder of a time when temperance workers battled to replace demon drink with pure water, and one bare breast was more acceptable than two.

WILLIS TOWER

(FORMERLY SEARS TOWER)

233 SOUTH WACKER DRIVE

With the development of steel-frame construction and improvements in elevator design, the last decade of the 19th century saw skyscrapers rising higher and higher. A writer for *Engineering News* may have been the first to notice there was a contest of sorts going on. In reporting on the proposed 26-story Park Row Building in New York, the journal noted on October 8, 1896, "The rage for phenomenally high office-buildings still continues unchecked in New York city, and there seems to be at present some rivalry here as to who shall build the highest structure."

It was a race that would continue into the 21st century.

The Park Row Building was passed by when the Singer Building was completed in 1908, topping out at 36 stories, making it the tallest in the world. It lost the title when in 1913 the Woolworth Building reached 60 stories. The Chrysler Building and the Empire State Building rose simultaneously in 1928. Their architects secretly changed the plans of both during construction in efforts to be "the tallest in the world."

The Empire State Building had held the title for three decades when the plans for the World Trade Center were unveiled in 1964. Even before the Twin Towers were completed, the bragging rights were in jeopardy. On July 27, 1970, *The New York Times* reported, "Sears, Roebuck and Company, the world's largest retailer, announced today that its new central headquarters in downtown Chicago would be the world's tallest building and the largest private building in the world." The plans by the architectural firm Skidmore, Owings & Merrill called for a 110-story tower 1,450 feet tall. The height would surpass the Trade Towers by 100 feet and the Empire State Building by 200.

The obsession to be the highest was so intense, and the civic pride of New York to retain the glory so fervent, that as the Sears Tower rose in 1972, there was talk about adding floors to the Empire State Building in retaliation. According to *The New York Times* on October 11, "The owners of the 102-story Empire

State Building, the Colossus of the skies for almost 40 years and about to be relegated to the indignity of third place among the world's highest buildings, are exploring the possibilities of adding 16 stories and making the building once again the world's tallest."

Although plans were drawn and financial plans formulated, that project never went forward. Instead the Sears Tower continued upward, eventually claiming the prize. For a while, anyway.

The vertical road was not without its bumps. Ground had barely been broken before television stations and citizens groups protested that the building's height would interfere with broadcasts from atop the John Hancock Center. The battle continued and in February 1972, a request was issued to the Federal Communications Commission to study the issue. The following month, on March 17, the first suit to stop construction at the 50th floor was filed by the Lake County State's Attorney. It was followed by another, 11 days later, by the communities of Skokie, Northbrook, and Deerfield, Illinois. The cases stretched on until September 20, 1972, when the Supreme Court of Illinois granted Sears the right to continue construction.

On May 3, 1973, steelworker Richard Gumber was at the controls of the crane that hoisted the final beam to the top. At that moment the Sears Tower officially became the world's tallest skyscraper. The 2,500-pound beam had been signed by 1,200 citizens, including Mayor Richard J. Daley, who was watching in the crowd below.

The tower was completed later that year. The architect on the project, Bruce Graham, had worked with structural engineer Fazlur Rahman Khan to design what were essentially nine clustered buildings. It was the first structure to utilize Kahn's "bundled tube" method. Nine square-cornered "tubes" rose together to the 50th floor. There the tubes at the southeast and northwest corners were capped. The others continued to the 66th floor, where the southwest and northeast ones ended. The central bundle of five rose to the 90th floor, after which only the core tube continued to the 108th floor.

Newspapers covering the opening of the building filled their columns with superlatives and figures. There were 102 high-speed elevators and 16 escalators, for instance, and 16,500 persons—the population of a village—would work in the building. Four million pounds of aluminum were required in its curtain walls and extrusions.

Despite Khan's far-reaching structural innovations, there was one issue that seems to have been overlooked. Had the Sears Tower been erected in Boston, known as "Bean Town," or Philadelphia, the "City of Brotherly Love," there might not have been a problem. But Chicago is the "Windy City."

On April 20, 1973, the California newspaper the *Desert Sun* reported, "Police cordoned off streets around Sears Tower because high winds reportedly were breaking windows in the skyscraper." The following winter, on February 23, 1974, the *Daily Illini* advised, "Wind gusts clocked at 60 miles per hour popped more than a score of windows in Chicago's Sears Tower, the nation's tallest building", and on January 11, 1975, the *Desert Sun* again reported, "Winds knocked out at least five windows in Chicago's Sears Tower and sent debris flying down city streets." It was a nagging, dangerous problem that would plague the building into the 21st century.

In October 1974, Alexander Calder's colorful 33-foot-tall motorized sculpture *Universe* was installed in the lobby. Described by art critic John Russell in 1976 as "one of Calder's most complex and least resistible inventions," it required seven separate motors to keep the seven sections in motion at seven speeds.

Of all the building's modernity innovations, Americans (obsessed with the Space Age) were perhaps most enthralled with the robots that picked up and delivered the mail. Each of the motorized carts had a name—like Malachi or Egore—and their photoelectric sensors followed an invisible fluorescent path sprayed on the carpeting. The carts were programmed to pause and then continue as employees retrieved or dropped in their mail.

The prestige and fame that come with being the world's tallest building have their drawbacks, as Sears, Roebuck & Company first discovered in 1978. Thrill seekers, in the form of urban mountaineers as well as political activists with a message, were lured by the soaring edifice.

Bent on saving the whales, 25-year-old Joseph E. Healy started climbing the tower on May 1 that year. He carried with him an enormous banner written in Russian and Chinese that urged a halt to whaling. He made it to the 19th floor, where strong winds "forced him down, into the hands of police," as reported in *The New York Times*. He nevertheless successfully attached his banner. That the Russian and Chinese whalers were paying as much attention as pedestrians and police is doubtful.

Two years later, on August 25, 1980, James McLaughlin made it 18 stories up. The inspiration for the 26-year-old Connecticut man's climb was not so political as Healy's. He told police he "just wanted to get to the top." City officials were not pleased with his rush-hour spectacle; the crowds that formed below forced the partial closing of Wacker Drive. Vertigo-defying firefighters were lowered on a window-cleaning platform to the 21st floor where they convinced McLaughlin to give up. The *Columbia Missourian* described the scene: "After he agreed to come inside, firemen removed a sealed 18th floor window and he stepped inside."

Sears executives signed a complaint, alleging he had slightly damaged the facade. A company spokesman, Ernest Arms, told reporters that while the climb was "an interesting novelty … we really don't need further mountaineering attempts on the tower."

Nonetheless, nine months later Daniel Goodwin made it all the way to the top. On May 26, 1981, the *Chicago Tribune* noted, "A 26-year-old Las Vegas man dressed in a custom-made blue and orange Spider-Man suit Monday climbed to the top of the 110-story Sears Tower, becoming the first person to scale the world's tallest building."

Once again, three of the city's firefighters boarded a window-washing platform, but this time the climber was determined. And because he repeatedly warned his rescuers not to touch him, saying it was dangerous, they didn't. Instead, they took the 110-story trip alongside him. One, Art Kieldyk, told a

Willis Tower dwarfs its neighbors, which are reflected only part way up its bundled tubes.

reporter, "It was cold up there and he was freezing. He told us he was tired—but not enough to quit."

The following day men in hard hats were back on scaffolding, this time making repairs to the damage Goodwin had caused. He pleaded guilty to disorderly conduct. Given the costs of repairs, the closing of traffic, and the many police and fire personnel required by his stunt, his $25 fine seems lenient.

On Monday, August 19, 1985, a Sears Tower security guard suspiciously eyed two men and a woman loitering outside. What caught his eye was the parachute one carried under his arm. They were ordered away.

Undaunted, they were later spotted scaling a 20-foot wall on the Jackson Boulevard side of the tower. Police were called and the trio, equipped with the parachute, three walkie-talkies and ropes, were arrested. It was soon discovered that Nicholas Feteris was the same daredevil who had parachuted from the World Trade Center a year earlier.

When Sears, Roebuck & Company had first laid plans for its monumental headquarters, it was the world's leading retailer. Much of the space being leased to outside firms upon the tower's opening was intended to handle Sears's growth and expansion. The firm's optimistic projections, however, ignored the big-box stores like Walmart and Target, which were changing the personality of retail selling. On November 7, 1974, the year Sears moved in, the *Daily Collegian* disclosed, "The company discharged 3,400 employes in its new Sears Tower offices in Chicago."

The building sat half empty through the 1980s, so there was little surprise when the firm announced that it intended to sell what Eric N. Berg, writing in *The New York Times* on November 1, 1988, described as "a sleek, black building with view on a clear day extending to Michigan, Indiana and Wisconsin." A buyer was found six years later in Boston-based AEW Capital Management. The skyscraper changed hands two more times before a group of investors purchased it in 2004 for a reported $840 million.

The terrorist attacks of September 11, 2001 in New York understandably caused tension and concern to tenants of the Sears Tower and Chicagoans in general. On October 8, already-nervous fliers were terrified when a passenger invaded the cockpit of an American Airlines jetliner screaming, "Save the Sears Tower! Save yourselves!" Two military jets appeared within minutes and accompanied the plane to its landing. Tensions were only heightened in March 2003, when the Sears Tower appeared on al-Qaeda's list of targets.

That uneasiness seemed apparently warranted when the FBI announced it had foiled a plot to bomb the tower in 2006. Seven men, known as the Liberty City Seven, were arrested and accused of "conspiracy to levy war against the United States and to provide material support to al-Qaeda." The ensuing trials lasted through May 2009, ending with convictions of five of the men.

That year the tower's owners initiated a series of changes, including installing the all-glass boxes called "The Ledge" which protrude from the Skydeck on the 103rd floor; painting the entire structure silver (a plan which was thankfully scrapped); and a name switch. In March 2009, the London-based insurance firm Willis Group Holdings agreed to lease 140,000 square feet of office space, including naming rights. The official name change to Willis Tower came about on July 16, 2009. Chicagoans firmly and vocally rejected the new name, but as it became clear that the change was going to happen, they simply ignored it. Overall, Chicago residents to this day steadfastly call the building the Sears Tower.

A controversy arose the following year. A court battle ensued after Sears, Roebuck & Company wanted Calder's *Universe* back. The firm pointed to a 1994 option agreement which, according to *The New York Times* on October 13, "would allow Sears to purchase the art for half its appraised value." The owners' attorney, George B. Collins, insisted the sculpture was part of the property. He dismissed the $250,000 cost of moving the piece, saying, "we don't plan to move it. We plan to win the case."

The owners' hard-fought victory meant little to Blackstone Group LP, which purchased Willis Tower in 2015. In 2017, it embarked on a $500 million renovation which, surprising to most, did not include *Universe*. On February 1, *Chicago Tribune* journalist Blair Kamin lamented, "That's a shame because the abstract, motorized work lends a sense of playfulness and movement to Willis Tower's high-ceilinged, ultra-sober lobby. In addition, because that lobby is heavily used by office workers and tourists, the piece, while privately owned, forms a significant part of Chicago's renowned collection of public art." Lynne Warren, curator of the Museum of Contemporary Art Chicago, added "I think it's a serious loss." *Universe* was dismantled and removed in March 2017.

The title held by Willis Tower (or Sears Tower, if you ask locals) as the tallest building in the world was relinquished in 1998 when the finished Petronas Towers in Kuala Lumpur measured 33 feet higher. That fact did not diminish the striking tower's importance in the minds of Chicagoans or on the personality of the skyline.

NEAR NORTH

VENICE ON LAKE MICHIGAN: ARTHUR T. ALDIS HOUSE

1258 NORTH LAKE SHORE DRIVE

Arthur Taylor Aldis was born far from the Midwest, in St. Albans, Vermont, in 1861. By the time he met Mary Reynolds (who was 11 years younger), he had established a highly successful real estate development business. One has to wonder, if Arthur Aldis had not met the artistically passionate Mary Reynolds, how much different the cultural history of Chicago would have been.

The couple was married on June 8, 1892, and within three years considered creating their permanent home. Despite the gap in time, the *Chicago Tribune* noted their planned residence was "a wedding present to Mrs. Aldis by her father." North Lake Shore Drive with its cooling breezes and lovely views had already attracted many of the city's wealthiest citizens. The Aldis mansion, however, would be like none other on the drive.

The Chicago architectural firm of Holabird & Roche was designing the Marquette Building downtown for Arthur's brother Owen Aldis in 1895. It was likely this connection that resulted in their commission to design the residence at 1258 North Lake Shore Drive. William Holabird and Martin Roche had been in partnership since 1880 and, before the century was out, would produce dozens of tall commercial buildings. For Arthur and Mary Aldis, they stepped out of their comfort zone.

On a block lined with chunky Romanesque Revival "castles," the Aldis house was a Venetian Gothic fantasy. Holabird & Roche had produced a near carbon copy of the 15th-century Palazzo Contarini Fasan in Venice, known as the House of Desdemona, because legend holds that it was here that she was murdered by her jealous husband, Othello.

Above a planar base, the red-brick and limestone upper stories sprouted the same unusual stone balconies and the identical pointed Gothic openings and cornice brackets in the shape of fearsome beasts of the original. Subtle differences were the omission of the Contarini coat of arms, replaced with a square window, and the substitution of a peaked roof for the original hip roof to accommodate a wide dormer on the servant level.

This photograph, taken in 1912, shows the derided "square" door.

An 18th-century owner of the Palazzo Contarini Fasan altered the Gothic doorway on to the canal. Holabird & Roche copied the resulting rectangular opening. It was an anachronism that still offended an architectural purist seven years after the Aldis house was completed. Parisian art critic Antoine Borel spoke on civic art at the Chicago Woman's Club on the afternoon of November 18, 1903. The following day, the *Chicago Tribune* reported, "Architectural Chicago was placed in a bake over of criticism and done to a crisp." Borel started off his tirade saying, "There is no use of talking civic beauty until your skyscrapers are torn down." After stating that Americans "do not feel the same love for home as the French," he attacked the Arthur Aldis house. "The house of Desdemona was built in Venice in the 15th century. In the 18th century its owner, a man of the name of Contarini, spoiled it because he wanted to enlarge its entrance. He changed the Gothic door into an awkward square door and made the side windows much smaller…[and now] your Mr. Arthur T. Aldis has had the house reproduced on the Lake Shore drive with its square door."

The artistic countenance of the mansion would be reflected within its walls. Passionate about the fine arts, Arthur was a governing member of the Art Institute of Chicago, and was nearly single-handedly responsible for bringing the "Armory Show" to Chicago.

On February 17, 1913, the International Exhibition of Modern Art opened in New York City's 69th Regiment Armory. Around 1,300 works by painters and sculptors including Cézanne, Gauguin, Picasso, John Sloan, Edward Hopper, and George Bellows were exhibited. Popularly known as the Armory Show, it is generally credited with changing the direction of art in America.

Four months before the exhibition opened, in October 1912, Aldis had already convinced the organizers to include a Chicago venue in its plans. He met with Walt Kuhn and Arthur B. Davis of the American Association of Painters and Sculptors in Paris and guaranteed them that the Art Institute of Chicago would be available for the show.

Immediately after the Armory Show closed in New York, it opened at the Art Institute. Although only about half the size of the Manhattan show, the Chicago version was added to with works by the local Cubist artist Manierre Dawson. Not everyone who paid the admission price was as forward thinking as Arthur Aldis. As had been the case with New Yorkers in Manhattan, the radical modernity confused and shocked some Midwesterners. The controversy ignited outrage in some, parodying by others, and loud dismissal by many. Nevertheless, just as it had done in New York, the Armory Show changed the course of Chicago art forever, thanks to the efforts of Arthur Aldis.

Mary Aldis was personally involved in the arts as well. Following other socialites, she incorporated music into her entertainments, like the dinner party given for her sister, Mrs. H. S. Hodges, on January 11, 1901, which ended with singing by the well-known soprano Jeanne L'Hommedieu. The Aldises acquired a permanent summer home in Lake Forest that same year, and their compound would become a summer refuge for writers and artists, such as poet Edgar Lee Masters and literary critic, poet, and art patron Harriet Monroe. In 1911, Mary founded the Aldis Playhouse of Lake Forest there. In 1915 she wrote the play *Mrs. Pat and the Law*, and would publish the novel *Drift* in 1918.

Writing would temporarily be put on hold in the summer of 1915. While everyone was asleep on the night of June 4, sneak thieves made off with $2,000 in Mary's jewels. The theft was big news. Even the *Chicago Livestock World* reported, "Included in the loot were heirlooms and letters which Mrs. Aldis treasured more highly than her jewelry."

When police seemed to be getting nowhere, Mary gathered her well-dressed friends and the women turned to detective work. The *Chicago Tribune* ran a headline on June 6 that read, "Society Women A-Sleuthing Go." One of Mary's guests was Mrs. Ray McWilliams, who also lived on Lake Shore Drive during the winter season. "The two women…decided to start out on the trail of the robber, the identity of whom the police had been unable to secure a single clew [*sic*]."

Apparently acting on a hunch that a burglar might escape town on a freight train, Arthur joined the determined women as they headed toward the railroad tracks. This seemingly pointless search was, in fact, slightly successful. "The results were rather discouraging for an hour or more, until finally Mrs. Aldis spied the box of family letters, highly valued as an heirloom, reposing at one side of the highway," reported the *Tribune*. "The letters were written by my parents, many of them being dated before the civil war, and I am most glad to regain them," Mary told reporters.

Before long Arthur and Mary Aldis stopped returning to the Lake Shore Drive mansion each fall. They leased it furnished to Charles B. Pike for several years, and then in February 1920 sold it to Landon C. Rose, president of the North Avenue State Bank. In reporting on the sale on February 11, the *Chicago Tribune* called the "replica of a residence in the city of gondolas...one of the finest examples of Venetian architecture in the country." Rose remained in the house following his divorce from his second wife in 1925. He maintained a country house in La Porte, Indiana, and it was there that the 59-year-old banker died suddenly in December 1931.

The timing of Landon C. Rose's death did not look good for the mansion. The 1920s had already seen many of the grand private homes along Lake Shore Drive demolished and replaced with apartment buildings. Now the Great Depression made maintaining the large residences even more cumbersome. Yet the house survived by being divided into high-end apartments by the president of Howard Blum & Company, a businessman and real estate mogul.

Blum and his wife, Sylvia, lived in the duplex on the third and fourth floors. The financial status of the residents was evidenced on March 30, 1956, when burglars ransacked their apartment and that of Florence Kuttner, who lived on

Other than the attic story, little has changed outwardly on Chicago's replica of Desdemona's house.

the first floor. Miss Kuttner, a 39-year-old advertising executive, was on a world cruise; the Blums were in Miami Beach. The crooks got away with nearly $10,000 worth of Kuttner's possessions; and they stripped the Blum apartment of furs and other valuables of about the same amount.

In April 1960, the 55-year-old Blum was vacationing when he suddenly died. The mansion was returned to a single-family home prior to 1987. Outwardly there is little change to the fanciful home that might be more comfortable looking on to a Venetian canal than Lake Michigan.

RANSOM R. CABLE HOUSE

25 EAST ERIE STREET

America's Successful Men of Affairs, published in 1896, was frank in its depiction of Ransom R. Cable as a self-made man. "With a scanty education, he began life in the lumber business, which he followed until 1856," it said. The son of Ohio pioneers Hiram and Rachel Cable, Ransom indeed started his career with next to nothing. At the age of 21, in 1857, he moved to Rock Island, Illinois, where his uncle was in the mining and railroad business. Aggressive and ambitious, Ransom Cable made a name for himself. He rose to become superintendent and then president of the Peoria & Rock Island Railroad.

On May 9, 1871, the directors of the similarly named Rockford, Rock Island & St. Louis Railroad met in New York City. The *Evening Argus*, of Rock Island, reported, "Since the completion of this road, it has been evident that the men who had control could not run it to the satisfaction of the people, nor with profit to the owners." Ransom Cable was elected president of the reorganized railroad that day. On the new board of directors were his father and brother, Hiram Cable and George W. Cable, as well as his father-in-law, Benjamin Stickney, a St. Louis banker. Also sitting at the table was James M. Buford, a banker from Rock Island.

Cable had married Stickney's daughter, Josephine, on February 15, 1865. The couple would have four children, Hiram, Josephine, Fanny, and Benjamin.

On January 15, 1875, Josephine died from what the *Daily Argus* described as "nervous rheumatism." She was 34 years old and the oldest of the children was just eight. In sentimental Victorian prose the newspaper lamented, "Her youth, her extraordinary loveliness of character, and her sweet little children combine to render her death a crushing blow to her husband and friends."

Five years later, Ransom Cable was president of the Chicago, Rock Island & Pacific Railroad and had amassed a sizable fortune. On February 2, 1880, he married Jane Buford (called Jennie by friends), daughter of his colleague James M. Buford. The wedding took place in the Buford mansion. "After the ceremony the company present sat down to a splendid collation," reported the

Rock Island Argus, "after which a general social time followed." The newspaper deemed the wedding presents "on a scale of magnificence." The palace train car Columbia had been specially provided for the newlyweds' honeymoon trip to Chicago. (George Pullman's "palace train cars" were the last word in comfort and luxury.)

By now, Cable's business interests included several centered in Chicago, such as the Union Stock Yards & Transit Company of Chicago. Founded in 1865, the importance of that firm (and Chicago as a cattle market and meat packing center) skyrocketed with the invention of the refrigerator car in 1868. In 1880, the Union Stock Yards butchered nearly 500,000 head of cattle and a staggering 5.7 million hogs. All of the meat traveled to outlying cities on Cable's railroad.

Gradually Cable realized that moving his home from Rock Island to Chicago would not only be convenient from a business point of view, but would establish the Cables as social players.

The Near North Side area was seeing the construction of mansions of some of Chicago's wealthiest citizens. In 1885, Cable commissioned the architectural firm of Cobb & Frost to design his residence on the building plot at the southwest corner of Cass (later renamed Wabash) and Erie streets.

Construction of the house was completed the following year. The architects had produced an imposing Romanesque Revival pile of rough-cut stone with all the bells and whistles expected in the medieval-inspired style. It featured an obligatory turret with a coned cap, variously sized dormers and chimneys, and an entrance porch with three heavy arches. The choice of light-colored Kasota sandstone gave a pink hue to the hulking house, which softened the weightiness of the architectural style and made the residence more approachable and homelike. The architects strayed from a strictly Romanesque motif by splashing the edifice with Queen Anne elements—clustered chimney pots, quiltlike designs in the stone of two of the upper eaves and in the front bay, and stained-glass transoms.

The *Chicago Tribune* called the house "elaborately constructed," and said, "In interior finish and exterior design it is ranked among the leading residences in Chicago."

The Cable house would be one of the last collaborations for Cobb and Frost. In 1887, the trustees of the newly formed Newberry Library settled on Henry Ives Cobb as its architect. He left the firm in 1888 to devote his entire focus to designing the new building.

A rail magnate's medieval-style mansion.

Twelve years after the Cables moved into the house, they left Erie Street and Chicago. On July 2, 1897, the *Chicago Tribune* reported that Cable "and other members of the household will take their departure for Rock Island, Ill., in a few weeks where they will live in the future." Among the reasons they gave for moving was Jennie Cable's deteriorating health.

Edward G. Mason, an attorney, had already purchased "their beautiful home at Erie and Cass streets" at the time of the article. In payment, he transferred title to his own house at the southwest corner of Michigan Avenue and 12th Street, valued at $125,000—about $3.5 million today. This would provide Ransom Cable a place to stay when he came to Chicago for business.

Mason was described by the *Rock Island Argus* as "one of Chicago's most prominent and successful lawyers." The neighborhood into which his large family would be moving was as fashionable, or more so, than it had been when the mansion was constructed. On the opposite corners were the mansions of H. H. Porter, president of the Chicago & Eastern Illinois Railroad; and S. M. Nickerson, president of the First National Bank.

Tragically, Mason would never live in the Erie Street house. Just as a year-long renovation was being completed, he died on December 18, 1898, of Bright's disease—a kidney condition diagnosed today as acute nephritis. The *Chicago Tribune* explained that he "intended moving into it with Mrs. Mason and the 13 children just before he died."

Mason's 15-member family and domestic staff would have filled the cavernous home, but, the *Chicago Tribune* noted, it "is much too large for a family of moderate size" and therefore it sat for another three years, boarded up and vacant.

Finally on May 6, 1901, the *Tribune* reported that "Judge and Mrs. Barnum, their son, and the Misses Edna and Alice Barnum" had moved into a section of the mansion; "The Cables have been out of their house four years now and it has not since until this month been occupied."

William H. Barnum was a partner in the legal firm Barnum & Barnum and had served as a judge from 1879 to 1884. When his name was considered for judge of Superior Court in 1902, the *Broad Ax* was elated: "In all probability there is not one lawyer within the state of Illinois nor in any part of this great country, who is more favorably known than ex-Judge William H. Barnum."

The *Chicago Eagle* chimed in, "He is a refined and cultured gentleman, of equitable temperament, a deep thinker, a scholar, and a profound and able lawyer." The newspaper felt that his "name is respected by every good citizen of Chicago, independent of race, creed, party or politics."

Around the same time, plans were being laid for the lavish wedding ceremony of Robert Hall McCormick Jr. to New York socialite Eleanor Russell Morris. Robert's parents purchased the Erie Street mansion as a wedding present, even though the couple initially intended to live most of the time in New York City.

Chicago and New York society filled the fashionable St. Bartholomew's Church in Manhattan on January 22, 1903 for the couple's wedding. The reception afterward was held in the mansion of the bride's parents at 12 West 53rd Street, just off Fifth Avenue.

Robert McCormick made his own way in the world, despite his father's boundless wealth. He had met Eleanor while working for a while in New York as a lawyer. They moved to Chicago during the 1904 presidential campaign. After making a few speeches, according to the *Chicago Tribune*, and appearing that he might take on politics, McCormick walked into the office of John J. Healy, the state's attorney, in the Criminal Court Building and asked for a job, emphasizing to Mr. Healy, "I don't ask for a salary. I want to work here for the experience."

In April 1908, Robert McCormick became assistant United States district attorney. On May 10, the *Tribune* remarked on his remarkable work schedule and ethic. He was at the office by 9 a.m., "lunch often is snatched hastily," and he "leaves for the big mansion, the Cable house…when his work is done, and not before."

McCormick's busy schedule was put on hold the following year, when he took his wife to Europe. The *Chicago Tribune* reported on August 15, 1909, "They will spend the summer touring in their automobile, the machine having been shipped ahead of them. Most of the time will be devoted to France."

Entertainments in the grand home were often lavish. When Robert's unmarried sister Mildred came for the winter season of 1909-10, she met all of Chicago society. On Tuesday, January 11, 1910, the McCormicks hosted a dinner dance for 70 guests. To provide additional fun, "Milani, a prestidigitator," performed magic tricks. A cotillion ended the evening.

Many of Eleanor McCormick's social events surrounded her charity work. Following Germany's invasion of Belgium in 1914, a large number of wealthy women in Boston, Philadelphia, New York, and Chicago threw themselves into fundraising to aid the victims. On April 27, 1915, Eleanor hosted a raffle of Belgian laces to raise money. Among the items most coveted was a black lace shawl that was sent by Belgium's Queen Elisabeth through her representative, Countess Marie de Hemptinne.

The *Tribune* wrote, "Mrs. McCormick had opened her reception room, out of which winds a most exquisite old English stairway, and her library, and the walls were beautified with the most beautiful bedspreads of Cluny combined with linen, delicate cloths of Battenberg designs. There were aprons and caps and laces by the yard, and there were designs the like of which, probably never before has been gathered together in one exhibition."

In 1925, the focus of entertainments would turn to the McCormicks' debutante daughter, Eleanor. Her formal introduction to society began on December 23 with a dinner party. It would be nearly a decade before Eleanor would marry at the family's summer estate in Bar Harbor, Maine.

The changing tenor of the neighborhood was evidenced in May 1941 when the Robert Hall McCormick residence was sold to brothers Eugene J. and John J. Carroll for just $43,000, in the neighborhood of $700,000 today. Partners in the undertaking firm John Carroll Sons, they contracted architect Albert A. Schwartz to renovate and rebuild the old mansion as a funeral home.

John Carroll was one of the city's first undertakers, opening his business in 1851. When Abraham Lincoln's funeral cortège reached Chicago in 1865, it was John Carroll who drove the team of horses pulling the hearse along Michigan Avenue.

The venerable firm would remain in the former Cable mansion for decades. Mourners would file through its doors for the wakes and funerals of everyday and celebrated Chicagoans. When Cardinal Samuel Stritch died in Rome in May 1958, thousands lined the 18-mile route from O'Hare International Airport to the Erie Street funeral home to glimpse the hearse. In 1965, the home received the bodies of former Olympic swimmer George Herbert Taylor and Cardinal Albert Meyer. In 1966, the funeral of Chicago Bears' attorney Charles F. Short Jr. was held here.

Today the Cable-McCormick mansion is home to Driehaus Capital Management. The firm commissioned the architectural firm Antunovich Associates to renovate and restore the mansion for its corporate headquarters. The sympathetic project resulted in the restoration of the peach-colored exterior to its 1886 appearance.

Too large for a family "of moderate size", the Cable House is now an unusual corporate headquarters.

CHICAGO WATER TOWER AND PUMPING STATION

806 AND 821 NORTH MICHIGAN AVENUE

Around the globe, certain structures, some of them rather quirky, have become icons of their locations. Among them are the Eiffel Tower, the Statue of Liberty, Tower Bridge, and the Sphinx. By the turn of the last century, the fanciful but functional Chicago Avenue Water Tower, as it was known then, had become the symbol of the city's resilience and determination.

Chicago has the natural advantage of sitting next to the waters of Lake Michigan; but as the city rapidly grew, officials struggled to extract adequate supplies of fresh water for its inhabitants.

On May 1, 1840, a New York engineer, John P. Foss, arrived in Chicago. His foresight and genius would help transform the settlement into a thriving metropolis. That year, seven years after Chicago was incorporated as a town and just three as a city, he helped organize the Chicago Hydraulic Company, which constructed the first pumping station and reservoir at the corner of Michigan Avenue and Lake Street. The city's first water pipes—hollowed-out cedar logs joined by iron bands—distributed fresh water for a distance of two miles.

In 1854, 591,000 gallons were being pumped daily for the city's 65,000 residents. By 1866, even with the addition of a second pumping station, the needs of the growing city were not being met. There were by now more than 300,000 citizens needing as much as 21.7 million gallons every day.

To solve the problem, city engineer Ellis S. Chesbrough (who had already designed Chicago's sewer system, the nation's first) devised a five-foot-diameter tunnel that burrowed two miles into the lake, at a depth of 60 feet, thereby avoiding pollution by the shoreline. Almost simultaneously, construction of a pumping station and water tower got under way on shore. On March 25, 1867, the cornerstone of the tower was laid. The tower and

In October 1871, the Water Tower stood among the devastation of downtown Chicago after the Great Fire.

the pumping station were designed by 49-year-old William W. Boyington, who had trained in New York as both an engineer and an architect. He had settled in Chicago in 1853 and was by now one of the city's chief architects.

Victorians saw no reason why decidedly utilitarian structures should not be visually appealing. Boyington's Gothic Revival pumping station and tower reflected the influence of New York architect James Renwick Jr., whose many similar designs included the Smithsonian Institution Building in Washington, D.C. Square-headed Gothic moldings, crenellated rooflines and turrets, and lancet windows made the industrial, limestone-faced structures romantic fantasies (although the tower itself clothed a mundane 138-foot standpipe, used to equalize water pressure from the pumping station).

The two harmonious structures were completed in 1869. Two years later, in October 1871, the tower and pumping station would stand above the ruins of a Chicago devastated by the Great Fire, two of the few buildings to survive in the area. Chicagoans embraced them as symbols of hope, and rebuilt the city at a furious pace around them.

Not everyone was so moved. Irish playwright, poet, essayist, and novelist Oscar Wilde was well known for his often acerbic tongue. During his

American tour of 1882 he visited Chicago, and in May described the water tower in the *Pall Mall Gazette* as an affront to good taste and "a castellated monstrosity with pepper boxes stuck all over it."

In 1896, the massive engine in the Chicago Avenue Pumping Station was showing its age. On April 17, the *Chicago Tribune* reported that it had been shut down for repairs, and as a result, "everything higher than the second floor on the North and Northwest Sides is experiencing a water famine." The smaller engines were still in operation, but were unable to keep up the supply. "The big engine has been in service night and day for

The Pumping Station today, with its machines and pipes, makes a surprisingly appropriate setting for theatrical productions.

many years," said the article, "its daily task being to force 36,000,000 gallons of water through the mains, and this is its first extended vacation."

Even an overhaul of the engine could not bring the pumping station up to the necessary capacity. On August 27 the following year, the commissioner of public works inspected the station. He reported, "The pumps have not been working well, and I wanted to see what was the matter. There is only one pump at that station worthy of being called a pump. A new station will have to be built there sooner or later, and in my opinion the sooner the better."

Two months later, city chemist William Maharg tested the water in all the pumping stations. The results were not good for the Chicago Avenue plant. He described the quality of water as "bad." Improvements were urgently needed to supply the city with fresh water. On November 4, 1897, city engineer Erickson completed his plans for remodeling the Chicago Avenue Pumping Station, with two new 20-million-gallon pumps and one 30-million-gallon pump to be installed. The plans, thankfully, did not include visible changes to the structure.

The romanticism of the neo-Gothic exterior of the Pumping Station belies its no-nonsense, industrial interior.

On May 22, 1901, John Ahern "danced a jig," according to the *Chicago Tribune*, in front of the Chicago Avenue Pumping Station. He was aided in celebrating his 48th anniversary as a pumping station employee by Mayor John Wentworth (who apparently did not jig). Now more than 80 years old, Ahern had been hired in 1855 at the original pumping station. The *Tribune* noted, "During the period when the tower of the water works was selected by many as a convenient place from which to leap into eternity, Ahern was relieved from his work as oiler and stationed in the tower to watch those suspected of suicidal intent. No suicides occurred during his vigil."

City engineer Erickson was back to update the Chicago Avenue station in 1906. The *Chicago Tribune* was outraged that within the half-million-dollar outlay $18,000 was allocated for two visitors' galleries, added so Chicagoans could see the giant turbines at work. Erickson was unapologetic. "We are spending about $500,000 on improving the Chicago avenue station, and I believe something should be done for ornamentation as well as utility," he said.

Despite the improvements, danger of disease had still not been eliminated. Residents of Chicago's North Side were terrified in 1914 when an outbreak of typhoid fever erupted. On December 18, the *Chicago Tribune* reported, "Altogether there are about forty cases in the city, and half of these are in the relatively small area supplied by the Chicago avenue station."

Inspectors visited the pumping station, where they found that three workmen repairing a leak all had typhoid fever. After a week of investigation, health commissioner Dr. George B. Young announced, "We finally came to the conclusion the

The Water Tower as it appeared around the turn of the 20th century.

spread of the disease must be due to the water." He pronounced the water from the Chicago Avenue station to be "the worst in the city." The water in the pumping station was treated with chemicals, and consumers were cautioned to boil it before drinking.

By mid-century, Chicago's number of pumping stations had grown to 12, and today they pump more than 357 billion gallons into the mains every year. None commands the affection reserved for the pre-Fire Chicago Water Tower and Pumping Station, now retired as an art gallery, theater, and tourist office.

Once the tallest building in the city, the 154-foot Chicago Water Tower and its accompanying Pumping Station are dwarfed by the soaring steel-and-glass skyscrapers of modern Chicago, yet these mid-Victorian survivors are more symbolic of the city that refused to quit than almost any other structures.

ENGINE COMPANY 98
FIRE STATION
202 EAST CHICAGO AVENUE

The *Power Wagon*, a journal for motorized vehicle enthusiasts, published the article "Chicago the Pioneer User of Motor Apparatus" in April 1913. In it, the author described the district covered by Engine Company 98.

The area included the properties "between North Avenue, Lake Michigan, the Chicago River and Milton Avenue, an area of perhaps two miles. This section includes many fashionable residences and $1000-a-month apartments along Lake Shore Drive at the north end, and millions of dollars' worth of warehouse and dock property at the south." The article added, "Along the western side of the territory are hundreds of old fire-traps where the poorer classes live and these contribute toward making the fire risk very high."

The "old fire-traps" may have contributed to the high fire risk, but it was the fashionable residences that had everything to do with the design of Engine Company 98's firehouse. At the turn of the last century, the mansions of some of Chicago's wealthiest citizens filled the two-mile area, and the threat of fire was a constant fear. The Department of Public Works requested bids for a brick and stone fire station for a new fire company in the neighborhood. The department's annual report promised, "This building will be, when completed, one of the finest in the City."

Indeed, the plans drawn by municipal architect Charles F. Hermann far exceeded other fire stations in the interior details (described by the 1903 annual report as "first-class in every particular"), architectural beauty, and cost. Traditional speculation suggests that wealthy residents, if not the millionaire Potter Palmer alone, personally provided the funds for a structure in keeping with their fine residences.

The newly formed Engine Company No. 98 moved into the new station house in October 1904. A quaint, neo-Gothic fantasy faced in rough-cut gray limestone, it had cost $19,975 to build (about $550,000 today). A miniature castle for a single horse-drawn fire engine, its central truck bay sat within a gaping pointed Gothic arch. Corner turrets clung to the second story and

The quaint neo-Gothic fantasy fire station originally also housed horses to pull the fire engine.

square-headed Gothic drip moldings crowned the openings on the front elevation. Blind arrow slits in the turrets and crisp crenellations above the cornice readied the structure for imaginary battle.

Along with the fire engine, the company's horses were housed on the ground floor. Glazed brick walls on this level assured sanitation and provided easy cleaning. Upstairs, the firefighters had the comforts of a marble-manteled fireplace and top-of-the-line oaken lockers.

As is the case today, firefighters dealt with far more than battling blazes. On September 5, 1912, for instance, the men found themselves temporary nursemaids when a two-week-old baby girl was left in a basket outside the firehouse.

The dangers of their job were apparent when the vacant Armour & Company tannery building on Wade Street caught fire on June 3 the following year. Homeless men had been sleeping in the boarded-up structure and it was surmised that they had accidentally caused the blaze. The inferno was so intense at one point that residents in the cottages across Wade Street frantically hauled their furniture on to the street, fearing their homes were next to go. Flying sparks did momentarily set several roofs on fire.

Pipeman Charles Nigg was inside the burning tannery when a portion of it collapsed. A timber crashed down on him, breaking his left leg. By the time he was removed to the hospital, his injuries were considered severe. The three-block-long, two-story building was a total loss.

Another pipeman with the company, Ed Ryan, narrowly escaped a different type of jeopardy on August 14, 1914. He was called before the Civil Service board on the serious charge of being drunk on duty. The lucky fireman walked away relieved when the board dismissed his case for "insufficient evidence."

During the summer of 1924, the men of Engine Company 98 spent much time in the side yard, tending their vegetable garden. Early that year, *Fire Magazine* launched its "first annual vegetable garden contest." In September, judges visited the various participating stations, taking into consideration "Neatness, carefully planned plots, and keeping the garden clean with every inch of ground utilized from the beginning to the end of the season."

The *Chicago Tribune* reported on September 14, "Fighting mosquitoes, weeds, bugs and worms all summer won the first cash prize of $25 for Engine Company No. 98, 202 East Chicago Avenue." Assuming that the 14 company members who worked on the garden shared the prize equally, they each got $1.78 for their troubles. And free vegetables.

One of the engine company's most colorful jobs involved motion picture star Ronald Colman's wife, Thelma. On the night of November 25, 1927, she and her poodle attended a party near Michigan and Chicago avenues. Prohibition did not dull the festivities, and champagne and liquor flowed. Thelma overindulged.

She later explained that she left the party to hail a cab, but finding one standing empty at the curb, she "took a sudden notion to drive it herself." Thelma Colman flashed up Lake Shore Drive at a great speed. She had neglected, however, to release the parking brake. The heat of the friction ignited a fire, prompting the *Tribune* to report the following morning, "Gold coast residents may be interested in learning that what appeared to be a comet sweeping along Lake Shore drive last night was in reality nothing more than a young woman driving a blazing taxicab with her poodle dog as the sole passenger."

The police and Engine Company 98 were successful in stopping the vehicle and extinguishing the flames, "but failed to extinguish her enthusiasm to go places and do things," said the newspaper. The poodle barked ferociously at the uniformed men while its mistress protested her arrest. The incensed woman would not cooperate at the police station and refused to give a local address. "Police said, however, that any fan mail will be delivered to her in the matron's quarters until future notice," explained the *Tribune*.

A multi-alarm conflagration on May 19, 1934 resulted in, according to the *Chicago Tribune*, "103 companies at the fire, consisting of 102 pumpers and 22 trucks." Among those responding was Engine Company 98. The massive fire destroyed the entire complex of early 20th-century stockyards buildings on the city's Southwest Side. The Stockyards Inn, the Saddle and Sirloin Club, and the Great Pavilion, which had been home to international livestock shows since 1900—all were gutted, despite the firefighters' valiant efforts. Lost in the art gallery in the Saddle and Sirloin Club were portraits of 300 livestock breeders, agriculture leaders, packers, scientists, and educators.

Every firehouse, at least by reputation, had a mascot and in 1942 Engine Company 98 adopted a one-year-old bulldog puppy, Libby. On March 15, the dog ventured outside the bay doors and suddenly disappeared. Manly firefighters despaired over their lost mascot. Stories appeared in the Chicago newspapers. Three days later, Libby was back. A stranger had returned the puppy, explaining that he thought it was a stray. Domestic contentment returned to the fire station.

The firehouse got a new mascot, of sorts, in the 1960s. Around 1909, a boy named George Inar Anderson began hanging around the city's fire stations. By the second half of the century, according to the *Chicago Tribune*, "Just about every fireman in the city" knew him; the newspaper called him "one of the greatest fire buffs the city has ever known."

For six decades George visited a station house every day, talking to the firefighters, learning the fire codes and regulations. In the early '60s, he started dropping into Engine Company 98. Every morning he would share morning coffee with the men and talk fire talk. But then, one morning during Christmas week in 1969, Anderson failed to show up. He did not come by the next morning either. Firefighters from Engine Company 98 called at the seedy Marshall Hotel where he lived to make sure everything was all right. They were informed he had died and his body was in the morgue.

The 77-year-old handyman had no family and no money. Word of his death spread rapidly throughout the fire department. One fireman, Louis DePinto, lamented, "We loved the old guy. We had no idea so many firemen in all parts of the city knew him." Firefighter Howard Johnston donated a space in his family plot for George, so he would not be buried in a pauper's grave. On December 29, 1969, the funeral of a lonely old man, who had seemed to have no friends, was crowded with men in uniform.

Charles F. Hermann's charming utilitarian structure continues as a firehouse today. The horses and old steam engine are, of course, long gone, and the bay doors and windows have been replaced. Yet the quaint limestone castle is otherwise little changed.

FOURTH PRESBYTERIAN CHURCH
126 EAST CHESTNUT STREET AT NORTH MICHIGAN AVENUE

The Fourth Presbyterian Church of Chicago was organized through the merging of the North Presbyterian Church and the Westminster Presbyterian Church on February 12, 1871. The joined congregations shared the existing North Presbyterian Church building, on the corner of Wabash and Grand avenues.

Renovations to the church were initiated and the rededication was held on Sunday, October 8, 1871. The timing could not have been worse. Even as the congregants celebrated their refurbished church, the first sparks of the Great Chicago Fire were igniting. The *Continent* reported later, "The evening services were just concluded when the heavens were alive with an increasing and horrifying tempest of wind, smoke and burning brands sweeping away homes, churches and possessions in the great historic fire…. The church building, of course, was a total loss."

For months afterward, the congregation worshipped in borrowed parlors and rooms, until a new structure was erected on the northwest corner of Rush and Superior Streets. The congregation worshipped uneventfully in that church for more than three decades, until the departure of the Reverend William Robson Notman in 1908. Fourth Presbyterian's search for a new pastor would cause waves from the Midwest to the East Coast.

On December 19 that year, the charismatic and highly regarded Reverend Dr. John Timothy Stone arrived in Chicago from Baltimore, where he was pastor of the Brown Memorial Presbyterian Church. Stone met and impressed officials of Fourth Presbyterian, who offered him the vacant position. The news quickly leaked back to Baltimore and a firestorm of a different sort ensued. Two days later the *Chicago Tribune* reported that "Baltimore public officials, labor unions, and the congregation of the Brown Memorial Presbyterian Church" were embarking on "strong efforts" to stop Reverend Stone from taking up his new appointment. "Seldom has so spirited a contest as that over Dr. Stone been waged between leading churches," it said.

Reverend Stone was to preach to the Fourth Presbyterian Church congregation on the evening of December 21, but before the service even began, telegrams were being delivered to his hotel room, including one from the Mayor of Baltimore. The *Tribune* said they all, in effect, pleaded that he "stand by Baltimore."

It had been assumed that Stone would accept the position on Sunday night; but the pressure from Baltimore was so great that he delayed his trip home while he reconsidered. In the end, Baltimore was crestfallen to lose its pastor, and the Fourth Presbyterian Church of Chicago, where Reverend Stone took the pulpit in the spring of 1909, was elated.

The Near North Side continued to grow, as did the programs of Fourth Presbyterian under the Reverend Stone. The *Continent* explained later, "Growing congregations and membership, need of larger and better equipped facilities for worship and work, and neighborhood problems made it advisable in the spring of 1911 to consider new and larger structures to carry out the work." "New and larger" they would indeed be.

Land was acquired three blocks away at what is now Michigan Avenue and East Chestnut Street. At the time, and until the opening of the Michigan Avenue Bridge in 1920, the site was far less prominent than it is today. The cornerstone was laid on Tuesday afternoon, September 17, 1912. Among the items in the box placed inside it were two volumes of the Holy Bible (the King James and the American Revised versions), various religious tracts and the latest issue of the church monthly newsletter, photographs of Reverend Stone and of the existing church building, copies of that day's local newspapers, an American flag, coins and stamps minted in 1912, and the silver trowel used in laying the mortar.

Church officials had turned to ecclesiastical and collegiate architects Cram, Goodhue & Ferguson of New York, and Chicago architect Howard Van Doren Shaw, to design a quadrangle of related structures. The church was, of course, the focal point of the complex. Connecting it to the manse, or rectory, would be a charming cloister. Around the open courtyard with its playing fountain (a gift of Howard Van Doren Shaw), were the Bible school building, and the men's and women's club house.

Dr. John Timothy Stone reads the service before the lowering of the cornerstone into place on Tuesday, September 17, 1912.

In 1914, Fourth Presbyterian Church sat in isolation on the future Michigan Avenue before the 1920 bridge over the river encouraged many neighbors.

On October 6, 1913, as the group of buildings neared completion, the *American Stone Trade* commented, "The whole exterior presents an impressively beautiful picture in Gothic art, spires and pinnacles marking the church structure and cloister, gables and dormers distinguishing all of the buildings." The *Chicago Tribune* predicted on January 14, 1914 that among Chicago's 1,000 churches, this would be "the largest, most costly, and most cathedral-like of them all."

The Fourth Presbyterian Church of Chicago and its related buildings were completed in 1914 and dedicated in May that year. Faced in limestone, the massive Gothic Revival church structure spread 95 feet wide and stretched back 103 feet. The ornate stone steeple rose nearly 204 feet from the sidewalk. Above the entrance, a carved stone screen in the French High Gothic Revival style sat before a deeply recessed arched opening for the immense stained-glass window.

Inside were accommodations for 1,150 worshippers on the main floor and 350 more in the three balconies. The cost of the project, estimated at $650,000 at the time of the cornerstone laying, had risen to $1.25 million— nearly $30 million today. The magnificence of the structure was possible only because, as the *Chicago Tribune* put it, it was "backed by the almost limitless wealth of its congregation."

The imposing church and the fashionable tone of its congregants attracted some celebrated out-of-town visitors. The *Chicago Livestock World* reported on August 2, 1915 that "Col. Theodore Roosevelt stopped off in Chicago between trains yesterday to scratch the back of Rajah, the biggest tiger in Lincoln Park Zoo, and to have a good time generally in Cy De Vry's menagerie. Mrs. Roosevelt, who had been reported ill in dispatches, accompanied her husband

and was sufficiently recovered from her indisposition to attend services at the Fourth Presbyterian Church."

Other observers were less impressed by affluence and influence. Five months later, when Fourth Presbyterian hosted an event for the United Charities, the *Day Book* was sarcastic in its reporting. "The Fourth Presbyterian church, where the millionaires and 'esses of Lake Shore drive go every Sunday to be comforted, is 'honored' by an exhibit of the United Charities. The church, located at Chestnut st. and Lake Shore drive [*sic*], covers half of a city block and houses the wealthiest congregation in Chicago—a fitting place for a charity exhibit."

The following year, on February 12, 1916, the same newspaper published a letter to the editor from A. Johnson that read, "To the Rev. Dr. T. Stone, Fourth Presbyterian church: Is it true that your parishioners presented you with a $5,000 automobile last Christmas and at the same time reduced the scrub woman's wages $1 per week?"

The family of R. Hall McCormick was among the affluent congregants of Fourth Presbyterian Church at the time. His daughter, Mildred, was introduced to society that fall. Young and beautiful, she caught the eye of another congregant, 26-year-old Roy Noland. Originally from New York, he had come west to study at the University of Chicago and later at the Moody Bible Institute.

Mildred caught his attention in the vast sanctuary during services and, although she never noticed Roy, he was smitten. In time he was obsessed. The *Day Book* reported, in florid terms, on February 23, 1917, "Finally maddened by the haunting memory of her whom he worshipped from a distance, he penned his love." When Noland's avalanche of love letters could no longer be ignored, Mildred's father had him arrested. The *Day Book* said he now "told his love to the other people of brilliantly painted illusions in the psychopathic hospital." He had been committed to the hospital awaiting trial.

Five years later, it would be a McCormick who was dejected because of love. On January 2, 1922, Alister McCormick prepared for his wedding to heiress Mary Baker. The pews of Fourth Presbyterian Church were filled with Chicago's most socially prominent citizens, the assembled guests and the dashing groom awaiting the arrival of the bride. She never came. She left, instead, for Europe with her mother. Later that year, Alister McCormick caught up with them in Paris. The *Chicago Tribune* said, "There were reports that he and Mary soon would be wed. This time the ceremony might be in England, where Alister's brother lived."

But it was not to be. Mary Baker continued her travels and romances. She later quipped, "A wise girl should always obey her hunches and I always will."

The on-again off-again romance was publicized worldwide. And at least one newspaper, the *Coconino Sun* in Arizona, had had enough by July 14 and remarked, ungrammatically, "Mary Langdon Baker is still gaining notoriety every few weeks as she changes her mind about marrying Alister McCormick. The waiting world is almost halted and are getting wild-eyed over this flip-flopping flapper whose personality a good, solid hair brush should be applied vigorously, until she forgot all about money and marriage."

Following McCormick's humiliation at the altar and the widespread publicity, a new phrase was used when someone failed to show up at a party—the host had been "Mary Bakered."

Fourth Presbyterian Church was the scene of the somber funeral of Senator Joseph Medill McCormick on February 27, 1925. A co-owner of the *Chicago Tribune*, the 48-year-old had lost his party's nomination for reelection in 1924. He was found dead in a hotel room in Washington, D.C. on February 25. While the family kept the circumstances of his death private, it was eventually revealed as a suicide.

The *Urbana Daily Courier* announced that the ceremony would be carried out "with utter absence of the pomp of high office which he held at the time of this sudden death." McCormick had left strict instructions that there was to be no funeral oration; only prayer, scripture reading, and singing by the choir.

The McCormick funeral was followed six months later by another subdued service for an esteemed congregant. The United States Ambassador to Japan, Edgar A. Bancroft, died in office in July; his funeral was held in Fourth Presbyterian on August 17, 1925. Despite the attendance of the Vice President of the United States, high-ranking Japanese officials, and American diplomats, the service was "of the utmost simplicity," according to a newspaper. That simplicity, however, did not extend to the family's decorating the sanctuary with twelve 20-foot-tall pine trees, brought in from the Great North Woods, and "great vases of flowers ten feet high."

Among the most illustrious funerals held in the church was that of Marshall Field, the entrepreneur and philanthropist, on the afternoon of September 21, 1965. Those sending tributes included the President and First Lady, Lyndon B. and Lady Bird Johnson.

On December 9, 1936, the congregation received an unexpected and precious relic. When the Great Fire raged in 1871, Charles M. Howe, then an elder of the Northminster Presbyterian Church, grabbed the silver chalice from the altar. As many other Chicago families were doing, the Howes buried their family silver in the backyard. Charles placed the chalice in among their items.

By the time the Howes dug up their things, church officials assumed the chalice was lost and had purchased a replacement. They gave the old chalice back to Charles Howe as a token. Now, more than 65 years later, Howe's daughter, Mrs. F. W. Crosby, presented the chalice to the Fourth Presbyterian Church.

A striking testament to the spirit of acceptance of the congregation came during World War II. With anti-German and anti-Japanese sentiment rampant throughout the nation, Fourth Presbyterian's nearly 150 Japanese members worshipped in the main church (albeit in separate services). Each Sunday following the Japanese services, 1,450 naval cadets housed at Northwestern University's Abbott Hall filed into the church for their service.

Another example of Fourth Presbyterian's outreach occurred in July 1971. A group of Native Americans had taken over the abandoned Belmont Harbor Nike missile site on June 14. "All we've done," explained one protester, "is to make a military reservation into an Indian reservation." The *Chicago Tribune* reported the following day, "The Indians say they have been smoldering for a long time because of the need for low-cost housing in their North Side community."

Negotiations ended badly on July 1, when officials lost patience. What the *Tribune* deemed a "skirmish" ended with a dozen Native Americans arrested, several complaining of minor injuries, and about 80 taking up temporary residence in the basement of Fourth Presbyterian. Church elders acted as go-betweens between them and state officials. The *Tribune* noted, "The Indians said they would spend the night in the church and continue their search for 'suitable housing' today."

The Fourth Presbyterian Church continues in its concern for the community by maintaining the Replogle Center for Counseling and Well-Being, which the church describes as "an oasis for those seeking direction in the midst of chaos, loss, or trauma." It stages art exhibitions and, in 2004, established the Fine Arts Council to support art-related initiatives.

The passing of a century has not harmed the magnificent building; the clinging ivy and weathered lines have perhaps made it that much lovelier. The charming complex is a welcomed urban oasis among the retail stores and modern structures that crowd in around it.

Skyscrapers in the 21st century replace the sky of 1914 behind Fourth Presbyterian

A cloister connects the church to the manse.

CARL C. HEISEN HOUSE

1250 NORTH LAKE SHORE DRIVE

Chicago historian John Drury recalled in his 1941 *Old Chicago Houses*, "When the Near North Side began to decline as a bon ton neighborhood, the Gold Coast along Lake Shore Drive began to rise. Here was a wide, quiet thoroughfare, shaded by rows of trees, that paralleled the shore of the lake for almost half a mile before reaching Lincoln Park. It was an ideal residential street, fronting on a blue inland sea. One after another came new mansions on either side of the Potter Palmer 'castle,' until Lake Shore Drive was solidly built with fine houses."

Among those new mansions was that of Carl Constantine Heisen at 65 Lake Shore Drive (later renumbered 1250). Heisen contracted Ohio-born architect Frank Bion Abbott in 1889 to design his new home, which according to the *Columbian Exposition Dedication Ceremonies Memorial* four years later, cost "upward of one hundred thousand dollars." The book noted, "Mr. Abbott has designed some of the handsomest buildings in Chicago."

Abbott turned to the immensely popular Richardsonian Romanesque style for the project. Architect Henry Hobson Richardson's personal take on Romanesque Revival resulted in romantic, medieval-looking structures of chunky, rough-cut granite or brownstone. His houses, churches, and civic structures often included robust arches, fanciful turrets, and battlements.

Completed in 1891, Heisen's fortresslike residence rose three stories above an English basement. Abbott rounded every corner and managed to make the mansion both imposing and charming. A flight of stone steps spilled to the sidewalk from the forbidding arched entrance within a corner tower. At the third floor, the tower transformed to a round, open balcony with a conical cap. The deep loggias of the parlor and second-story levels were perfect for sitting on warm summer nights and taking in the lake view.

The Heisens had four children, William (known as Willie), Carl Jr., Myrtle Celia, and Mamie. The family had barely moved into their new home when it was the scene of a funeral. Willie was 19 years old and had fallen in love with a 21-year-old woman named Le Claire. He became the victim of blackmail, in which she seemed to be somehow involved.

Realizing his predicament, the teen confided in his father in October 1891. Carl later told authorities, "When Willie and I talked about his troubles in my office, I asked him who was this man who was persecuting him. He intimated that he was a West Side lawyer, but refused to give his name or address."

On Sunday afternoon, October 11, Willie visited Miss Le Claire, who lived in the boarding house of Mrs. Strong at 373 Superior Street. The *Chicago Tribune* noted, "Miss Le Claire is said to be of prepossessing appearance, tall, handsomely formed, and 21 years old; such a person as might readily be supposed to make an impression upon a youth of 19." It appears that Willie Heisen proposed to the woman he loved, yet who was blackmailing him. He left with neither an acceptance nor a rejection, but with some hope.

Later that day a man called on the teen. The *Tribune* reported, "It is believed that he was the go-between for funds for the blackmailing woman." Whatever they spoke about, it was too much for Willie to bear. That night, he committed suicide in the Wellington Hotel downtown.

The *Tribune* ran the headline, "Heisen Died For Love," and reported that detectives found a note in his pocket, which read, "Called at Strong's on Superior street at 2:30 p.m. and met Miss L. She promised to wait six months before giving answer." The journalist had already decided, "Unrequited love is undoubtedly the cause of the suicide of young Heisen." His father had another theory. "I believe that Willie, who was very sensitive, had been goaded by his persecutors until he was insane."

The "strictly private" funeral services, according to the *Tribune*, were held in the new Lake Shore mansion.

Following the expected period of mourning for Willie, things slowly returned to normal in the Heisen household. In April 1897, society pages noted that Mrs. Heisen had returned to town after spending the winter season in Colorado Springs. The *Chicago Blue Book* informed socialites that her "Receiving Day" was on Mondays.

Tragedy seemed likely to repeat itself in 1906 when daughter Myrtle contracted a severe case of rheumatic fever. The recent debutante recovered, however, and on May 29 that year she was married to Malcolm Graeme Bruce in the mansion's drawing rooms. The *Tribune* reported, "Throughout the house the decorations were done in pink and white, roses and swansonia [*sic*] predominating, with masses of greens as a background." Following the ceremony, a reception was held in the house before the newlyweds left on their "wedding journey."

Now intimidated by a high-rise apartment building, the Heisen House, along with other mansions, once lorded over a fashionable stretch of Lake Shore Drive.

Carl C. Heisen Jr. had moved to New Haven, Connecticut by 1907. He fell so seriously ill in December that year that his mother left Chicago to take care of him. She sat at his bedside through the Christmas and New Year's holidays. He seemed to be improving and there were hopes that he could accompany his mother back to Chicago for his sister Mamie's wedding on January 7, 1908, but he relapsed.

No doubt torn, Mrs. Heisen arrived alone in Chicago on January 6, just in time for the second wedding in the mansion. The *Chicago Tribune* called the bride, "one of the handsomest of the Chicago women." Most likely because of Carl Jr.'s absence and ill health, the newspaper noted the marriage would be "quietly celebrated."

Nevertheless, the Heisens threw a dinner party later that day "for the bridal party and out of town guests, later taking the company to the theater." Mrs. Heisen returned to New Haven and her ailing son within the next few days.

Four months later, on April 29, 1908, society pages reported that Mamie "planned a pleasant surprise for her parents... by arriving unexpectedly yesterday to be their guest during the week." And the following year, in October, both daughters came for a month's stay.

Glittering entertainments in the Lake Shore Drive mansion that next winter season would not be hosted by the Heisens. They leased the furnished house to the esteemed author Hobart Chatfield-Taylor and his wife, Rose. On February 18, 1909, 80 guests heard the former Shakespearean actor George Riddle here. The *Cambridge Tribune* said of him, "Mr. Riddle has been content to rest upon his youthful laurels as an actor, and to please the public with frequent tastes of his quality as a reader." Riddle's readings of Shakespeare were accompanied by classical music. Prominent Chicagoans in the drawing room that afternoon included Mrs. Harold McCormick, Mr. and Mrs. John Alden Carpenter, and Dr. and Mrs. Henry Hooper.

Carl Heisen Jr. married Dorothy Dickson in 1914. The 21-year-old bride was the daughter of a well-known newspaper man (he had scooped other journalists by interviewing Jesse James) and an American feminist. The newlyweds became enthralled by the ballroom dance craze popularized by Irene and Vernon Castle. Dancing initially for fun, they became so accomplished they were soon dancing professionally in nightclubs and vaudeville theaters. No doubt to protect his family's reputation, Carl changed the spelling of his surname to Hyson.

By 1917, the couple had relocated to Manhattan where they appeared in Broadway shows and the Ziegfeld Follies. At one point Carl was considered America's top male ballroom dancer. Eventually, however, Dorothy stole the limelight. After English impresario Charles B. Cochran relocated the couple to London, Dorothy Dickson became the sensation of the West End, performing without her husband. They divorced in 1936.

Well before then, at least by 1912, the former Heisen mansion had become home to the George B. Harris Sr. family. Harris had retired as president of the Burlington Railroad in 1910, but stayed on as its chairman of the board.

On the afternoon of November 7, 1912, Mary Rose Harris was alone in the mansion. While she busied herself downstairs, a brazen burglar entered a second-floor window. Before the two surprised each other, the well-dressed robber had pocketed $700 of Mary Rose's jewelry. "Mrs. Harris, according to the police, became hysterical when she discovered the burglar on the second floor of the house," reported the *Chicago Tribune*. She described him as "about 28 years old and wearing a stiff black hat, tan shoes, and a light suit of clothes."

Mary Rose Harris died on June 1, 1917, leaving her husband the bulk of her $250,000 estate. The following year, in May, the 70-year-old Harris suffered a stroke, which "his friends believe will not prove serious." Despite their optimism, he died in the Lake Shore Drive house on June 11, 1918.

The mansion became home to former state senator George W. Dixon and his wife, the former Marion E. Martin. Dixon's parents, Arthur and Annie Dixon, had been Chicago pioneers. His broad career also included being president of the Arthur Dixon Transfer Company, president of the Wesley Memorial Hospital, president of the Chicago Temple Methodist Episcopal Church, and holding directorships in numerous concerns.

The house was the scene of the wedding of his sister, Edna, to Paul Walker on October 6, 1920. But most entertainments centered on his and Marion's many charitable involvements. When Marion died in January 1926, her funeral in the mansion was a civic affair. On January 8, the *Chicago Tribune* reported, "A detail of police stood at the entrance of the home while the traffic was detoured from Lake Shore drive to the side streets."

The house was filled with floral tributes from across the city. "The spacious residence was a bower of flowers. Roses, Easter lilies, forget-me-nots lined the walls, from the floor to the ceiling, extending up the sides of the stairway and down the hall corridors."

The second half of the 20th century was not kind to private homes along North Lake Shore Drive. Most were demolished for modern apartment buildings, and those that survived were mostly abused. In 1990, the Heisen house had sat empty, with a For Sale sign on it, for years. The *Tribune* described it as "uninhabitable on three of its five sprawling floors."

It was purchased by developer Art Frigo that year, along with 1254 Lake Shore Drive, for the combined price of $3.75 million. The *Tribune* revealed his plans "for gutting and rebuilding everything inside," with the exception of the entrance hall and formal staircase, in a conversion to apartments. Landmark status required his preserving the exterior appearance.

Frigo broke through common walls of the two mansions, joining them and creating four luxury residences—the largest being 6,700 square feet. The sympathetic treatment of the facades resulted in the Carl C. Heisen mansion—a rare survivor of Lake Shore Drive's palmy days—appearing essentially as it did when the family moved in in 1891.

BRYAN LATHROP HOUSE

120 EAST BELLEVUE PLACE

In his 1933 book *Chicago Welcomes You,* Alfred Hoyt Granger commented, "Bellevue Place has always been a favorite residential district, and immediately west of the Borden Chateau—such is the incongruity of our American architecture in Chicago—stands the most perfect piece of Georgian architecture in Chicago, the personal design of Charles McKim for his great friend, the late Bryan Lathrop."

Architectural hair-splitters may prefer the term neo-Georgian over Granger's "Georgian," but they cannot argue with the classic beauty and proportion of McKim's handsome design.

Bryan Lathrop was a highly cultured Southerner who arrived with his family in Chicago from his native Virginia during the Civil War. Educated by private tutors in France and Germany, he brought with him a refined appreciation of art and music. With his uncle Thomas B. Bryan, he developed a successful real estate business that garnered him a vast fortune.

Lathrop married his cultural equal, Miss Helen Lynde Aldis, the daughter of a Chicago judge, in 1875, and along with her would promote the arts in Chicago throughout his lifetime. Having been an early trustee of the Art Institute, Bryan Lathrop's importance in the cultural growth of Chicago continued. He became a trustee of the Chicago Orchestral Association, then its vice president, and as president spearheaded the construction of Orchestra Hall. He was a trustee of the Newberry Library and sat on the Board of Lincoln Park—eventually rallying support for extending the park to the north.

Construction began on the Lathrops' new home at 77 Bellevue Place (later renumbered 120) in 1891. Bryan Lathrop not only had a personal relationship with Charles Follen McKim of the prestigious New York architectural firm McKim, Mead & White, but an ongoing professional relationship with Holabird & Roche. While McKim personally designed the Lathrop mansion, he commissioned Holabird & Roche as associate architects, who most likely concentrated on the interiors.

LEFT The most perfect piece of neo-Georgian architecture in Chicago

RIGHT The interior rooms, likely by Holabird & Roche, were spacious enough for the Lathrops' frequent entertaining.

Robert Bruegmann of the Chicago Historical Society said in the 1918 volume *The Architects and the City: Holabird & Roche of Chicago, 1880-1918*, "The Lathrop house, with its elegant classical exterior and highly developed plan, undoubtedly made the Romanesque houses of the day, including those by Holabird & Roche, look heavy and old-fashioned."

Indeed, the neo-Georgian residence exuded elegance. Red brick, contrasted with white stone, was laid in Flemish bond with charred, blackened headers to give the illusion of age. Although the entrance was offset, the perfectly matched openings of the ground floor did not upset the strict symmetry of the structure. Rather than a stoop, or porch, McKim's stairs led to a spreading terrace protected by a handsome stone balustrade.

The bowed sections flanking the central portion, the splayed lintels with layered keystones, and the stone balustrade above the cornice (now lost) gave the Lathrop home the air of a decorous 18th-century New England residence.

McKim, Mead & White were simultaneously at work on buildings for the Columbian Exposition. The firm designed both the Agricultural Building and the New York State Building, and was significantly involved in the design of the Court of Honor, the focal point of the fair grounds.

In 1892, a year before the exposition opened, the mansion was completed and the Lathrops moved in. Like other millionaires, the Lathrops filled their home with art and antiques. Their collection of James Abbott McNeill Whistler etchings grew to be what was considered the largest in the country.

The house would be the scene of notable receptions and entertainments over the years. On March 11, 1903, the *Chicago Tribune* noted that, "While there is a strict observance of Lent, so far as formal entertaining is concerned, there is a great deal of going about to small informal affairs." One of those was in the Bellevue Place mansion. Although the Lathrops had no children, the house was filled with the sound of young voices that month when they entertained their nieces, Minna and Florence. Bryan's sister, also Florence, had married Henry Field, brother of Marshall Field. "Mr. Bryan Lathrop, Miss Florence Field's uncle, will give a young people's party Friday evening at his residence," said the newspaper.

As war erupted in Europe, the gatherings in the Lathrop residence became more serious. On November 10, 1915, according to the *Tribune*, Enid Yandell spoke to a group of women, while "seated against the dull green velvet pillows of a couch that graces the fireplace corner of Mrs. Bryan Lathrop's drawing room at 120 Bellevue place."

"I went to Paris to work out a fountain for Watch hill—that was why I was there with my sister, Maude, when the war broke over us," she said. "After the war started there was no art. There was nothing but agony and sorrow and a great striving to help."

Yandell was a noted sculptress who had done work for the Columbian Exposition's Women's Building. She had gone to Paris in connection with her commission to design a statue for Watch Hill, Rhode Island. Now she turned her attention to war relief, specifically *La Société des Orphelins de la Guerre*, which was currently taking care of 1,000 French orphans.

Her involvement came, she recalled, when a French soldier brought his two children to her and her sister. He was leaving for the front, their mother had been killed, and he had nowhere to leave them. Before long, the two women were caring for ten children.

Enid Yandell was as talented in the art of oratory as she was in the art of sculpture. "Could any one forget the eyes of four little children who saw their father shot and their mother die within the hour from the shock of it?" she appealed. "He was a French customs officer. Why was he shot before his children?" Another of her examples was even more egregious. "I remember the story of one French mother who went to a German officer in utter despair. Her six children were starving and their father had been shot. The officer told her to bring the children to him the next day. He stood them up against a wall, all in a row. With his own pistol he shot four of them down before her and then said, 'There you are; perhaps you can care for the two I've left for you.'"

Enid Yandell's impassioned pleas for donations in Helen Lathrop's drawing room that afternoon no doubt opened many pocketbooks.

Bryan Lathrop died in the Bellevue Place house on May 13, 1916, at the age of 72. He bequeathed $700,000 to the Chicago Symphony Orchestra—a staggering $15.6 million today. His vast collection of books was to go to the Newberry Library, upon the death of Helen.

Helen Lynde Aldis Lathrop stayed less and less in the Chicago house, spending much of her time in Italy, Maine, and Florida. In 1922, it was purchased by The Fortnightly of Chicago, one of the city's oldest and most exclusive women's clubs, on the organization's 50th anniversary.

In 1941, Chicago historian John Drury, in his *Old Chicago Houses*, noted that the club had made few changes to the interior. "The rooms still retain their simple, dignified atmosphere, with here and there the decorative touches of the Four Georges era. And in keeping with the tasteful atmosphere of those rooms are the pieces of genuine Biedermeier furniture with which they are outfitted.

"If Bryan Lathrop, with his familiar white beard and quiet cultivated manner, were to visit his house today, he would undoubtedly be highly gratified at the way it has been preserved and its twenty-three rooms maintained with the same decorative charm as when he lived there."

Under the operation of The Fortnightly, Bryan and Helen Lathrop's home continued to be the scene of elegant entertainments. On October 9, 1933,

Since 1922, the Lathrop House has been home to a prestigious women's club, The Fortnightly of Chicago.

for instance, Judith Cass reported in the *Chicago Tribune* that "During the next few weeks the distinguished Georgian home of The Fortnightly club at 120 East Bellevue place will be the scene of two interesting parties." The "interesting parties" were a debutante tea for Jean Hyman, and a "buffet supper and dancing party" for the son and daughter of Mr. and Mrs. Edwin W. Sims. The location was quite convenient for the Sims family—they lived next door.

The club offered lectures and readings as well. Another women's group, the Friday Club, had been established in 1907 for the purpose of promoting "literary and artistic culture". This club held its meetings in the former

Lathrop billiard room. One of the few rooms altered, it had been converted by Rue Winterbotham Carpenter to The Fortnightly's ballroom. Judith Cass described it in 1937 as "now a gray room with many mirrors and flame hangings of satin. At the north end is a dais framed in old Chinese Coromandel screens." In these surroundings, women authors and poets read from their works.

As had been the case 25 years earlier, war in Europe brought a different type of speaker and cause within the gracious rooms of the Lathrop house. On May 15, 1940, Mrs. Mary Breckinridge addressed the Chicago Committee of the Frontier Nursing Service, which she had founded in 1925. Following the death of her first husband and both her children at an early age, she had dedicated her life to improving the health of women and children. Her group of "saddlebag nurses and midwives," so called because they traveled on horseback, brought medical care to the remote hills of eastern Kentucky. The work of the Frontier Nursing Service was credited with cutting the high rates of infant and maternal mortality. Now women from Scotland and England traveled to Kentucky to get training from Mary Breckinridge on setting up similar organizations of traveling nurses at home.

The Fortnightly of Chicago remains in the venerable McKim, Mead & White neo-Georgian mansion—a fact that is responsible for its astonishing preservation. The house, which was given Landmark status in 1973 and listed on the National Register of Historic Places in 1974, is dwarfed by two high-rise structures. They make it seem an anachronism, a relic of a much more genteel period on this block of Bellevue Place.

"ELOQUENCE IN STONE AND STEEL": TRIBUNE TOWER

435 NORTH MICHIGAN AVENUE

In 1922, the year of the *Chicago Tribune*'s 75th anniversary and just months after the completion of the south tower of William Wrigley's massive headquarters, *Pencil Points*, a "journal for the drafting room," announced an architectural competition. The competition demonstrated that the development the chewing gum magnate had begun—changing the northern riverfront from dilapidated shacks to magnificent commercial palaces—had gained noteworthy momentum.

Such contests for substantial commissions were not uncommon, but this one stood out. The journal said it was "of unusual interest," not only because of the $100,000 in prizes, but "because of the opportunity it affords to produce a distinctive solution of an interesting problem." Architects who submitted plans for the new *Chicago Tribune* building would compete for $50,000 for the winning design, a $20,000 second prize, or $10,000 for third. Ten architects specially invited to participate were guaranteed $2,000.

The *Tribune* publishers had already chosen the site for the new structure—the 13,500-square-foot vacant lot in front of its printing plant on Michigan Avenue and directly across the avenue from the new Wrigley Building. *Pencil Points* felt that the far-reaching effect of the contest would be "unquestionably, the awakening of a great deal of interest in architecture on the part of the public and a new appreciation of the value of architectural character in the buildings of our great cities."

That was apparently just what the newspaper's executives sought. In announcing the competition the *Tribune* noted, "It is hoped that the winning design will enable the *Tribune* to erect one of the most beautiful buildings known to men." The newspaper implored the architects to design a skyscraper that would impress. "The monumental beauty of New York is amazing to appreciative Europeans, who see what American architecture can do with the flexibility of steel." Now, it said, it was Chicago's turn. "The development of

Michigan Avenue as a majestic thoroughfare is the possible gift of the future to the city, and the *Tribune* hopes to do its part."

The three-month competition began on August 1, 1922, and submissions were accepted until November 1. *American Architect and Architecture* anticipated that a masterful plan would be the outcome. On June 21, it contended, "At the very outset a result is assured, that will secure the erection in Chicago of a building that will be a fine adornment in a city that is so earnestly striving to achieve the very highest ideals of monumental beauty." It added, "The enthusiastic approval of the citizens of Chicago of the *Tribune*'s great project shows a fine civic spirit."

Among those who planned to enter the competition was the successful New York architect John Mead Howells. A friend of his, 41-year-old Raymond W. Hood had not accomplished a great deal in his career. The two met while studying architecture at the École des Beaux-Arts in Paris. Hood, after working for Cram, Goodhue & Ferguson, found himself designing radiator covers for the American Radiator Company. Howells convinced Hood to collaborate on the *Tribune* project.

Inspired by the notable neo-Gothic structures by Cram, Goodhue & Ferguson with which he was familiar, Hood worked with Howells to create a spectacular neo-Gothic tower design. On November 2, 1922, the five-member jury, composed mostly of *Tribune* officers and assisted by an advisory committee, was faced with more than 260 designs from 23 countries.

Looking back on the competition years later, on May 21, 1930, Earl H. Reed Jr., head of the department of architecture at the Armour Institute of Technology, would tell members of the American Institute of Architects that it changed the course of American architecture. "This competition, cast as a hero in a stupendous melodrama, resulted in the production of a series of designs which have profoundly affected American architecture. It would be difficult to overestimate the favorable influence of this great competition."

Within a month of the competition's closing, the plans of Howells and Hood were unanimously awarded the commission. There was only one snag that the *Tribune* had to overcome. On December 28, 1922, the *Columbia Evening Missourian* reported, "The new Chicago Tribune building will soar to a height of 650 feet if the board of aldermen will dispense with the 400-foot rule, Tribune authorities announced."

The city and the Tribune Company apparently arrived at a compromise, and in 1925 the 36-story edifice was completed at under 500 feet. As Cass

Under orders from McCormick, the *Chicago Tribune*'s correspondents sent back relics from all corners of the globe to be embedded in the first floor facade. The publisher had his impressive office two-thirds of the way up Tribune Tower.

Gilbert had done a decade earlier in Manhattan's monumental Woolworth Building, the architects brought the medieval style into the modern age. And, like Gilbert, they introduced nearly hidden details into the elaborate facade.

Artist Rene Paul Chambellan executed the sculptural elements—gargoyles and grotesques, ornate tracery, and the now-famous Aesop's Screen above the main entrance doors. Here nearly twenty of the ancient Greek fables are depicted in stone. Cass Gilbert had represented himself in the Woolworth Building as a marble grotesque. Howells and Hood followed suit in a subtler, more tongue-in-cheek manner. Near the main entrance the architects were represented by depictions of a baying canine (a dog who "Howells"), and Robin Hood.

During, and even before, the three-year project, the *Chicago Tribune*'s principal owner, publisher, and editor, Colonel Robert Rutherford McCormick had tasked his foreign correspondents to bring back rocks and masonry from historically important sites. These were incorporated into the street-level facade and labeled for the passerby.

The Tower officially opened on July 6, 1925. *Tribune* journalist John Herrick wrote, "Everything was prepared to handle a crowd of perhaps 2,000 persons. Twenty thousand came, it was estimated."

Chicagoans from all walks of life "swarmed over every one of its thirty-four [*sic*] floors" and paused outside "to read the bit of carving beside some of the famous stones that are set into the walls of the Tower."

A telegram was received from Charles H. Wacker, head of the Chicago Plan Commission, and his wife. It read, "There is eloquence in stone and steel. There is inspiration in good architecture. There is character building in good surroundings."

Not everyone was as enthusiastic. McCormick and Australians did not have a friendly relationship. The editor was notoriously blamed, perhaps rightfully so, with distorting facts about the continent and with refusing to publish letters from the Australian press that attempted to correct or clarify *Tribune* reports. He wrote to one Australian, "yours is a nation of criminals' descendants." It was, therefore, not especially surprising that the Tribune Tower got some less-than-glowing reviews there.

The Australian press mocked McCormick's prized souvenirs. On November 3, 1926, the *Construction and Local Government Journal* of Sydney wrote, "In order to endow its new-world 473 feet high [*sic*] Gothic building with old-world associations, the Tribune Newspaper Company, Chicago, has embodied a great number of stones from old buildings of historical or architectural fame. There is a stone from Hamlet's Castle in Denmark; a stone from Westminster Abbey, London; a stone from Edinburgh Castle; a stone from the oldest part of Cologne Cathedral; one from the gables of the windows of a chapel in the nave of Notre Dame Cathedral, Paris; a stone from the Taj Mahal, India; a stone from the Great Wall of China; one from the Parthenon"; and continued with a seemingly endless list of rocks and their origins—including one from an old Chinese graveyard, which was brought as ballast by Spanish ships at the beginning of the century.

The newspaper accused McCormick of using the stones to lure tourists and creating "a lucrative visitors' trade." The writer said it "reminds us of the way the ancients carried off the spoils of architecture…of fallen cities." The threat was, he said, that historic structures "would soon be dismembered" and elements "would be scattered wide over the earth," while the removed pieces were replaced with new, non-historic materials.

The same newspaper was less than thrilled with the Howell and Hood design overall. "As will be seen, gross liberties are taken with the supposedly Gothic architecture and one sees here the admixture of principles in the semi-circular, arched opening [of the main entrance] with splayed mouldings and applied fretwork carving in Moorish-Spanish style, together with depressed arches, statuary, enrichment and other features in Gothic feeling."

Few architectural critics, however, shared the *Journal*'s opinion. Doris Johnson, secretary of the English-Speaking Union in South Australia, gushed, "If the Tribune Building were a Campanile attached to an enormous cathedral it would probably be considered the most beautiful Campanile in the world."

The *Tribune* newspaper's massive presses were located below ground. Space elsewhere in the Tower not used by the publisher was leased to a variety of tenants, the largest of which was the Union Trust Company, a financial institution.

McCormick's own lavish office on the 24th floor was paneled floor-to-ceiling in walnut. The stone mantel was inscribed with a quotation by the publisher himself, and despite his staunchly American persona the plaster ceiling (inspired by Robert Adams) included royal elements such as *fleurs-de-lis* and Tudor roses.

Colonel McCormick's genius at marketing did not stop with historic stones embedded into the masonry of his new headquarters. Even before the building was opened, thousands of onlookers crowded Michigan Avenue as veteran catcher of

The massive entryway of the tower, shown decorated for the holidays, is three stories high and has a screen depicting Aesop's Fables over the doors.

the Chicago White Sox, Ray Schalk, prepared to catch a baseball thrown from the Tower on May 11, 1925.

The publicity stunt was not entirely new. Three players—William Schriner of the Cubs, Gabby Street of the Senators, and Billy Sullivan of the Boston Braves—had all caught baseballs thrown or dropped from the Washington Monument. But never before had the exploit been attempted from a skyscraper.

The *New York Times* reported, "Three balls were thrown from the tower. The first was wide, the second was fumbled as it struck Schalk's mitt, but he managed to hold the third one. The ball traveled a distance of 460 feet and its speed was estimated at approximately two miles a minute."

The opinions and personality of the *Chicago Tribune*, called by one journalist a "trumpet-voiced paper," were a direct reflection of McCormick. A fist-pounding conservative, he was feared and admired, hated and loved. No one on either side of the fence questioned his power and authority.

Described by many as an eccentric or, more often, a "lone wolf," he became a vehement isolationist despite having fought in World War I, and railed against the country's involvement in World War II. He pointed to George Washington's doctrine against being ensnared in the affairs of other countries as support.

By 1945, the world at large had seen fundamental change. The means by which the war had been brought to a close was a double-edged sword. It ushered in not only peace, but the terrifying threat of atomic annihilation. On September 26, 1947, the Associated Press reported, "An Atom Bomb shelter would be built under the Chicago Tribune building, the Newspaper has announced." The article was triggered by a notice in the *Tribune* that read, "Measures are being taken to protect as far as possible employees and tenants in the event of an atom bomb attack on Chicago." Two years later the newspaper reported that a steamboat whistle had been installed within the light court "to inform the Tribune population and others in the neighborhood that an atomic bomb attack is imminent."

The Adelaide *News* had scoffed, in 1946, "As for the colonel, he will eventually find, no doubt to his surprise, that he is neither invulnerable nor immortal." That "surprise" came to pass on April 1, 1955, when the bigger-than-life publisher died at the age of 75.

The New York Times said of him, "In American newspaper history there have been many controversial figures, but few more controversial than Col. Robert Rutherford McCormick, powerful editor and publisher of that powerful and controversial newspaper, The Chicago Tribune…. Indeed, that headstrong, pugnacious, trumpet-voiced paper during his leadership was but an extension of his own strong-minded, strong-willed personality. A dogmatic, intensely partisan, unpredictable man, he boldly stamped it with his own likeness, impregnated it with his own vitality and virtuosity, and through it made his dynamic impact felt on American life."

One can only imagine what Colonel McCormick's reaction would have been when, in the fall of 2016, Tribune Media sold Tribune Tower to developers CIM Group and Golub & Company for $240 million. The *Tribune* reported on September 28 that the buyers planned "to transform the historic North Michigan Avenue property into a mixed-use redevelopment."

Less than two years later, the *Tribune*'s staff packed boxes and prepared to move to the modernist One Prudential Plaza, south of the river. That skyscraper's lack of ornament led journalist Blair Kamin to say it "could be the box Tribune Tower came in." In his article about departing on June 8, 2018, he commented, "I will miss the visual poetry of the tower and its hushed, churchlike Michigan Avenue lobby."

Even without its namesake newspaper, the tower's Gothic elegance outshines anything in its Michigan Avenue neighborhood, a physical reminder of the colorful publisher who envisioned it in 1922. And, incidentally, with its masterful plan under his belt, Raymond Hood returned to New York, not to continue devising covers for the American Radiator Company, but to design that firm's stunning 1924 skyscraper headquarters in midtown Manhattan and, later, Rockefeller Center.

WRIGLEY BUILDING

400–410 NORTH MICHIGAN AVENUE

In 1919, William Wrigley Jr. had every reason to be proud of his accomplishments. Born in Philadelphia during the Civil War, he moved to Chicago in 1891 with savings of $32. He began by selling scouring soap (manufactured by his father), then baking powder. For every can of baking powder a customer bought, he would give two packages of chewing gum. Before long he realized that the gum was more popular than the baking powder, so he concentrated on the manufacture of chewing gum.

In 1893, he introduced a new brand, Juicy Fruit. It would quickly make the Wrigley Company the most successful chewing gum manufacturer in the world. Now, 26 years later, Wrigley was about to change Chicago's skyline.

The *Real Estate Record & Guide* reported on August 2, 1919, "Wm. Wrigley, Jr., Co. are erecting two buildings on a site of 22 acres where they plan the largest chewing gum factory in the world." The report was just a bit erroneous. William Wrigley Jr. was indeed planning two massive edifices; but they would serve as the headquarters of his company. Architects Graham, Anderson, Probst & White had been given the commission for the mammoth structures; and it was Ernest R. Graham and Charles G. Beersman (who had just joined the firm that year) who put pencil to paper to design the magnificent buildings.

Graham had been the original partner of renowned Chicago architect Daniel H. Burnham. Now partnered with William Peirce Anderson, Edward Mathia Probst, and Howard Judson White, his firm was a powerhouse among Chicago architectural concerns.

The site for the new headquarters was unexpected. *Building Management* magazine noted in 1921 that real estate operator Bertram M. Winston of Winston & Company had first proposed the seemingly unlikely location to Wrigley. "Although the boulevard was not opened and the improvements on the ground were just a dilapidated old dock house, Mr. Wrigley and Mr. Winston both realized that upon completion of the Boulevard Link project the lot in question was so located that a building situated thereon would appear to be in the very center of Michigan Avenue."

The Boulevard Link project was the widening of Michigan Avenue and construction of "a double-decked bridge" connecting the north and south sides, first announced in *Chicago Commerce* in May 1914. Once completed, the bridge would unite Michigan Avenue and Pine Street, the latter losing its name.

The half-completed Wrigley Building, from Michigan Avenue, south of the river.

The first building to go up was the south tower, sitting at the edge of the Chicago River. As Wrigley anticipated, it evinced a stately presence when viewed from the opposite side of the river. Completed in April 1921, it dazzled both by its terra-cotta cladding and its 398-foot-tall tower, the design of which was influenced by the Giralda Tower (originally a minaret) of the Cathedral of Seville, Spain. The architects used graduating hues of terra-cotta tiles, as explained in *Building Management* that year in December: "The color is graded from the base to the top of the tower in five shades, the top being almost a clear white, and the base slightly darker, so as to more nearly match the stone facing around the base of the piers."

The *Clay-Worker* magazine described the new skyscraper: "As a magnificent snow-capped pinnacle caps the grandeur of a mountain range, so the new Wrigley building with its lofty tower of snowy terra cotta dominates the skyline of Chicago's waterfront along Michigan avenue and entrances the gaze of Chicagoan and visitor alike."

Chicagoans and visitors alike were even more entranced at nightfall. Wrigley wanted his new skyscraper to be illuminated from head to toe. *Architecture and Building* wrote, "Mr. Wm. Wrigley, Jr., in considering the flood-light of this unique building at night, wanted it to surpass anything that he had ever seen and to say the least, that was a problem to solve." It was an expensive problem to solve. Floodlights were installed in the setbacks and on surrounding buildings. *Engineering and Contracting*, on February 22, 1922, placed the total cost of installation at $30,000, and estimated the nightly cost of lighting the building from dusk to midnight at $80—more than $1,000 in today's terms.

The Wrigley Building by moonlight, but still illuminated, unlike an evening hour of October 21, 1931, when all the lights were turned off for a minute in tribute to Thomas Edison, who was buried on that day.

With his nearly $4 million building completed, William Wrigley announced that he intended to spend another $3 million to construct the north tower. On August 9, 1922, the *Chicago Tribune* reported, "The new building, to conform architecturally with the present structure, will rise sixteen stories above the boulevard level.... The total floor area of the new office skyscraper will be about 22,000 square feet, or 9,000 square feet more than that of the present building."

In announcing the proposed structure, and while stressing his confidence in Chicago and the future of Michigan Avenue, Wrigley dredged up the long-running feud between the Windy City and New York. "Chicago is ludicrously far behind New York in municipal improvements," he complained. "For instance, we had fuss and fume interminably to get our new Michigan avenue bridge link through, whereas New York has within a few years built two wonderful bridges and is planning a third, which is to be the world's greatest." (The "world's greatest" referred to by the chewing gum mogul was apparently New York's planned double-decked George Washington Bridge, still the busiest motor vehicle bridge in the world.)

Wrigley quite openly intended his magnificent joint project to surpass anything in Manhattan. His sense of competition arose from his love of the city. Years later a close friend, capitalist and sportsman John Hertz, said Wrigley had two great loves: Chicago and his baseball team. "He once told me that he would not take the throne of England if it meant he had to leave Chicago."

Just two years later, in May 1924, the "annex," or north tower was finished. The anticipated 16 stories had grown to 21, just nine floors shorter than its fraternal twin. The two buildings—clad in 250,000 tiles, more than any other building at the time—were joined by a common courtyard, with a mammoth arched entrance, and a pedestrian sky bridge at the third floor. (Another walkway would be added at the 14th floor in 1931.)

Beersman and Graham had freely melded several architectural styles in designing the buildings. Along with Spanish Gothic for the clock tower, they ornamented the edifices with touches of Spanish Revival and French Renaissance Revival, the latter responsible for the spiky finials that detonate from the roofline.

William Wrigley Jr. was beloved by his employees. In his triangular-shaped office a framed motto was hung: "Nothing great was ever achieved without enthusiasm." To foster enthusiasm in his workers he allowed his female employees a free manicure and shampoo on company time once a month. They were provided linen dresses and free laundry, and ate in the company cafeteria, which operated at a loss. The Wrigley Building was equipped with a small "hospital," staffed with a doctor and company nurse for the employees.

The 1920s was a decade of dance marathons, goldfish swallowing contests, and myriad other zany attempts at being "the most," "the longest-lasting," or "the best." In 1922, 17-year-old Olive Belle Hamon used the new building to get in on the trend. On August 29, the *Chicago Tribune* reported that Olive, "daughter of the late Jake Hamon, Oklahoma oil millionaire, and heiress to his vast estate, will give a unique violin recital this afternoon at 2 o'clock for the benefit of the Camp Algonquin fund."

Unique it was. Olive played her "specially made violin" continuously while climbing the stairs to the top floor of the skyscraper and descending again. She never stopped playing.

The site became a destination for tourists the world over. Despite being two distinct structures, the floodlit twin towers took on the joint name Wrigley Building. A 1922 rental pamphlet said the "revolving light at the tower's tip [served] as a beacon to the mariners on the lake as well as the navigators of the air," and noted the floodlights created "an ethereal beauty." The revolving light could reportedly be seen for 20 miles into Lake Michigan.

There was one night, however, when the lights went dark. At 9:00 on the night of October 21, 1931, the date Thomas Alva Edison was buried, every electric light in the nation was to be turned off for 60 seconds in tribute to the inventor. For the first time in a decade, the floodlights of the Wrigley Building were shut off.

The following morning, the *Chicago Tribune* wrote, "When Chicago and the nation put out lights, Chicago and the nation partially reverted to a night of darkness which Edison, alone, changed.... Along Michigan avenue, State street, Randolph street, Wacker drive, and other downtown thoroughfares, skyscrapers illuminated in brilliance plunged suddenly into a mellow darkness."

The lights would also go out during the blackouts of World War II; and yet again in November 1946—this time more begrudgingly. That fall, 400,000 Pennsylvania soft-coal miners walked out, refusing to go back to work without a contract. The strike resulted in violence, with two miners dead less than 24 hours after the walkout. On November 22, the *Daily Illini* reported, "The Wrigley building, brilliantly flood-lighted Chicago nighttime landmark, returned to its wartime darkness last night because of the coal crisis." Philip K. Wrigley, owner of the building since his father's death in 1932, told reporters the lights "were turned off voluntarily for the duration of the coal strike as a power conservation measure."

Earlier that year, structural restoration was done on the south tower. The terra-cotta parapet, exposed to Chicago's brutal winters and hot summers, was entirely replaced. Four years later, the parapet of the north tower was restored. "The $400,000 job includes replacement of the parapet wall and finials," explained the *Chicago Tribune* on August 17, 1950. Exact reproductions of the architectural elements were cast and installed.

On Monday, July 12, 1965, the *Chicago Tribune* ran a huge banner headline that read "BOMB JARS WRIGLEY BLDG." In what today would be called a car bombing, a "black powder bomb" had been hidden in the wheel well of an automobile parked outside the skyscraper the night before. When it detonated, the car was demolished and 30 windows of the Wrigley Building were shattered. It was the third such attack within five days in the downtown area.

The Wrigley bombing came just 26 hours after a similar bomb exploded at the Meyer Building (designed by Louis H. Sullivan and Dankmar Adler). Despite the tense civil, political, and racial unrest in the city and nationwide, the assistant deputy superintendent of police, Merlyn Nygren, did not feel the bombings were domestic terrorism. He said instead that they "appear to be senseless."

The Wrigley Company initiated a modernization, partly to lure new tenants, in 2010. Everything above the first floor was gutted and renovated into modern offices; and in a shockingly unsympathetic makeover, the street-level facade

The south tower and annex or north tower of the Wrigley Building are linked by walkways at the third and 14th floors.

was encased in what *Chicago Tribune* architecture critic Blair Kamin described as an "antiseptic, refrigerator-style wall."

The resulting outrage was instantaneous. When BDT Capital Partners, an investment and financial advisory firm, purchased the property in 2011, Goettsch Partners was brought in to undo the architectural insult. The lost and damaged terra-cotta elements were recast or repaired at a cost of $300,000. The facade was carefully cleaned and 2,000 windows were replaced. The $70 million full-scale restoration was completed in 2013.

This meticulous rehabilitation brought William Wrigley's showpiece to its original appearance; and, as it did in the 1920s, it once again "entrances the gaze of Chicagoan and visitor alike."

NORTH AND NORTHWEST

THE ALARM STATUE

LINCOLN PARK, AT WEST WELLINGTON, EAST OF NORTH LAKE SHORE DRIVE

Martin Ryerson was a very wealthy man in the 1880s, but that had not always been the case. The son of a New Jersey farmer, he had struck out on his own in 1834 at 16 years of age. The adventurous boy sought the vast opportunities in the West he had read about in magazines and books.

Ryerson traveled along the Erie Canal, and then through Lake Erie to Detroit, where he found a job with Richard Godfrey, an Indian trader. They continued on to the small Michigan village of Grand Rapids. Here young Ryerson became familiar with the trappers and traders. He worked for a year with Louis Campau in 1835, and then for three years with Joseph Trottier, both also Indian traders. In the meantime, he formed friendships with the Ottawa Native Americans with whom they traded goods.

Decades later, in 1892, *The Encyclopaedia of Biography of Illinois* would recall, "While with these traders Mr. Ryerson made many trips among the Indians, and became very familiar with their language and customs. His experience with the Aborigines was a most happy one, and he acquired a deep admiration for their character."

In 1841, Ryerson started a sawmill in Muskegon; and in 1851 he settled in Chicago, where he co-founded a lumberyard, Williams, Ryerson & Company, at the corner of Canal and Fulton streets. By the last quarter of the 19th century, his lumber business was one of the largest in the West.

As Chicago changed from an outpost to a city and the Ottawa nation was pushed farther west, Ryerson was disturbed by the misconceptions regarding Native Americans that the urban population was accepting as fact. Americans were learning about the Indians through Wild West shows, pulp novels, and tall tales. He wanted to provide a depiction of Native Americans as the noble and honest people who had befriended him.

In Paris in 1880, Ryerson commissioned the 29-year-old New York sculptor John J. Boyle to execute a bronze grouping. Boyle had studied at the Franklin Institute, the Pennsylvania Academy of the Fine Arts, and the École des Beaux-Arts in Paris. This would be his first major commission.

It is possible that Boyle was influenced by the work of another New York sculptor, John Quincy Adams Ward, whose *Indian Hunter* had been unveiled in Central Park in 1869. The statue presented an Indian youth with his dog—among the first works to break away from the formal Neoclassical style. His subject, in a naturalistic pose, was also among the first representations of Native Americans.

By November 1883, Boyle's model of *The Alarm* was completed. A purely American subject by an American artist, *The Alarm* was groundbreaking in several respects. It was the first public depiction of Native Americans in Chicago. Like the Ward statue, it presented the subject in a dignified, unposed light, devoid of Victorian sentimentalism. Frank Leslie's *Illustrated Newspaper* praised the work, saying, "The Indian group of the sculptor John J. Boyle, designed for Lincoln Park in Chicago, is in every respect a masterpiece." Working with Ryerson's recollections, the sculptor portrayed a family at the moment the father senses danger.

The newspaper described the group: "A majestic specimen of Indian manhood is the centre figure, having apparently just risen to his feet. His long pipe is in his hand, and his bow and arrows lie on the ground. Across the man's chest are the folds of his buffalo robe, but the arms are bare, showing the swelling muscles, every line of the anatomy being graven with complete fidelity. The keen, wistful expression on the Indian's countenance cannot

be misinterpreted. There is no sign of fear on the bronzed features. The searching glance in the direction of where a branch had been heard to rustle, perhaps, or the sound of an approaching footstep detected, means haughty curiosity, almost indignation, at the possibility of domestic privacy being intruded upon by a stranger."

The completed 6-foot statue was delivered to the Lincoln Park Zoological Park on April 25, 1884, and placed on its 8-foot granite

Visitors admire the new statue in the zoo in the 1880s.

base, "on the high drive near the cage of sea-lions," according to the *Chicago Tribune* that morning.

Eleven days later, on May 5, it was unveiled. The *Tribune* reported, "With but little ceremony the beautiful group of bronze statuary in Lincoln Park was yesterday presented to the Park Commissioners by Mr. Martin Ryerson, whose gift it is, to the City of Chicago."

Boyle's naturalistic grouping sat on a decidedly formal granite base, on which Ryerson had inscribed, "To the Ottawa Nation of Indians, my early friends." On the sides were bronze tablets depicting Ottawa everyday life: *The Peace Pipe, The Corn Dance, Forestry,* and *The Hunt.* The sculptor had successfully captured the dignity of his subjects, prompting the *Chautauquan* to say in typical 1880s terms, his "bronze Indians commemorate so well the 'noble red man.'"

During the ceremony Martin Ryerson explained his purpose: "I have caused the construction of this statue to commemorate the Ottawa race of Indians, with whom I spent several years of my early manhood. While with them I saw much that was good and noble, and I looked upon them as my friends. There are but few white people now living who understand that race as I did half a century ago. I present this monument to the citizens of Chicago, trusting that the Commissioners of Lincoln Park and their successors will keep it in good condition, so that it may afford those who are to come after us a memento of a noble race."

OPPOSITE, LEFT The 29-year-old John Boyle's magnificent statue was the first in Chicago to portray Native Americans.

OPPOSITE, RIGHT The *Forestry* panel, like the other three, was reproduced in granite after thieves stole the bronze originals in the 1950s.

LEFT More than 130 years after its unveiling, the bronze group still conveys a sense of dignity, vigilance, and bravery.

More than sixty years later, the *Chicago Tribune*'s Claudia Cassidy complained about the statue's location in the zoo. On January 18, 1951, she wrote, "Its Indian family, more alert than alarmed, would be more effective in a better Lincoln park setting, and minus that incongruously classic pedestal." In the same article, Cassidy remarked on the disturbing amount of vandalism plaguing Chicago public artwork. It was a prophetic note. Within the next decade thieves pried three of the side panels off the pedestal for their bronze, breaking Ryerson's 1884 trust that it be kept "in good condition." The resultant blank scars would remain until 1975.

When park commissioners realized in November 1974 that *The Alarm* had to be relocated, a restoration was built into the move. The *Chicago Tribune*, on November 7, reported that "The site it occupied for 90 years is needed for the new primate house to be built in the near future to accommodate the gorilla population explosion in the zoo."

The newspaper noted that the grouping's new location would be north of the Lincoln Park Gun Club and east of Lake Shore Drive, between Diversey and Belmont harbors where "It will rest on a grassy plot of land between the Drive and the rocks of the lakeshore."

By the time *The Alarm* was installed in its current position, the one surviving bronze plaque had been removed and the four original scenes had been reproduced in the granite, not only eliminating the possibility of future metal robbers but fulfilling the requirement of Martin Ryerson.

SAVED BY CIDER?
RICHARD BELLINGER COTTAGE
2121 NORTH HUDSON AVENUE

On October 12, 1871, two days after the last flames of the Great Chicago Fire were extinguished, the *Chicago Tribune* summarized the damage to the North Side. "The line of destruction ran northeast from the Newberry school, striking Webster avenue near Lincoln place and continuing thence to the lake... A few solitary houses stand. One of these, on Lincoln place, is a small white cottage, which remains unscathed in the midst of the dreary waste surrounding it."

The modest Italianate-style frame house had been built two years earlier, designed by architect William W. Boyington (also responsible for the Chicago Water Tower). One-and-a-half stories tall over a high basement, its charm was enhanced by the decorative shake shingles of the second floor, the paired wooden brackets upholding the eaves, the elliptical arched windows, and the high stoop leading to the porch. Policeman Richard Bellinger had purchased the house shortly after its completion and moved in with his bride.

As the inferno worked its way north in October 1871, Bellinger and his brother-in-law worked furiously to clear away all the flammable materials around the cottage. The *Tribune* revealed the curious reason the house still stood. The article explained that Bellinger, "hauled up the sidewalk, as far as possible isolating his home. Then he poured water over the building until none was left and when the water was gone, he took his cider out of the cellar and used it in the same way."

Later that year, Elias Colbert and Everett Chamberlin published *Chicago and the Great Conflagration*. Their retelling of the story seared it forever into Chicago folklore. With a passion for the dramatic, they described the events of that day in florid Victorian prose:

"[Bellinger] stood his ground manfully until the red demon approached threateningly near, and then he redoubled his vigilance. Of this there was need, for now the sparks and brands fell thicker and faster, and his scant ladlefuls of water hissed and went up in puffs of steam as they struck the

The Bellinger Cottage, as it appeared when the Kirschten family lived here.

blistering shingles. By and by the last ladleful was gone, and the flames had not yet ceased to rage around him.

"If he only had a little more water—a bucketful merely—he thought he could save a home for his wife... the home which he had been struggling so long to build.... The wish did him honor, and the divine source of it sent him a thought which proved the wish's realization. In the cellar was a barrel of cider, which he had lately got in to drink with the winter's nuts and apples.

"He called to his wife to draw and bring him all the contents of the cask. It was done. The libation was poured out (in the right spots) and the home was saved."

Thirteen years later, in his *History of Chicago*, Alfred Theodore Andreas also expounded the story. He wrote, "There were vacant spaces contiguous, and Policeman Bellinger, who lived there, was encouraged to believe that he could preserve his home. He tore up the wooden sidewalks, raked the leaves in piles and burned them, and prepared for a battle with the flames in every conceivable manner. When the fire reached him, he covered his house with blankets and carpets, which he kept moistened. But when the fiercest wave of destruction came sweeping upon him, he found his cistern dry. Even then his courage and presence of mind did not forsake him. His cellar contained a store of cider, and with that fluid he fought his foe, and triumphed. His hands were burned, his cider was gone, but his home stood amid the general ruin, and he had won the victory in the face of fearful odds."

The story of the cider that saved one of the two houses that survived on the North Side was told and retold. It was printed in the public school books as part of Chicago history; and schoolchildren were often brought to the house on Fire Anniversary Day to hear the tale.

Lincoln Place was renamed North Hudson Avenue and the Bellinger Cottage was given the number 2121. The wooden dwelling remained unchanged into the 20th century; and in 1912 it became home to the family of postal clerk, Joseph J. Kirschten.

Kirschten had been three years old in 1871. When the fire approached his family's home near North Avenue and Wells Street, his mother grabbed framed religious pictures from the walls. The house was destroyed, but now those same pictures hung on an upstairs wall in the former Bellinger Cottage.

Mrs. Kirschten received an unexpected visitor one afternoon in 1915. A "small, white-haired, elderly lady" walked up the front steps and knocked on the door. She identified herself as Mrs. Richard Bellinger, the widow of the now-famous policeman. She asked if she could possibly look around her old home.

According to Chicago historian John Drury, Mrs. Kirschten later explained, "I was glad to show her the house. She looked eagerly around, felt the old-fashioned sliding doors, and went into the basement and touched the arched window frames. She appeared to be happy. The visit seemed to bring back memories of her girlhood romance."

As the two women talked, the widow told in detail how her husband had, indeed, exhausted the water in their cistern. He then ran across the street to a small truck farm where he got more water. When that was gone, he pulled water from the Ten-Mile Ditch, about a block east of the house.

Then came the startling truth about the cider myth. "The history books say that my husband put out the fire with cider, but that is not true. We did have a barrel of cider in the basement, sure enough, but we didn't use it because we were able to get enough water from the dugout across the street." Mrs. Bellinger did not offer any theories on how the quaint legend was started.

She did say that when the threat was over, she and her husband fed and sheltered 21 victims in the neighborhood who had lost their homes to the fire. She said they stayed in the crowded cottage until they could get relief from outside sources.

The Kirschtens remained in the wooden house for decades. In October 1938, its story was retold by the *Chicago Tribune*, which added, "The little white honeymoon cottage still stands, prettier than ever, flanked by towering American linden trees, surrounded by flowers, well-kept shrubbery and hedges, and embellished with a rock garden, in which are stones from many historical spots."

Mrs. Kirschten died in the late 1930s, and Joe remained in the house until his death in 1952, at the age of 83. His estate sold it in 1953 to architect Albert A. Liebrich and his wife, who owned lots next door. Mrs. Liebrich later explained,

A rare relic of Chicago's Great Fire of 1871, the Bellinger Cottage still looks pristine in the 21st century.

"We wanted it partly to make our property larger and partly because the other people who were negotiating for the place seemed pretty weird to have for neighbors. I couldn't have cared less about its history."

But Liebrich did care about its history and, according to his wife, "we did a few things as concessions to history." She related, "My husband had a wire mural made depicting Bellinger pouring cider on the roof, we let them put a plaque up out front, and we built a wine cellar to keep a little cider around."

In 1971, during the centennial of the Great Fire, a movement started to designate the cottage a Chicago historic Landmark. Mrs. Liebrich, now a widow, was not having it. She complained to a *Chicago Tribune* reporter, "It may be history to you, but to me it's a place I've paid for. There is no mortgage. It's unencumbered and I want to leave it to my son." To emphasize her stance, she added, "I guess you could say that 100 years later we're still trying to save the place."

She was successful for six years; and then in 1977 the cottage was given Landmark status. Subsequent owners remodeled the interiors, breaking open the living room ceiling to make it double height, adding a den and a "country kitchen," as a real estate agent would later describe it. The wooden house that had cost Officer Bellinger about $500 was sold for $1.4 million in 2005. Disregarding nearly 150 years of change elsewhere, the charming Hudson Avenue block is still mostly lined with freestanding homes built in the boom after the fire, and the Bellinger Cottage survives with an architectural charisma equal to the urban myth that some would prefer had never been disproved. As Mrs. Liebrich confessed in her later years, "I prefer to believe the cider story."

A TOUCH OF THE TROPICS
IN LINCOLN PARK:
ALFRED CALDWELL LILY POOL

125 WEST FULLERTON PARKWAY

Fanny Copley Seavey, writing in *Modern Cemetery* magazine in 1896, commented on the lily pond that had been introduced to Lincoln Park in 1889. A Victorian showpiece, it was the work of J. A. Pettigrew, then superintendent of the Lincoln Park Commission. Pettigrew, the article explained, had had to fight for the lush pool. He had become fascinated with an enormous type of water lily, the *Victoria regia* (now *Victoria amazonica*). In 1882 he began growing the plants in wash tubs at his home, where they reached diameters of nearly two feet. His concept of a public lily pond, where the extraordinary plants could grow even larger, met with resistance from the parks department. Called "tender aquatics," the lilies likely could not endure Chicago winters.

The magazine explained, "In the introduction of tender aquatics in the Park there were ... doubts to be dispelled, and it required strenuous efforts to secure an appropriation for purchasing the plants and providing suitable quarters for them. The money was, however, finally forthcoming and a low swale among the sand dunes was selected." The plants required warmer water than natural, and Pettigrew chose his site carefully—it was near the park's engine house so "steam for heating the water was easily supplied." Additionally, machinery was installed to keep the water constantly moving to ensure it would not freeze and irreparably damage the lilies.

Pettigrew designed his lily pond to be more formal than the unheated ponds already in place. Fanny Copley Seavey said of those, "The ponds are larger than those that are warmed; their setting is naturalistic, and the planting along the shore adds much to the good effect."

She pointed out, "The plants met with various misfortunes and for a time the result was doubtful. Indeed the ponds were facetiously referred to at this stage as 'Pettigrew's frog ponds.' But the plants finally redeemed themselves, and beginning about July 12 [1895] the flowering of the Victoria was for some

Well-dressed admirers of Victoria regia visit Caldwell's lily pond at the end of the 19th century. Named for Queen Victoria, the plant's veiny underside inspired the design of the Crystal Palace in London.

time announced in the evening papers and hundreds visited the Park to see the flowers by electric light."

Lincoln Park and its exotic lily pond drew Chicagoans and tourists for decades. The location near the lake and the shady trees provided a welcomed respite from the summer heat and a pleasant place for an outing. On the afternoon of October 28, 1909, however, the lily pond was the scene of a near tragedy.

Four-year-old George McNary and Leona Koehler, just two years old, were playing by the pond unattended. The *Billings Gazette* explained that "the children had strayed away from home." Along with the beautiful plants in the pond was a family of ducks that fascinated the toddler.

The newspaper reported, "Leona fell into the pond while trying to catch one of the ducks." Her playmate acted with bravery and resources beyond his years. He waded into the pond and caught hold of her dress. It was enough to pull her into the shallower water, but he was unable to pull her out.

George instructed Leona to hold on to a branch while he ran for help. He found Police Officer Martin Burns in the zoo's nearby aviary, and he rushed to the scene. The *Gazette* reported on the happy ending: "Leona was wrapped

The water lilies are decidedly smaller in the restored lily pool and the emphasis is on native plantings rather than the exotic.

in a warm blanket and an officer took them both to their homes."

At the time of Leona Koehler's near drowning, Alfred Caldwell was six years old. By the time he went to work for landscape architect Jens Jensen in 1926, Pettigrew's lily pond was suffering. As predicted nearly three decades earlier, the tropical plants did not survive, and the ponds were becoming unsightly.

Jensen was a proponent of the "Prairie Style" of landscape architecture—the antithesis of J. A. Pettigrew's Victorian reining in of nature. The Prairie Style sought to foster an appreciation for natural landscape and to encourage conservation of naturally occurring plant life. Jensen passed on to the young Caldwell respect for natural environments and "the relation of living things to each other and to the soil." Caldwell was also influenced by the work of Frank Lloyd Wright, who sensitively harmonized his architecture with its environment.

Following the onset of the Great Depression, the Works Progress Administration was formed as part of the ambitious New Deal, through which millions of unemployed Americans were hired by the government to carry out public works projects. Along with laborers were skilled workers, including hundreds of artists, who created works like murals in government buildings. The WPA hired Alfred Caldwell to redesign the neglected lily pond, and to refurbish other areas of Lincoln Park.

Caldwell embraced the project. He designed a naturalistic setting of meandering paths, indigenous plants, a waterfall, and circular stone seating he called "the council ring" and "friendship circles." Wright's influence was evidenced in the two wooden pavilions that nestled among the trees and jutted slightly into the pool. Horizontal planes mimicked the stone-slabbed bases, which pretended to have always been there. Unlike Pettigrew's hourglass-shaped pond, Caldwell's more naturally shaped pool imitated the atmosphere of a quiet river, meandering through a Midwestern prairie.

Caldwell was struck a major blow in 1938, just as the project was nearing completion. The Park District cut his budget for wildflower plantings by a significant amount. Unwilling to allow his design to suffer, Caldwell cashed in his $5,000 life insurance policy, receiving only a fraction of its value – $250. He spent the money on thousands of plants, which he brought back from Wisconsin and, with the help of four friends, personally planted around the lily pool.

Caldwell viewed his creation as an escape from what he termed "the Megalopolis." The public was thrilled. As a matter of fact, the response was so favorable that thousands of feet trampled plantings and caused significant erosion. Then, as had happened with Pettigrew's lily pond, Caldwell's gradually fell into neglect and desolation as the century progressed.

At mid-century the deteriorating pool was taken over by Lincoln Park Zoo as part of its avian exhibit, the Rookery. The new role simply furthered the decline of the once-glorious lily pond. Eventually, weed-choked and with broken stonework, it was abandoned and closed.

Alfred Caldwell lived to be 95 years old. Shortly before his death in 1998, he visited his lily pool and was devastated at what he saw. A restoration had been planned in 1993, but stalled. Caldwell reportedly lamented that his pool had become "a dead world."

He did not live to see the beginnings of the resurrection of the Alfred Caldwell Lily Pool in the new century. The Friends of Lincoln Park (later renamed the Lincoln Park Conservancy) raised $1.1 million for the restoration. Another $1.3 million from the Chicago Park District went toward the project.

In May 2000, *Chicago Tribune* staff writer Jon Anderson had reported on the "place of dead trees, drooping branches, pond scum and, in the water, the lifeless shell of a turtle lodged against soggy driftwood…It was not a happy sight." But, continued the article, "All that, happily, is about to change."

"Weed trees," which had made themselves at home over the decades, were removed. Caldwell's detailed notes and old photographs were used to ensure that historic plantings and trees were preserved. Non-historic features, like 1960s stonework, were removed. Then restoration of the pavilions and waterfall, replacing stonework, resetting of the paths, and careful replanting resulted in the Alfred Caldwell Lily Pool reemerging much as it looked in 1938.

The $2.4 million project was completed in 2002, when the pond's name was officially changed to the Alfred Caldwell Lily Pool. The 2.7-acre site was designated a Chicago Landmark in 2002, and a National Historic Landmark in 2006. Nearly lost, it survives as a rare example of Prairie landscape architecture.

RESCUING AMERICAN ARCHITECTURE FROM THE BOW-WOWS: EDWIN M. COLVIN HOUSE

5940 NORTH SHERIDAN ROAD

Architect George W. Maher told the Chicago Architectural Club in March 1906, "If the architecture of this country is to be kept from going to the bow-wows, in which direction it is headed just now, Chicago must do it.… New York and other cities which, architecturally speaking, [have] bound the United States on the east, are powerless to take the initiative. They are to be rescued."

When millionaire Harry M. Stevenson commissioned Maher to design his North Sheridan Road mansion in 1909, the architect took the opportunity to rescue American design. The completed home at 5940 North Sheridan Road

The fine house brought no happiness to its inhabitants.

stood in stark contrast to the Beaux-Arts and neo-Georgian mansions being constructed on the East Coast.

The substantial beige Roman brick and stone house featured a hipped roof, punctured by a single arched opening, sitting deeply within an overblown dormer. Despite the austere facade, relieved only by a pair of sober inset columns at the second floor and a rather forbidding stone entranceway, Maher's design, assisted by a sweeping stone entrance plaza, managed to exude grandeur and class.

Atypically, it was unencumbered by the porte cochère traditionally at the front or side of grand houses, because the architect placed that to the rear, unseen from the street. The *Chicago Tribune* described the mansion as "one of the handsomest homes in North Edgewater, the house being a three story brick structure finished in walnut, oak, and mahogany, and containing twelve rooms and three baths." Edwardian millionaires often strutted their wealth in the form of expensive, custom-built pipe organs. The Stevensons were no exception and theirs was built into the massive entrance hall.

Stevenson was president of the H. M. Stevenson Company, a merchant tailoring firm. He and his wife, Genevieve, would not live in the new home for long. The *Chicago Tribune* reported on October 23, 1912, just three years after they moved in, that the Stevensons had sold the mansion to Edwin M. Colvin, vice president of the William F. Hall Printing Company, and also president of Photoplay Publications and vice president of the Central Typesetting Company. At the time of the sale, the house was valued at $75,000 (in the neighborhood of $1.9 million today).

Harry and Genevieve moved into 706 North Sheridan Road where 1920s Prohibition brought an end to their marriage. Genevieve was awarded a divorce on Friday, October 26, 1923, after explaining to the judge, "As soon as prohibition came Mr. Stevenson started excessive drinking, and he has been most consistent."

Judge Sabath was confused. "Was it after prohibition, did you say? Don't you mean before?"

"Oh, it was rather bad before," Genevieve replied, "but nothing as compared to the last few years. He became very abusive." She said that Harry's "contempt for the Volstead act" (as the National Prohibition Act was informally known) made him determined to drink more.

In the meantime, the 45-year-old Edwin M. Colvin moved into 5940 North Sheridan Road with his wife, the former Clara Fuller, and their four children: Jay Austin, Edwin Richard (who went by his middle name), Willard

Otis, and Ruth Elizabeth. As the Colvin boys grew to young adulthood, they sometimes brought unwanted publicity to the respected family. Such was the case in July 1921 when Richard was arrested in Clear Lake, Indiana where the family maintained their summer home. Motor Policeman Jackson nabbed Richard for speeding along West Front Street. The *South Bend News-Times* reported that he pleaded guilty and was fined $9.40.

Clara Colvin was no doubt devastated when "elaborate plans" for a fashionable wedding "went glimmering," according to the *Chicago Tribune* on September 1 the following year. Willard was to be married to Hally Isobel MacLeod in what the *Tribune* deemed "a smart society wedding" on October 10. But it would not come to pass. The couple "slipped away" to Valparaiso, Indiana for a civil ceremony. The newspaper explained that Hally's trousseau had been purchased—"six of everything"—"But the thought of an orange blossom laden atmosphere, the white gardenias in the ushers' buttonholes, the friendly enemies criticizing the length of her train, urged her to slip away Wednesday to the Indiana courthouse."

As had been the case with Harry Stevenson, liquor would bring an end to Willard's marriage. Hally testified that Willard was a good husband until his father's death in 1926, but for the previous six or seven years, "he has been intoxicated five days a week." On September 15, 1934, the *Chicago Tribune* reported, "Mrs. Hally McLeod Colvin was granted an uncontested divorce yesterday from Willard Otis Colvin, sportsman and heir to the million dollar estate of his father, Edwin M. Colvin."

Losing his wife was sufficient cause to make Willard give up the bottle. He moved to San Francisco and determined to reform. His rehabilitation convinced Hally to reconcile, but an ironic accident ended it all. News of it traveled the world. The Australian newspaper the *Examiner* reported luridly on August 29, 1936 that, "After nine years of constant intoxication, wealthy Willard Colvin, of San Francisco, successfully went on the water wagon to win back the affection of his wife, who had wearied of the eternal triangle of the husband, his insobriety, and his bottle.... [But] after five months of absolute abstinence he crashed into a truck loaded with liquor and was killed instantly in a terrific smash, thus dying in the fumes of whisky vapour." The newspaper deemed the accident "Fate's Cruel Joke."

Following the Colvins in the mansion was the Baris family, who undertook an extensive interior remodeling. Maher's designs were replaced with the then-trendy Spanish Colonial style.

The porte cochère was placed discreetly in the rear.

Although designated a Chicago Landmark in 1994, the house suffered neglect by subsequent owners. When the once-elegant home was put on the market in 2015 for $1.2 million (and, according to one journalist, "a lot of elbow grease"), plaster had fallen from the ceilings of some rooms, water was seeping into the structure, and decorative ceiling brackets in the entry hall were missing. Nevertheless, the ghost of former elegance remained. The real estate listing described the house as "a beautiful woman in the morning who hasn't yet put on her makeup."

Despite the abuse, George Maher's dignified mansion survives outwardly much as it looked in 1909, when Harry and Genevieve Stevenson first walked in—a handsome relic of North Sheridan Road's glory days.

"THE DREAM LADY": EUGENE FIELD MEMORIAL

LINCOLN PARK ZOO, NORTHEAST OF HELEN BRACH PRIMATE HOUSE

The unveiling of the charming Eugene Field Memorial in Lincoln Park Zoo on October 9, 1922, concluded a fundraising project that stretched back before the turn of the century, not long after the writer's death in 1895.

As a young man, Eugene Field's career prospects looked bleak. His mother had died in 1856, when he was six years old. He was 19 and attending Williams College in Williamstown, Massachusetts when his attorney father died. He dropped out; later enrolled at Knox College in Galesburg, Illinois, where he again walked out after a year; then entered the University of Missouri in Columbia.

He failed at acting, at law, and wrote for the university newspaper with limited success. After traveling through Europe for six months, the young man returned to the States destitute. In 1875, the same year he married Julia Comstock, he landed a job as a writer for the *St. Joseph Gazette* in Missouri. A string of other newspaper positions finally led him in 1883 to Chicago and a job writing "Sharps and Flats" for the *Chicago Daily News*. The daily humor column started the day over morning coffee for hundreds of Chicagoans.

It was perhaps the fact that Eugene and Julia had eight children that caused him to pen his first children's poem, "Christmas Treasures," in 1879. *The New York Times* later wrote, "The children of the family were the father's chief delight. His love for children was strong, and it inspired some of his daintiest lines."

While he pressed away at work writing pithy newspaper columns, he continued to write children's verse on the side. Eventually he would publish more than a dozen poetry books. His most memorable poems were the "Dutch Lullaby" (otherwise known as "Wynken, Blynken, and Nod"), "The Duel" (more often recognized as "The Gingham Dog and the Calico Cat"), and the sentimental "Little Boy Blue."

Eugene Field fell ill on November 1, 1895, when he was just 45 years old. He went to bed as normal two days later and slept soundly until about 5:00 the next morning. Then, according to *The New York Times*, on November 4, his son "heard his father groan, and, putting out his hand, discovered that his father was dead." A headline in the newspaper that morning read, "A Remarkable Character is Gone."

Almost immediately Chicagoans united to honor their cherished citizen. The Eugene Field Memorial Association was founded to raise funds for a fitting monument. Because much of the money came from schoolchildren, the project would be a long-running one. And because the money came from pennies and nickels from children's allowances, when a thief was caught stealing from it in 1898, the nation was especially outraged. The news made it to Kansas, where the *Hutchinson Gazette* reported on December 22 that "C. W. Griffin, a Chicago letter carrier, who has robbed the mails of small sums, the aggregate of which is several hundred dollars, during the past six months, was arrested by government inspectors Monday. The thefts consisted mostly of money taken from letters addressed to the Eugene Field Memorial Association."

The devastating Financial Panic of 1907, one of the most difficult economic depressions the country had yet faced, was possibly one reason that the Eugene Field Memorial fundraising ground to a halt. On January 2, 1914, the *Ogden Standard* explained, "Money was collected and placed in a bank…. But the time was not ripe for the movement and it languished. The money, however, remains intact and will be added to the funds to be raised in the future."

"The future" had been triggered when the cause was taken up again in September 1913. Personal friends of Field, Will J. Davis, Slason Thompson, and Harry J. Powers, joined forces to reenergize the fund drive.

For the first time a concept of the memorial was offered and publicized nationally by the trio in newspapers. "The first purpose of the fund will be to erect a shaft or monument over the grave at Graceland Cemetery, and if the fund is sufficiently large a portion of the money will be used to erect a memorial in a Chicago park," reported the *New York Sun* on September 4, 1913.

On the other side of the country, the *East Oregonian* quoted Will Davis two weeks later: "It is a sad commentary for us not to have erected this memorial before and it certainly should appeal to everyone to make up for past neglect." He added, "It shows how we, in our busy commercial life, are quick to forget."

Within the month, another cad plagued the drive. The *Day Book* reported on October 6, the "Eugene Field Memorial Ass'n. warns people against giving money to a man posing as a collector for the poet's monument."

The following year, after a monument to Goethe was erected in Lincoln Park, Will Davis appealed to American patriotism and guilt. A communication was reprinted in *Chicago Commerce* that read in part, "It has often been said by American people that our parks are filled with tributes to foreign heroes. Has America none?" Davis pointed out that the German-born residents had had no problem raising the funds for the Goethe statue; yet the Eugene Field committee "is having difficulty in raising its necessary amount, $10,000—scarcely half having been subscribed." He ended by saying that the support of American citizens, particularly Chicagoans, would "refute the charge that we are slow in remembering our best citizens."

It would take another six years before the funds were such that submissions from sculptors could be considered. By then, the idea of a cemetery memorial had been scrapped in favor of a monument in

Children's pennies contributed largely to the memorial for their poet, Eugene Field.

Lincoln Park, where hundreds of Field's greatest fans, the children, played. The $10,000 goal Davis had announced in 1914 had been surpassed. The *American Stone Trade* reported in December 1920, "The trustees of the Art Institute of Chicago have the fund of $25,000 for the purposes of the memorial."

The article mentioned that New York sculptors Johannes S. Gelett and Edward Francis McCartan had already submitted models. It was McCartan who won the commission. Finally, 27 years after his death, Eugene Field received the honor he deserved. On October 9, 1922, Melville E. Stone, former general manager of the Associated Press, spoke at the memorial's unveiling in the zoo grounds.

Two of Eugene Field's grandchildren, six-year-old Jean Field Foster and Robert Eugene Field, pulled the cords to unveil the touching sculptural grouping, which sat on a raised stone plaza, flanked by two marble benches. A 7-foot bronze fairy-like figure bent protectively over two sleeping children, sprinkling "the sand of dreams into their eyes." (The "sand of dreams" was actually poppy dust, and the opium reference would no doubt cause controversy today.)

The figures were placed on a limestone plinth, designed by New York architects Delano & Aldrich. McCartan had taken his theme from Field's poem,

"The Rock-a-By Lady." On one side of the base were carved the first lines of "Wynken, Blynken, and Nod:"

Wynken, Blynken, and Nod one night
Sailed off in a wooden shoe,
Sailed on a river of crystal light
Into a sea of dew.

On the other side of the sleeping children were the opening lines of "The Sugar-Plum Tree:"

Have you ever heard of the Sugar-Plum Tree?
'Tis a marvel of great renown!
It blooms on the shore of the Lollipop Sea,
In the garden of Shut-Eye Town.

Panels above the pedestal depicted scenes from the two poems, carved by New York sculptor John Donnelly. A drinking fountain was built into each end of the memorial. Above each, verses from Field's poems were carved into the granite. The whole project cost $35,000—about half a million dollars today.

Following the unveiling, Edward McCartan talked about the project with Blythe Sherwood of *Arts & Decoration* magazine: "It was not simple to design this monument. I was told by the Commissioners that I would have to put some of Mr. Field's poems into granite. Consider all of the poems, and try to figure out which of their subjects lend themselves to sculptural design!"

After studying Field's works, he said, "The Rock-a-By Lady is the gist of all of Mr. Field's songs…. So I decided to make The Rock-a-By Lady the central figure of the monument." Rather than cover the figure with poppies, as the poem described her, McCartan simply placed the flowers in her fingertips, over the children's heads. But then came the problem of "What *is* the life-size of a fairy?" The sculptor asked the two children who posed for the grouping how big they thought a fairy was. They agreed the proper size was no taller than 10 inches. "Another sculptural obstacle!" exclaimed McCartan.

Then there was the matter of the wings. "When I put the wings on The Rock-a-By Lady I knew that I would have to mold her so that she could not be mistaken for an angel." Edward McCartan was no doubt crestfallen when he read newspaper accounts of the unveiling. Despite his care to create obvious fairy wings, a single journalist's account described the figure as a "brooding angel," and it was repeated nationwide.

"The Dream Lady" still gives the nod to the winkin' and blinkin' sleepy children.

One publication, Dearborn, Michigan's *America To-Day*, did get it right. And the writer perhaps first coined a term that would attach itself to the memorial forever. The article noted, "The sculptured group includes the figure of a dream lady, with delicate wings suggesting not so much the angelic as the butterfly fancies of childhood. At her feet are two reclining young figures, a drowsy boy and girl, who wait for the dropping of the poppies which the dream lady holds by her finger tips."

In September 1947, the park's board of commissioners announced that the Eugene Field Memorial would be moved. The statue's location near the entrance of the zoo's small animal house was problematic. Thousands of people passed by and "Many children have tripped and been hurt on the steps leading to the monument," explained the general superintendent of the Chicago park district, George A. Donoghue. The monument was moved slightly north within the zoo grounds, at a cost of $4,000.

"The Dream Lady", as the memorial came to be widely known, continued to enchant Chicagoans and tourists. Claudia Cassidy, writing in the *Chicago Tribune* about Chicago fountains on January 15, 1951, digressed to mention, "while charm is on your mind you will invariably go back to the Eugene Field memorial in central Lincoln park, the gentlest of monuments with the dream lady whose wings are so like a guardian angel's watching over the children sprawled in sleep."

Just as it did in 1922, Edward Francis McCartan's gentle grouping not only enchants thousands of children each year, but adults as well. The ethereal sculpture is a fitting memorial to the man who created so many timeless children's verses.

GATEWAY THEATRE

(COPERNICUS CENTER)

5216 WEST LAWRENCE AVENUE

Even though the migration of the motion picture industry from the East Coast to California was well under way in 1926, Adolf Zukor planned his Paramount Pictures headquarters in New York City, directly in the middle of Times Square. He chose the Chicago-based brothers Cornelius W. and George L. Rapp to design the 33-story Art Deco tower and theater.

While Manhattan had its share of well-known theater designers, the firm of Rapp & Rapp had made a significant name for itself as motion picture house architects. Eventually it would design more than 400 theaters; and if the Paramount commission seemed it would be the firm's crowning glory, it was in some ways just the beginning.

Following the release of the first full-length talking film, Warner Brothers' *The Jazz Singer*, in October 1927, the course of the motion picture industry—and its theaters—changed. Two years later, Balaban & Katz, operators of a chain of theaters, hired Rapp & Rapp to design a theater in the Jefferson Park area of Chicago. It was to be designed especially for talking pictures, and have state-of-the-art acoustics.

On September 8, 1929, the *Chicago Tribune* reported on the proposed "new Gateway, movie-talkie playhouse and business block, to be erected at the northwest corner of Lawrence and Lipps avenues." The newspaper noted it would serve "a rapidly developing district of the far northwest side, as well as Park Ridge, Edison Park, Norwood Park, Des Plaines, and other suburbs and neighborhoods."

The *Tribune* noted, "The Gateway will be one of the first good sized Chicago theaters to be built since the talkies have become more than mere talk. The question of acoustics, therefore, has been considered by the architects, C. W. and George L. Rapp, as of prime importance and ranking with the problem of visibility in the design of this new movie-talkie house."

Balaban & Katz was formed in 1916 by two sets of brothers, Abe and Barney Balaban and Sam and Morris Katz. Choosing to erect their own theaters, they

Rapp & Rapp's
extraordinary theatrical
venue for the talkies.

had often turned to the Rapp brothers, who were responsible for the design of their premier movie house, the exuberant Chicago Theatre. Eventually Balaban & Katz would operate more than a hundred theaters in the Midwest, over half in the Chicago area.

The *Tribune*'s reporter, Al Chase, said of their latest project, "The new playhouse will be called the Gateway theater, a name chosen because it will be adjacent to several important thoroughfares." The theater, with a projected cost of $1 million, was slated to have an auditorium capable of seating 2,500 patrons and be designed in "the open air or garden effect, first used in this city, we believe, in the Cort theater and later on a larger scale at the Capitol moving picture house on Halsted, near 79th," wrote Chase. "Since then the idea has been carried out more or less elaborately in various playhouses."

Completed in June 1930, Rapp & Rapp's Gateway Theatre was an architectural sensation. The terra-cotta facade was designed in an Aztec-inspired Art Deco style, with an angled, electric-lit "GATEWAY" sign forming the main section of the prominent, headdress-like parapet above the marquee. Balaban & Katz referred to the theater as "A Garden of Dreams," and along the sides of the building painted trees and trellises were intended to give the parking lot a garden atmosphere.

Inside, the main lobby was ornamented with marble pilasters and "walls decorated with mirrors, sculpture relief ornament and paintings." The semi-domed ceiling was decorated by Chicago artist Louis Grell in vibrant Art Deco motifs, including Greek and Roman mythological characters.

The "garden effect" of the auditorium—what we call "atmospheric theater" today—transported patrons to another realm. The *Tribune* said the auditorium represented "an Italian garden with fountains, trellises, gateways, statuary, etc. around the sides and with the ceiling as sky. This atmospheric reproduction of the heavens will start from the floor of the auditorium and the theatergoer will be able to catch glimpses of it through the gateways and trellises on each side, as well as have a sweeping view above."

The proscenium was flanked by ornate Renaissance-inspired, engaged, twisted columns. Above these were busts of Diana, Apollo, Aphrodite and, curiously enough, Voltaire.

Rapp & Rapp's attention to acoustics paid off. The *Chicago-Herald Examiner* called the auditorium "the most acoustically perfect theatre in the world."

Despite opening in the first years of the Great Depression, the Gateway dodged the fate of many movie houses and survived for the next half century. It remained the flagship movie house of Balaban & Katz until the organization dissolved in 1970.

In 1974, the Gateway proved too successful. The operators had advanced Warner Bros. $150,000 for exclusive showing rights of *The Exorcist*. The gamble paid off, and in the first ten days of screenings the theater had taken in that much in box office receipts for the massively popular movie. But on January 22, 1974, Aaron Gold wrote in the *Chicago Tribune*, "It now looks as if Warner Bros. will ask the courts to invalidate" the Gateway's exclusive showings. He explained, "Residents of the Gateway Theater neighborhood are putting the pressure on officials to alleviate the massive traffic jams in the area so Warner Bros. execs are trying to ease the problem by making Bill Friedkin's controversial movie available at other theaters."

It was not merely residents who were dealing with the heavy traffic caused by the movie. The firemen of Engine Company 108, across the street from the theater, found it "virtually impossible" to get their engines out of the station on several occasions, due to the automobile backup on the street.

Despite the theater's success, its owner Henry Plitt decided to sell the Gateway in March 1979. Plitt was the head of the largest independent theater circuit in the country, with over 400 venues; and he was about to have one fewer when he signed a purchase agreement with the Copernicus Foundation. On March 23 that year, the *Tribune* reported that "the acquisition and renovation is estimated at $1.6 million. The not-for-profit center will include a 700-seat theater; Polish restaurant, banquet and meeting facilities; a library; a book store; and classrooms."

The Polish-American organization took possession in time for a visit to Chicago by the Polish-born Pope John Paul II. When it became known that on October 4 the Pope's car would travel to Lawrence Avenue, "through Polish, German, Italian and Irish neighborhoods," the Copernicus Foundation went into action. Although renovations of the building were still far from complete, the group made a request that the Holy Father stop briefly to bless their new building.

Michael Kobelinski, president of the foundation, told reporters, "There's a lot of hope in our hearts that he'll stop for a minute. We're going to have a big chorus out there and the parking lot will be filled with our members." James Yuenger of the *Chicago Tribune* felt, "It will be a minor miracle if the pontiff isn't impressed by the 40-foot high mural of himself on the wall at the site." Kobelinski added, "Not only is it visible from the street, you can see it from a half-mile away."

On October 4, the foundation stationed a trumpeter in a band uniform on the roof of the old theater. As the motorcade approached, he blew a call to alert the members below. Crestfallen, they watched as the Pope's vehicle drove past without pausing.

The following day the *Tribune* reported, "Probably the most disappointed group was the crowd that waited at the Gateway Theatre, 5216 W. Lawrence. The ornate building is being converted to a Polish cultural center named for the astronomer Copernicus, and the Polish American crowd had hoped the Pope would stop to bless the building, which is to contain a library named for the pontiff."

Among those crestfallen was 75-year-old Mary Rzeszot, who had waited five hours in the cold. "I heard someone say, 'Here comes the Pope.' By the time I looked around, he had passed by already." Sixty-nine-year-old Mary Paterek was understanding, if disappointed. "You can't blame the Pope. He

The exterior of the theater today has changed its costume from Art Deco Aztec to elegant Eastern European.

wasn't driving. If he had just stopped for one minute, it would have been fine."

The completion of the sale of the building did not end the ties between Henry Plitt and the Copernicus Foundation. On November 2, 1983, Plitt screened *Nights and Days* in the theater. Subtitled in English, the Polish film had been nominated for an Academy Award for Best Foreign Language Film.

By 1985, little of Rapp & Rapp's Art Deco exterior was left. The foundation had covered the building in mustard-colored stucco. Now it embarked on an ambitious project—the construction of what it would call the Solidarity Tower. Fundraising for the needed $350,000 started in March that year; construction was slated to begin in April.

The completed addition was a nearly exact replica of the 14th-century, 135-foot clock tower atop the Royal Castle in Warsaw. That tower had been demolished by the Nazis during World War II in retribution for the 1944 Warsaw Uprising.

Intended as a Polish cultural complex, the Copernicus Center today is broadly used. Other ethnic groups—East Indian, Korean, Hispanic, and others—use the space for concerts, plays, seminars, and many other events.

While the exotic Eastern European exterior gives no hint of the original 1929 Art Deco facade, inside, the Copernicus directors have carefully preserved Rapp & Rapp's priceless interiors, taking the visitor back to Balaban & Katz's "Garden of Dreams."

GOETHE MONUMENT

LINCOLN PARK AT WEST DIVERSEY PARKWAY

As the 19th century became the 20th, Chicago had 470,000 residents who were either born in Germany or who had at least one parent born there. Throughout the previous half century, the immigrants had established social and musical clubs, German dance halls and beer gardens, and German language newspapers and churches.

Founded in 1878, the Schwaben Verein was among the earliest of the German social organizations. The original purpose was to provide assistance for immigrants arriving from Swabia in southern Germany. Its members, unlike many newcomers to America, were for the most part financially comfortable. In 1886, the group raised more than $8,000 to erect a statue of poet, physician, historian, and playwright Johann Christoph Friedrich von Schiller in Lincoln Park. It would not be their last monument.

In August 1899, plans were coming together for a lavish celebration of the 150th anniversary of the birth of Johann Wolfgang von Goethe, scheduled for September 3. The committee promised, "The entrance to the park will be transformed into a high medieval portal, from which a festooned archway will lead to the stage, which will represent a Greek temple."

As the committee completed its program—a compilation of scenes from the writer's works—it received a letter from New York City. The *Chicago Tribune* reported on August 5, 1899, "Henry Baerer, a sculptor of New York, has sent the committee a photograph of the model for a Goethe monument designed by him and an offer to build the monument planned for Chicago."

Baerer's offer was somewhat premature. At the time, only $4,000 had been collected by the Schwaben Verein for a Goethe monument fund and no real plans regarding its appearance had yet been discussed. The group had amassed $50,000 by 1910 to pay for a statue and, as was often the case with public art, a competition for the design was held. The sculptors were restricted by the Lincoln Park commissioners who officially discouraged traditional portraiture.

The *Chicago Tribune* pointed out, "it was one of the conditions of the program of the competition that the monument should not be a mere portrait statue, but should be expressive of the genius of Goethe or significant of his works." The newspaper added that the Lincoln Park board felt that "the portraying of great men or national heroes by a sculptural duplicate of their outward appearances has become obsolete."

The nine participating artists now had to creatively memorialize the great German writer without sculpting his true likeness. It was most likely a frustrating condition for German-born Hermann Hahn, who had gained an international reputation for creating lifelike statues of important German figures. His public monuments graced the cities of Bremen, Weimar, and Chemnitz.

Hahn's winning submission transformed Johann Wolfgang von Goethe into an Olympic god—symbolic of the writer's "Olympic achievements." The nearly nude, muscular figure stood with his right leg perched upon a rock. A cape fell off his shoulders, covering his back, and an eagle, a symbol of Germany, stood on his knee. On the stone pedestal would be the Goethe quotation, "He took to himself the wings of an eagle." A few steps across a small plaza a complementary exedra featured a bas-relief portrait of Goethe (despite the commissioners' stipulation).

Hermann Hahn's somewhat surprising design both confused and offended citizens and critics. On October 1, 1910, the *Chicago Eagle* worried that the statue would die of pneumonia: "Judging from photographs of the proposed Goethe statue in Lincoln Park, it will be necessary to take up a collection to buy a suit of clothes for the figure to keep it from catching cold."

Harriet Monroe, writing in the *Chicago Tribune* on February 12, 1911, was merciless. She called the statue "another sad imposition upon the long suffering community." Her critique was accompanied by a sketch showing an "improvement" on the design. It was a shower head installed over the figure.

"Why the poet should be shown poised insecurely with one leg at a right angle with his body, and with a singularly wooden bird—is it a decoy duck?— perched squarely on his knee, is one of those mysteries which will puzzle the wisest heads as long as the threatened statue lasts, and bronze is sometimes too durable."

Monroe apologized to Germany, saying, "This model is by no means representative of modern German sculpture—I know, for I saw good work last summer."

One reader quickly responded, his letter to the editor appearing four days later. "The criticism of Miss Harriet Monroe in The Sunday Tribune of Feb. 12 in regard to the proposed Goethe monument deserves praise, as it expresses

LEFT Hermann Hahn posed in his Munich studio at the base of his gigantic statue before shipping it to Chicago. **RIGHT** The ghostly outline of the monument awaits its unveiling in the rain in June 1914.

the sentiment of many people. The proposed monument would be more fitting to the memory of a Hagenbeck than of a Goethe." (Carl Hagenbeck was Germany's version of P. T. Barnum; he is credited with creating the modern zoo.)

Famous New York sculptor Karl Bitter, also born in Germany, fired back at critics, especially Harriet Monroe. In an exhaustive rebuttal that took up the majority of a page in the *Chicago Sunday Tribune* on February 26, 1911, he reminded critics that the raised knee that had puzzled Harriet had ancient precedents.

He wrote, "If this competition is a failure, one so carefully studied and guarded, then we may despair of a good result in any conscientious effort to secure a worthy public monument." He described Hahn as "a man of the highest distinction, a leader of the Munich secessionists, the most progressive group of artists in Germany."

Harriet Monroe was only tepidly moved. She replied, "It would be premature, perhaps, to find fault with the modeling of Mr. Hahn's figure, as this preliminary design is merely a sketch, and the finished work probably would have more life and quality." She was quick to add, "But I cannot find in the sketch that power of imagination, that loftiness of idea, which Mr. Bitter seems to think has been achieved."

Whether critics liked the sketch and model or not, the project went forward. In December 1913, the *Chicago Eagle* announced that President Woodrow Wilson would be invited to the unveiling of the finished sculpture and anticipated that 75,000 members of German societies in Chicago would be in attendance.

The ceremony took place in a misty rain on June 14, 1914. The expected throng of 75,000 was reduced to 20,000, possibly because of the uncomfortable weather. Also absent was President Wilson. With political upheaval in Europe, Count Johann Heinrich von Bernstorff, German ambassador, took the opportunity to plead for "mutual understanding between the United States and his nation."

The monument sat within a 100-foot-diameter plaza, surrounded by six granite benches. The 18-foot-3-inch bronze statue stood upon a black Swedish granite base. Once unveiled, it prompted more criticism.

The trade journal *Monumental News* praised and denounced the monument in one sentence. It wrote that Hahn "has wrought a remarkably beautiful piece of sculpture, although the symbolism by which Goethe is represented is so far-fetched as to need considerable explanation."

As America was pulled into the Great War, anti-German sentiments strengthened the already antagonistic feelings about the Goethe memorial. On April 17, 1918, the Lincoln Park Board of Commissioners met to discuss the statue. The *Tribune* reported, "The bronze figure of the German writer has disturbed the patriotic senses of certain people living in the neighborhood who day after day read with mingled feelings the lettering on the statue, 'The master mind of the German people.'"

The board had received rumors that groups were plotting to destroy the memorial. Destruction would be a significant job; vandalism was simple. On the night of May 7, 1918, the monument was slathered in yellow paint from the knees to the base. The can was then upturned, allowing a yellow pool to disfigure the ground below. A placard was left that read:

An emphatic protest from a free people against the retention of what always has been an offense against art, and now is a challenge to loyalty. Shall this park, named for the illustrious Lincoln, continue to harbor such an enormity or will the people of Chicago insist on its immediately removal?—Two Americans

The *Chicago Tribune* noted that "Since it was installed there has been much controversy over it as an object of art…. Since America's entrance into the

Impervious to public opinion, the statue remained unmoved by anything less powerful than a lightning bolt.

war the element of patriotism has further irritated the situation."

The anti-German fervor would rise again when America found itself fighting in World War II. One level-headed Chicagoan, Mrs. Ethel Besset, berated those who lashed out at the Goethe statue as a symbol of the enemy. Instead, she insisted, they were acting like the enemy. She wrote to the editor of the *Chicago Tribune* on September 22, 1942, chiding that a reader's previous letter "urging that the Goethe statue be scrapped indicates a reappearance of the 1917-'18 war hysteria directed against the Goethe statue. Minds like Homer, Dante, Shakespeare, and Goethe belong to all mankind and to no one country. They are above nationality. 'B.O.G.'s' intolerance of the statue is of the Nazi pattern of intolerance, which we aim to put down in this war."

Ironically, it was neither war nor racism that did significant damage to the memorial—it was, apparently, Mother Nature. On September 14, 1951, a loud explosion was heard by hundreds near the park. The following day the statue and its base were found cracked, and the entire statue was twisted. Officials presumed it was a bolt of lightning that was to blame.

The greatest damage was to the left foot. It was so severe that the entire statue was removed in September 1953 while a replacement foot was cast and attached. During the time the statue was in the shop, German societies raised money for a full restoration. In July 1954, the $6,000 project was completed. The replacement foot, forged by the Chicago firm Artisans of Bronze, Inc., had been attached, the statue sandblasted and then recolored, and replaced on its granite pedestal.

Hermann Hahn's remarkable work of art no longer prompts public controversy or overt emotions. The Olympic figure has weathered two world wars and a lightning strike admirably. And despite one journalist's concern in 1910, it has reputedly never caught cold.

LOUIS SULLIVAN'S LAST COMMISSION: KRAUSE MUSIC STORE
4611 NORTH LINCOLN AVENUE

William P. Krause was a successful merchant in 1921, when he sought out architect William Presto to design his new music store. The plot Krause had chosen, 4611 North Lincoln Avenue, was almost directly across from his home at No. 4626. The commission came about, it seems, as a result of the two men being neighbors.

Two years earlier, William Presto had been loaned by his employer, George C. Nimmons, to architect Louis Sullivan to assist as a draftsman on the Farmers and Merchants Union Bank project in Columbus, Wisconsin. Unfortunately for Presto, shortly after that building was completed, Sullivan had to let him go for financial reasons. By now, despite his astonishing career and contributions to American architecture, Sullivan was receiving no new commissions, and he was plagued with emotional and financial problems, besides alcoholism.

William Presto, however, described his experience with the master architect as "wonderful." After he worked on floor plans for the Krause building, he took them to Sullivan. Presto later recalled that Sullivan looked them over, then picked up a pencil and sketched out a concept for the front elevation on the back of an envelope. It was the first step in the last facade Louis Sullivan would design.

Krause directed that his building would house his shop on the first floor, with a home for him, his wife, Olga, and their family on the second. Construction was completed in 1922 at a total cost of about $22,000, $3,770 of which was for Sullivan's extraordinary terra-cotta facade. The *Music Trades* magazine wrote, "When it became known that Louis H. Sullivan would design the facade of Mr. Krause's store, lovers of the beautiful in architecture looked forward to seeing a store that would be a landmark in the district. In this they were not disappointed."

Indeed they were not. Sullivan had lavished the green terra-cotta facade with his signature ornamentation. He strongly believed that architecture should be "organic"; that it should harmonize with the natural world through design. The facade of the Krause store overflowed with floral forms executed in the intricate motifs that had become Sullivan's hallmark. Above the deep-set show window was a robust bouquet or basketlike grouping of leaves from which sprouted two thin, engaged columns that blossomed into a treelike panel. This, in turn, exploded at the roofline into a wreath enclosing a shield with the Krause "K."

The *Music Trades*, on November 18, 1922, reported, "William P. Krause has set a high standard for retail music merchants with his new store at 4611 Lincoln Avenue.... No expense was

The newly completed building as it appeared in 1922 and . . .

spared to have the interior of the store in keeping with the architect's [elaborate] exterior design. Solid oak and gray is the predominating motif in the decoration of the first floor." The magazine was taken with the forward thinking of the owner and the architects. "An elaborate automatic pumping apparatus which virtually eliminates any possibility of damage to his stock has been installed in the basement by Mr. Krause."

Krause sold a variety of music-related products, including pianos, phonographs, and records. Rather surprisingly, he also offered sewing machines. Perhaps to Olga Krause's discomfort, he outfitted the apartment above as a sort of second showroom. The *Music Trades* noted, "Above the store is a five-room apartment, where Mr. Krause lives with his family. This is exceptionally beautifully decorated, with solid mahogany predominating. In his living room he has installed a grand piano, a talking machine, and other musical instruments from the stock carried in the store. The purpose of this, Mr. Krause explained, is to enable a customer to see just how a baby grand will look in an apartment."

The Krause music store continued to be a success until the Stock Market Crash of 1929. The Great Depression resulted in Americans cutting back on luxuries—from fur coats to motion pictures. Pianos and talking machines,

... as it looks almost a century later.

unfortunately for William Krause, fell into that category. With his business in sharp decline, Krause was found dead in his apartment. He had committed suicide.

Olga Krause leased the store, which was converted to a funeral home. She kept possession of it until 1958, when it was sold to Francis Wagner, who quickly resold it to James M. Coleman. Coleman was a founder and partner in the Arntzen-Coleman Funeral Home, which would remain in the building for decades.

Arntzen-Coleman was still operating here when the building was nominated for Landmark designation in September 1978. Architecture critic Paul Gapp was somewhat tepid in his assessment of Sullivan's facade at the time, saying, "though the effusiveness of its terra cotta ornamentation is a bit heavy-handed, we can forgive that."

James Coleman died in February 1988 at the age of 77, having been with the funeral home for more than half a century. He was responsible for several alterations to the Lincoln Avenue structure, including drilling holes in the terra-cotta to accommodate a sign, and replacing Sullivan's large plate-glass show window with three smaller windows. At some point, a misguided acid wash bleached the green tint of the terra-cotta.

Scott Elliott then opened his Kelmscott Galleries, which focused on the Chicago School of Architecture, and on 20th-century crafts. He restored the facade, returned the plate-glass show window, and replicated the original oak entry doors. A subsequent owner, Studio V. Design, a creative agency and marketing firm, initiated interior renovations in 2006.

The remarkable little store is crammed in among later commercial buildings along the block. They prompted Professor Hugh Morrison in his *Louis Sullivan: Prophet of Modern Architecture* to comment, "We only have to compare it with the conventional facades of the stores that have been built around it to realize, as forcefully as ever, that even in the least significant of his works, Sullivan was still a master."

THE WHISTLE STOP INN

4200 WEST IRVING PARK ROAD

By the end of the Civil War, Chicago had developed into a substantial city, holding its own with the metropolises of the East Coast. In 1869, Charles T. Race, his son Richard, and other investors embarked on a risky but potentially highly profitable scheme. They would build an idyllic suburb where families could enjoy comfortable homes, with porches that caught the summer breezes, away from the congestion and bustle of the city.

The men purchased land in Jefferson Township, north of the city, which they divided into building plots. A deal was struck with the Chicago & North Western Railroad for future train service, and an aggressive marketing strategy was put into place. The upper-middle-class tone of Irving Park (named after popular author Washington Irving) was evidenced when Richard and Susan Race's residence was completed on June 1, 1873. The bill from the contractor was $3,000 plus $359 for "extra work not embraced in the original agreement." The total outlay would be equivalent to about $70,000 today.

A year later, Everett Chamberlain, writing in *Chicago and Its Suburbs*, commented that Irving Park's houses were, without exception, of a "neat pattern, and almost endless variety."

As the community grew, it demanded other buildings and services— churches, firehouses, stores, and livery stables, for instance. In 1881, Henry E. Nichols purchased the plot at the northwest corner of Irving Park Road and Keeler Avenue for $750. But he would wait another eight years to develop it.

He borrowed $3,200 in 1889 to construct a frame grocery store and dwelling. Nichols and his family lived upstairs, while he operated his store, Nichols & Son, on the ground floor. His wooden commercial building made no pretenses of grandeur, yet it was handsome in its fine proportions and Italianate cornice. The shop entrance, recessed between show windows, was a precursor to the "arcade windows" that would gain popularity in the following decades.

Nichols operated his grocery store for only a year, selling it to another grocer, David D. Mee, in 1890. A small-town "grocery" in the 1890s was more a general store—selling not only canned goods and other foodstuffs,

The 20th and 21st centuries encroach the 19th-century structure.

but also dry goods, grains, and household items. Mee and his successors may have earned extra income when at least a portion of the building was used as the Irving Park Road tollhouse from 1891 to 1894.

The rapid turnover continued when Mee sold it 18 months later to Fred A. Brown. Brown's grocery store, too, would be short-lived. In June 1903, the building became home to William H. Brown's drugstore, which was formerly located at 1168 West Byron Street, about four miles to the east. Whether Fred Brown and William Brown were somehow related is unclear. In any case, William was no stranger to Illinois druggists. He was the former vice president of the Illinois Pharmaceutical Association.

A drugstore would remain in the building for about two decades, sharing space for one year, between 1911 and 1912, with the town library. As mid-century approached, however, the building received several attempts at modernization. The entrance was moved to the corner, the wooden balustrade that had capped the cornice was lost, and at some point the clapboards were hidden beneath asphalt shingles. The upper windows at the front were removed and grouped replacements installed.

By the early 1940s, the old pharmacy had been converted to a bar-room. It was the source of intense problems for one policeman from Albany Park in 1944. That was a presidential election year and Officer Cyrus Merrill was given the responsibility of taking election supplies to a warehouse on Monday,

November 6. Curiously, he never showed up. And later that day, when he was to report for Election Day instructions, he again was AWOL.

Fearing he may have been the victim of foul play, a search was initiated. The *Chicago Tribune* reported two days later that he "was found Monday night in a tavern at 4200 Irving Park Rd."

Officer Merrill's on-duty indiscretion could not have come at a worse time for him. The reputation of the current police commissioner, James P. Allman, was one of no tolerance for corruption, loafing, or "foolishness." It earned him the nicknames "Iron Man" and "Cleanup Man." Merrill was unceremoniously suspended from duty by Commissioner Allman.

By the 1980s, the old wooden building had suffered substantial abuse. New owners initiated a restoration of sorts, attempting to bring the vintage structure back to its Victorian appearance. Around 1987, with the project complete, the Whistle Stop, a bar and grill, opened. The clapboards had reemerged; a new storefront closely replicated the original with its centered entrance; and a several-hued paint scheme—popular among late Victorians— gave the grocery-turned-pharmacy-turned bar new life.

The proprietors no doubt wished they had omitted one modern item. Shortly after opening, in September 1989, the new tavern was raided by Chicago police, who confiscated an illegal video poker machine.

The unassuming wooden building is a charming relic of a time when Irving Park was still a suburb, and its restoration is a laudable nod to the city's past.

The Chicago Federals, precursors of the Cubs, playing at Weeghman Park, which became Wrigley Field.

WRIGLEY FIELD

1060 WEST ADDISON STREET

Professional baseball had been around for 45 years when Charles Henry Weeghman first envisioned a ballpark for his newly organized Chicago Federals (named for the Federal League in which it played) in 1914. Fans and the press popularly called the team the Chifeds.

Weeghman had made a fortune in lunch counters in the Chicago area. When he was foiled in his attempt to purchase the St. Louis Cardinals in 1911, he helped found the Federal League, and then formed his own professional team.

Weeghman and his partner W. M. Walker found the site they were looking for in land bound by Clark and Addison Streets, and Waveland and Sheffield Avenues. The property was almost entirely owned by a Lutheran evangelical college (it possessed all but a 16-by-100-foot swath). Weeghman acquired the plot and, since the adjoining strip was owned by a friend, he was unconcerned about getting possession of that as well.

But professional baseball was a cut-throat business and Charles Weeghman nearly fell victim to corporate sabotage. On January 19, 1914, the *Chicago Tribune* reported that the little strip of ground, "caused most of the chaos at the meeting of the Federal league baseball magnates Saturday afternoon." Weeghman explained the situation to reporters: "About a week ago this friend of mine was approached by some unknown man and offered $25,000 in cash for that bit of ground. Of course, that was a fabulous sum for it, and he came to me. I knew organized baseball was behind that offer."

Hoping that it was a bluff on the part of a rival to force him to abandon the project, Weeghman told his friend to accept the bid. The deal was agreed upon and the buyer agreed to meet at 4:30 the following Saturday to sign the papers. As Weeghman had suspected, it was all a ruse and the "buyer" never showed up.

The Iowa newspaper *Daily Gate City* commented, "Possibly it indicates real desperation when magnates such as Garry Hermann and others try to buy a strip of dry land sixteen feet wide…in hopes of blocking the scheme of President Weeghman of the Chicago team for the erection of a ball park."

Demolition of the old wooden buildings on the site began on February 23. Weeghman chose Zachary Taylor Davis (who had previously designed Comiskey

Park) as the architect of Weeghman Park. The single-story concrete-and-steel structure went up with dizzying speed and was completed within two months. Typical of early-20th-century ballparks, a brick wall surrounded the playing field and the stands were protected from sun and rain by a roof upheld by tall poles.

Opening day for the $250,000 park on April 23 was a pompous affair. Handy Andy, *Chicago Times* sportswriter, announced "It's the north side today, and all hail the Chifeds!" He deemed the new ballpark "up to date in every particular." The opening ceremonies were to be a patriotic affair: "A great American flag will be presented to the local Federal league club by the ladies of the G. A. R. [Grand Army of the Republic]. President Ida E. Wright will make the presentation speech in front of the grand stand, after which twenty women, members of the G. A. R. auxiliary, will carry the stars and stripes across the field to the flag pole. The ceremony is certain to arouse considerable patriotic feeling."

The article noted that "Arrangements have been made to care for over 25,000 fans. The seating capacity of the new park is about 18,000, and circus seats will be ready for the overflow crowd which the new leaguers are confident will be on hand."

Seats in the park cost 50 cents in the grandstand and 25 cents in the bleachers. But streetwise boys knew how to get in for free. Decades later, Irv Swoiskin recalled to a *Tribune* reporter, "In order to get a free pass, you'd get there early and pick up papers in the grandstands. Sometimes they would give you two passes. If you got two, you sold one. A 50-cent pass you sold for a quarter."

The season went well for the Chifeds and they ended in second place. The following year their name was changed to the Chicago Whales. Their jerseys sported a large "C" that encircled a whale. Despite winning the league championship, it was the end of the team. The Federal League disbanded following the end of the season. In response, Charles Weeghman and W. M. Walker merged their club with the Chicago Cubs, who had been playing on the West Side. Weeghman reportedly spent $500,000 to buy the team. The men were joined in the venture by chewing gum mogul William Wrigley Jr., who bought a minority stake.

On July 8, 1916, the *Tribune* stoked baseball fans' enthusiasm by declaring, "You know the players! You know the records of the clubs that are now racing for the pennant! You know before you go out that you'll see that kind of baseball which has made Chicago the greatest ball town in America—and which is going to make the new Weeghman Park a famous spot."

The article called the park "new" because the owners had remodeled it. The renovations included raising the right field wall ten feet. The *Chicago Tribune* noted, "A wire screen now perches on top of the wall and informs curious persons what the fence surrounds, besides making it harder to knock home runs into Sheffield avenue." By now ticket prices had doubled to $1—around $23 today.

Just as the 1917 season opened the United States entered World War I. A flood of patriotism swept the nation and its ballparks. Charles Weeghman was staunchly in favor of the draft and ensured that each of the eligible players had registered. On June 1, the *Chicago Tribune* reported, "Military propaganda will feature the home series of Chicago's Cubs, which begins today at Weeghman park with Brooklyn as the enemy, and one of the features will be a patriotic pageant on June 5, to do a bit to offset the anti-draft plotters." Two drill squads from the Great Lakes Naval Training Station were scheduled to perform, while the Great Lakes Band of 125 men would "lend music and color to the pageant."

Later that year, on September 10, the *Chicago Tribune* noted, "A big day is planned for Weeghman park tomorrow. It will be military day....Every soldier and sailor in uniform will be admitted free and there will be military bands as well as a special feature in the company of civil war veterans."

At the time Charles Weeghman was selling more and more of his stock in the team to Wrigley. Interest in his luncheon counters—which had garnered him a fortune estimated at $8 million in 1915—had sharply fallen off. No doubt with great sorrow, he sold the last of his stake to Wrigley in 1918. Two years later Wrigley dealt Weeghman the final blow by removing his name from the park. It was now Cubs Park.

During the Roaring '20s, Chicago would become a hotspot of bootlegging, gambling, prostitution, and other gangland crimes. On May 25, 1920, the *Tribune* ran a banner headline that read, "CUBS PARK RAIDED – 47 BETTORS ARE JAILED." At the end of the first inning of the Chicago-Philadelphia game, undercover police stormed the stands. The raid had been planned for a week after police learned there was an open-air gambling ring in operation in the park.

A battalion of cops, dressed as fans, was scattered throughout the crowd during that week. The article quipped, "They ate peanuts. They drank pop and lemonade and things. They kept the score. They rooted. They watched the betting men and got acquainted with them, and had a nice time. It was hard to take."

On May 24, things would be different. The 47 bet-takers were "basking in the sun, exchanging opinions and money, some writing down bets they had made. The next instant a horde of teamsters, sailors, soldiers, ice wagon drivers, sewing machine agents, boot blacks and farmers—seemingly—had rounded them up and told them, 'You're under arrest.'"

Of the men's fines, $1 each went to the widow and children of Policeman William Roberts who had been killed by a bandit who robbed an Illinois Central mail train.

In 1921, the Cubs got strange bedfellows. For half a century, following baseball season, the playing field would be reworked for the Chicago Bears football team. And then things would be a little more crowded between 1931 and 1938 when the Chicago Cardinals football team also called Wrigley home.

Between the football and baseball seasons in 1923, the grandstands were enlarged, and three years later the stadium was rechristened Wrigley Field. A second deck to the grandstand was begun in 1927 and completed the following year.

William Wrigley Jr. died on January 26, 1932. His son, Philip Knight Wrigley, took over the reins and would soon make changes of his own. In 1937, he erected new outfield bleachers and installed a new scoreboard. That same summer, the now-famous outfield wall ivy was planted.

An innovation in 1938 would become iconic to baseball parks nationwide. On June 15, the *Farmers' Weekly Review* announced, "Even the hot dogs at Wrigley Field have gone de luxe. No longer must the steaming little puppies wait for the fans to 'come and get 'em.' They now go after the fans." White-uniformed hot dog vendors now prowled the stands with steam-heated cases, hollering "Hot Dawgs!"

Another first came on August 26, 1941, when the park debuted its pipe organ. Organ music, like the hot dog sellers, quickly became a ballpark staple. In 1946, the first televised game was played here.

In the meantime, the Chicago Cubs tried valiantly (and vainly) to claim a title. They had not won the World Series since 1908, years before moving to Weeghman Park. In 1935, it looked like the prize was within reach. On September 23, the *Urbana Daily Courier* announced, "A dozen heavy trucks rumbled up to Wrigley field on the North Side at dawn today and workmen started unloading yellow pine planks, boards and uprights." The lumber was for the construction of 12,000 more seats for the World Series. One of the drivers remarked, "It looks like Mister Wrigley is sure our Cubs is going to

Fans enjoy a traditional day game in the iconic park.

win the pennant." Indeed, the Cubs won the pennant. But, once again, they lost the series.

Things were looking up for the fans when the Cubs were back in the World Series in 1945. But an incident in Game 4 would cement the team's fate (at least in most fans' minds) for decades. William "Billy Goat" Sianis came to watch the game that day. The owner of the Billy Goat Tavern had brought along the bar's mascot, a goat named Murphy, for good luck. And Murphy brought along the pungent perfume of goat.

As with all good urban legends, the story took on different renditions as it was told and retold. One version says that Sianis and Murphy made it to the stands, but shortly fans complained about the stench, so Sianis and Murphy were ousted from the park.

Another (and likely more accurate) tale is that although Sianis had purchased a ticket for Murphy, they were stopped at the gate by ushers who insisted, "No animals allowed." When things threatened to get heated, Philip Wrigley himself got involved. He told the ushers to admit Sianis, but not the goat. "Why not the goat?" asked the tavern owner. "Because the goat stinks."

Whichever way it happened, the ending was the same. William Sianis and Murphy never saw Game 4 and on their way out Sianis vowed, "Them Cubs, they ain't gonna win no more." And indeed, they did not. The Cubs lost the

Cubs fans remained loyal throughout 108 years of disappointment in the World Series.

series to the Detroit Tigers and the long drought dragged on. Fans were certain their team had been bedeviled by what became known as "The Curse of the Billy Goat."

By 1957, Wrigley Field was one of the few major league parks not to have lights. That winter a rumor circulated that night games would finally come to Chicago, but Philip Wrigley quickly squashed the tale. On January 24, he told reporters, "The story is ridiculous. There aren't any lights in Wrigley field now and no lights are planned. I'm finding it pretty irksome having to deny such silly stories." The *Daily Illini* added, "Wrigley has long insisted baseball is a day sport only."

One fan and stockholder, however, disagreed. In 1953, when he was 14 years old, William Shlensky had purchased two shares of Cubs stock. Now, in March 1966, he filed suit in Circuit Court "to force Cubs owner Phil Wrigley to install lights for night baseball at Wrigley Field." Despite Shlensky's intrepid attempt, it would be another two decades before the lights came on over Wrigley Field.

In 1981, the Tribune Company purchased the Cubs, ending a 66-year ownership by the Wrigley family. *The New York Times* commented, "The purchase began a series of changes that has increased attendance, made the premises more comfortable and the operation more efficient."

At 6:05 p.m. on August 8, 1988, a 91-year-old fan named Harry Grossman was set to flip the switch on the newly installed lighting system. It was no small affair. Anticipating throngs in the streets of between 40,000 to 45,000, police begged Chicagoans who did not have a ticket to stay home. One policeman said, "We expect traffic jams for hours. People are going to want to come down and see the lights."

One baseball fan who wanted a peek was former Cubs broadcaster Ronald Reagan—who happened to be President of the United States at the time. He was in Chicago that day and, according to Illinois Republican Representative Dennis Hastert, who accompanied him, he requested the helicopter pilot change course to pass over Wrigley Field.

Hastert told a reporter, "He believed that old man Wrigley's philosophy was to get people out in the sunshine." As the President looked down on the field, he sighed, "I guess, sentimentally, it ought to stay that way. That's what Mr. Wrigley wanted."

For the park's 100th anniversary on April 22, 2014 the team donned the old Chicago Federals jerseys. The first 10,000 fans to arrive got a cupcake. Outside, a 400-pound cake in the shape of the park from Carlo's Bakery in Hoboken, New Jersey was on display. The ushers wore pointy birthday hats.

The first pitch that night was thrown by Sue Quigg, the grandniece of Charles Weeghman. *The New York Times* noted, "Firing a strike from about 45 feet, Quigg tossed a 100-year-old ball that her grandmother once threw at a Federals game." The list of sports luminaries at the field that night was impressive. The pre-game ceremony included Ernie Banks, Andre Dawson, Ferguson Jenkins, Gary Matthews, Billy Williams, Ryan Dempster and Randy Hundley. Also on hand were Chicago Bears star players Gale Sayers and Dick Butkus.

In reporting on the centennial, *The New York Times'* Ben Strauss said, "The charm of Wrigley is more than just its longevity. The park is quaint, tucked into a residential neighborhood on the city's North Side. The hand-operated scoreboard in center field is a landmark, as is the ivy that sprouts on the outfield walls each summer."

Another journalist, Benjamin Hoffman, could not resist pointing out the Cubs' long title drought. "The team's loyal fans have spilled quite a bit of Old Style beer over the years, but the Cubs have had little use for Champagne, not having won a World Series since moving to Wrigley from West Side Park." And yet, it was not championships that kept Chicago fans coming back. "Wrigley has endured this long based on beer sales, mediocre teams and sunny days. There is no reason that formula could not work for another hundred years," said Hoffman.

That formula would not have to last another century. In 2016, the long-discounted Chicago Cubs broke the Curse of the Billy Goat by winning the World Series over the Cleveland Indians in seven nail-biting games.

A $575 million renovation by the Ricketts family, who bought the team and stadium in 2009, was revealed in January 2013. Ongoing, they are bringing the 21st century to the 1914 park—like a giant video scoreboard. But the ivy still clings to the brick and the signature red "Wrigley Field Home of Chicago Cubs" sign, installed in 1934, still welcomes fans who hope their next World Series win will come faster than the last.

WEST

FIRST BAPTIST CONGREGATIONAL CHURCH

1613 WEST WASHINGTON BOULEVARD

In 1851, the issue of slavery had smoldered for several years, driving a wedge between neighbors, clubmen, and business associates in the North. In Chicago, heated arguments over slavery would cause a religious schism and the creation of a new church. In May that year, 48 fervently anti-slavery members of the Third Presbyterian Church defected. They had come to an impasse with the General Assembly, which failed, in their estimation, to make a strong enough stand for abolition. Led by Philo Carpenter, the group broke off to form the First Congregational Church.

It was no doubt a difficult decision for Carpenter, who had arrived in the settlement that would become Chicago in 1832, and within the year had helped found the First Presbyterian Church. He operated Chicago's first apothecary in a log house near what is today Lake Street. Then in 1847 he was instrumental in the organization of the Third Presbyterian Church. Now he started, again, from scratch.

According to a church historian, writing in the *Manual of the Union Park Congregational Church and Society* in 1892, the first permanent building for what would become the Union Park Congregational Church was not completed until June 1858. That was the "Mission Sabbath School on West Washington street, near Wood, and in the following autumn the congregation erected a plain wooden building, designed with reference to its possible use, at some future time, as a place of worship."

In 1859, in an agreement with the Chicago Theological Seminary (which Philo Carpenter also co-founded), the little building was moved at the seminary's expense to Reuben Street (later renamed Ashland Avenue) and Washington Street (later Washington Boulevard). The mission structure was also enlarged. The seminary took possession in October, while the mission continued to hold services there on Sundays. When a meeting on April 18, 1860, resulted in the movement to organize what had been a mission into the Union Park Congregational Church, things moved swiftly.

All the while, the congregation continued with its abolitionist efforts, assisting escaped slaves on their way to Canada and becoming an important link in the Underground Railroad. It was a dangerous undertaking, even in the North.

As the membership and the surrounding population grew, the frame church was enlarged twice—in 1865, when it was moved again, from the north to the south side of Washington Street; and in 1867. But just as the congregation was assembling for worship on Sunday evening, February 21, 1869, fire broke out. A newspaper reported later, "The Union Park Congregational Church caught fire through a defect in the furnace and was almost entirely consumed. A costly organ purchased last spring shared the fate of the building."

Immediately, Reverend Charles D. Helmer laid plans to erect a substantial stone edifice. He turned to one of the best known of Chicago architects at the time—Gurdon P. Randall. A New Englander, he had been in Chicago since 1856, and by now, according to *Biographical Sketches of the Leading Men of Chicago* in 1868, had "designed and supervised the construction of more public buildings in the Northwest than any other architect." The author found it necessary to add, "He prides himself on never having fallen into any of the demoralizing, tobacco-using, whisky-drinking practices of the age, or into any of those vices which undermine the health or the morals of mankind. He is a rare exception to the Western rule in this respect."

Among Randall's chief contenders for architectural commissions was Otis Wheelock, another well-known and formidable Chicago architect, whom the Chicago Theological Seminary had hired to replace the mission building. As Randall worked out his plans, Wheelock's Carpenter Chapel—named obviously in honor of Philo Carpenter—was nearing completion next to the blackened ruins. Wheelock's limestone Gothic Revival structure was completed in 1869—just about the time that the cornerstone for the Union Park Congregational Church was laid.

The cornerstone ceremony was held on August 7 and construction would take two years. The "elegant and commodious edifice," as described in 1884 by A. T. Andreas in his *History of Chicago*, was dedicated on November 12, 1871. Randall had created a dignified limestone-clad Gothic Revival structure that so perfectly melded with Wheelock's Carpenter Chapel that they appeared to be designed by the same architect. Rough-cut stone walls were supported by hefty buttresses; and the corner bell tower, offset by a spindly, minaret-type spire, was capped by a soaring, angular steeple rising more than 200 feet.

Randall designed a nave with amphitheater seating, capable of accommodating 1,500 worshippers. Overhead, a network of carved wooden trusses supported the complex ceiling. The original 1851 pulpit furniture and communion table, rescued from the fire, were installed in the new sanctuary.

Active in the church was Mrs. Frances M. Scoville, who headed the Women's Personal Liberty League. She chaired a meeting of the women's group in the church on October 15, 1872. The women had decided that crime was not going to be eliminated by the government, and they must step in. Among the resolutions that afternoon was "That Intemperance and Licentiousness are twin brothers in evil and crime; that houses of prostitution are hot-beds of intemperance; and that any measures which shall tend to destroy one of these evils will help to remove the other, thereby materially diminishing crime."

The women were united in condemning Chicago officials. "The Mayor, Police Superintendent, and Board of Police Commissioners of our city have not only so far failed to enforce the 'New Temperance Law,' but have also, as we are informed, separately refused the offer of the Citizens' Committee of fifteen to supply a voluntary special police force to assist in its enforcement."

The police commissioners were blissfully unaware that the meeting closed with the selection of the committee of 15, charged with "devising some way by which the servants of the people can be forced to do the work demanded of them by the people and the exigencies of the hour."

Few of the congregants' activities were as confrontational. Music played an important part in Union Park Congregational Church and its musicians were high caliber and well known. On July 20, 1872, the *Ottawa* [Illinois] *Free Trader* reported on an upcoming concert of "superior music" to be held at the Turner Hall. "At this concert Mr. L. A. Phelps, the talented musician, will lead as tenor, and will be assisted by three very splendid artists from Union Park Congregational church, Chicago, viz.: Mrs. Carpenter, soprano; Mr. Bowen, basso; and Mr. Allen, violinist." The newspaper added, "The music will be of a very high order, and on the evening named expect to see a full house and to hear such music as will be remembered for a life time."

The Union Park Congregational Church was the venue of entertainments as well as religious services. On March 11, 1878, Alfred J. Knight gave "another of his costume recitals" here; on December 7 that year the *New York Clipper* reported in its "Musical Notes from Chicago, Ill," that "Musical circles were made interesting by the appearance of Mlle. Litta at the Union Park Congregational Church Thanksgiving night"; and a week later Mrs. Minnie G.

Otis Wheelock's Carpenter Chapel and Gurdon Randall's First Baptist Congregational Church are so harmonious they seem to be a single structure.

Slayton gave "the third entertainment of the West-side Lecture Course, with readings and impersonations, aided by Miss Zo Swisshelm in piano-solos."

Even after the Civil War ended, the Union Park Congregational Church did not forget its abolitionist roots. In 1879, the church lured Reverend Frederick A. Noble from New Haven, Connecticut as its pastor. Noble had a fiery anti-slavery reputation that went back years and was a member of the Beecher Council (the nationwide council of Congregational churches headed by Brooklyn abolitionist Henry Ward Beecher, whose sister wrote *Uncle Tom's Cabin*). The *History of Chicago* later said of him, "He took a decided stand in the pulpit and on the platform in favor of the maintenance of the Union and the destruction of Slavery."

In September 1879, the church staged a one-week presentation of *Uncle Tom's Cabin*. An advertisement noted that the production was "Endorsed by Mrs. Harriet Beecher Stowe," and called it the "Greatest Moral Dramatic Combination on Record." The play was presented every afternoon and evening, beginning September 8.

Reverend Noble's pointed sermons went far beyond anti-slavery issues. His topic on March 30, 1884 was "Conversation." After tiptoeing into the issue by speaking of truthfulness, kindliness, and purity, he got to the point: slang and cursing. The world would survive, he felt, if everything from slang to oath were omitted. "There is less excuse for foul words than for any other," he charged. "No syllable tainted with foulness should be allowed to escape the lips." He warned the congregation that "The vile person will speak villainy," and "If a man's conversation cannot please without entering into the vile borders of the obscenity, let him know that God never intended him for a wit."

When the officials of the Chicago World's Columbian Exposition proposed to have the fairgrounds opened on Sundays, the strait-laced Reverend Noble exploded. He joined other stalwart Christian pastors in lobbying to keep the World's Fair closed on the Sabbath (resulting in a staggering loss of receipts). On July 23, 1893, he informed his congregation that the fight was won: "I regard this day as a special vindication of the sanctity of the Sabbath and as a day of universal rejoicing among Christians because of the fact that the World's Fair is closed."

Five years later, after Commodore George Dewey occupied Manila during the Spanish-American War, Reverend Noble preached a rousingly patriotic sermon. The *Chicago Tribune*, on October 17, 1898, noted, "The Union Park Congregational Church…was elaborately decorated. The music was of a patriotic nature and the sermon was suited to the occasion. The Rev. Mr. Noble said: 'The guns of Dewey awoke the nation to self-consciousness and to a consciousness of its mission to the world.'"

In 1908, true to its inclusive roots, the Union Park Congregational Church offered its space for "a union meeting of members of colored churches of the west side," according to the *Chicago Tribune* on May 4.

In 1910, the church was renamed the "New" First Congregational Church. Its pastor in 1922 was as unabashedly opinionated from the pulpit as had been Reverend Noble. In August that year, Reverend W. A. Barlett declared that the anti-Prohibitionists were "anarchists" and that if Theodore Roosevelt were alive, "he would have them all in jail and take a chance at being supported by public opinion."

His sermon was quickly met with a reply by A. D. Plamondon of the Association Opposed to Prohibition. On August 22, the *Chicago Tribune* reprinted parts of his infuriated response. Half a million Illinois residents had signed a petition for a referendum on exempting beer and wine from the Volstead Act. Plamondon said they "will undoubtedly be shocked to learn from the Rev. Dr. Barlett, who preaches the gospel of the lowly Nazarene, how wicked they really are." He went on to point out that two of Theodore Roosevelt's sons were members of his organization. "Should they be put in jail?" he asked.

Even while the battle over imbibing continued, the congregation focused attention on music. In January 1927, work on installing the magnificent new organ in the church was begun. The immense size of the instrument—the largest enclosed pipe organ ever made, according to National Register of Historic Places documents—necessitated structural reinforcement to support it. Restoration of the deteriorating roof trusses and foundation strengthening were simultaneously undertaken. The $150,000 project carefully avoided altering the architectural elements. The organ, costing $125,000 ($1.7 million today), was installed in June and dedicated on October 9, 1927.

The name of the historic church would be changed again twice—to the First Congregational Baptist Church in 1970; and to the First Baptist Congregational Church in 1976. But a new name did not mean that the congregation was any less involved in the community or that its sometimes-fiery ministers were any less outspoken.

When the owner of a roller rink, the Grand Rollerena, at Laramie Avenue and Adams Street, decided to convert the property to a motel in April 1980,

Reverend Arthur D. Griffin made his opinion known. "We can live with the skating rink, but we sure don't need a motel," he told a reporter. "People who are traveling, they don't come into our neighborhood. We don't need to facilitate prostitution."

Seven years later when a new football stadium for the Bears was proposed in the area, Griffin spoke out again, calling it a "playground for the wealthy" that would displace thousands of low-income and elderly people. For weeks he led an opposition group against the plan and ultimately overturned it, rescuing the neighborhood.

While the neighborhood around the Landmarked church and chapel has greatly changed in the nearly 150 years since their completion, the two harmonious structures have not. And the church continues to be an integral part of the lives of its congregation and community.

HOLY TRINITY
ORTHODOX CATHEDRAL

1121 NORTH LEAVITT STREET

Prior to 1870, only a few thousand Russian immigrants had landed in America, but those numbers would soon swell, and by 1881 there were 10,000 Russians arriving each year. Between 1891 and 1900, more than half a million Russians left their homeland for America—many fleeing the devastating famine that began in 1891. The groups spread across the country, enough Orthodox Russians settling in Chicago to establish a parish, St. Vladimir's, in 1892.

According to an anonymous history written for the 50th anniversary of the parish, a church was erected at Center and Madison streets. Three years after its founding, St. Vladimir's welcomed 22-year-old Father John Kochurov, who was sent from St. Petersburg as pastor. Ambitious and energetic, Father Kochurov almost immediately focused on a permanent church structure for the congregation. The young priest's fundraising talents were apparently remarkable, for he not only garnered substantial donations from Chicago businessmen like Charles Richard Crane and Harold McCormick, but from Tsar Nicholas II (most likely with substantial help from Archimandrite Tikhon, later Bishop Tikhon). The Tsar's contribution of 5,000 rubles was equal to about $4,000 dollars—around $116,000 now.

Land was purchased at 560 North Leavitt Street (later renumbered 1121) in what is today known as Ukrainian Village, and one of the Midwest's preeminent architects, Louis Sullivan, received the commission. It would be one of only two churches he designed throughout his career. Sullivan looked to rural Russian churches for inspiration, completing his plans in 1899.

As construction got under way, the *Chicago Record Herald* commented on Sullivan's rendering: "A colored drawing that is calculated to arouse criticism is one by Louis H. Sullivan for an orthodox Russian Church. It is thoroughly Russian in character, and the exterior is painted in polychromatic colors, its domes embellished with gold. The color, which runs from ultramarine to red, is to be applied to plaster. It is to be hoped that this structure will

Louis Sullivan successfully melded provincial Russian Orthodox architecture with his signature style.

soon blossom forth like a flower amid the somber surroundings, and do for a city street what Mr. Sullivan's superb Transportation Building did for the Columbian exposition."

Construction took four years at a total cost of $27,104.37. On August 21, 1903, Louis Sullivan wrote to Prince Nicholas W. Engalitcheff, Imperial Russian Vice Consul, saying that their very pleasant interactions—"you as member of the Building Committee, I as architect, for the St. Trinity Russian Church—have now come to a close." Sullivan informed the prince that his normal charge was 10 percent of the structure's cost. However, he said, because of the cordial relations "and our mutual desire to see a beautiful little Russian Church erected in this city, so great and enthusiastic, that I consented to do the work for 5% commission—which means—practically—cost to me—and in money terms, a donation of $1250.70 to the church."

The resultant structure was, indeed, "thoroughly Russian in character." Sullivan's delightful country-style church featured a bell tower with open belfry to the front, and an octagonal dome over the sanctuary. Although the vivid colors and eccentric lines were unmistakably Russian, Sullivan managed to include his signature decorations, most notably in the exquisite openwork bonnet of the doorway.

The cathedral's interior is an explosion of colors and shapes. Rich stenciling covers the walls and a massive, art-glass lamp hangs from the soaring dome.

For parishioners, entering the building would be like stepping into the churches they had left behind in Russia. Brilliantly colored stenciling, art-glass fixtures, gilt-framed icons, and the sunlit dome echoed traditional Orthodox elements.

By the time the church was dedicated on March 30, 1903, the parish had been renamed Holy Trinity. *The New York Times* reported, "With the picturesque rites of a religion which has retained all the opulent symbolism of the ancient Byzantine civilization, the Russian Orthodox Church, which stands at Leavitt Street and Haddon Avenue, was consecrated to-day. Five hundred Chicago people, present as invited guests, witnessed the services side by side with the devout Slav peasants who compose the congregation."

Bishop Tikhon, by then Bishop of the Aleutian Islands and North America, presided, aided by Father Kochurov and 11 other priests. In the church that afternoon were Baron von Schlippenbach, Russian consul; Prince Engalitcheff, vice consul; Captain A. G. Butakoff, naval attaché at Washington; and Colonel N. W. Raspopoff, military attaché.

In the meantime, political, social, and military clouds were forming in Russia. The following Easter, on April 10, 1904, the congregation that packed the church was seriously concerned with conditions in their homeland,

While the neighborhood has changed, Sullivan's Russian-inspired house of worship looks much as it did in 1903.

most notably the Russo-Japanese War. The following day, the *Chicago Tribune* reported, "Prayers for the success of Russian arms in the war with Japan were said early yesterday morning at the Easter mass in the Church of the Holy Trinity... in which the Russians of Chicago worship. Nearly 1,500 Muscovites murmured response and wept with emotion while the priest prayed that 'victory might crown the efforts of the Christian czar [*sic*] and his Christian soldiers to drive back the unbelievers.'"

Father John Kochurov left Holy Trinity in 1907, while Russia was still in the turmoil of the Revolution of 1905. In 1916, he was transferred to St. Catherine's Cathedral in Tsarskoe Selo. On October 31, 1917, the Bolsheviks stormed the town and arrested Father Kochurov. He was taken outside of town and shot.

Father Vladimir Alexandroff had taken Father Kochurov's place at Holy Trinity; but agitation soon arose among the congregants. Chicagoans perhaps first got a hint of the problem on April 22, 1912, when the *Day Book* reported that police were necessary to guard the church while Father Alexandroff performed three marriages. The article noted that the "Congregation has been split into warring factions, one wing claiming [the] pastor has wrongfully administered finances."

The uneasy situation came to a violent end toward the end of 1915. Certain parishioners were outraged that Father Alexandroff had begun charging more to perform weddings, christenings, and funerals—services that were necessary for all congregants. The *Day Book* stated that a committee had asked him to account for the money he was collecting. He did so from the pulpit. "In the Russian church no one must speak but the priest," the newspaper explained on February 16, 1916, but "when Father Alexandroff told the people how he collected the money with his right hand and gave it away with his left, they began to talk among themselves."

"Aren't you satisfied?" he asked. "No!" was the reply and, fearing an uprising, Father Alexandroff turned in a "riot call" to the police, who arrested 100 people. Already disgruntled, they were irate when they appeared in court and Father Alexandroff "denied that they were his parishioners, saying that he never saw them before."

The "warring factions" of 1912 now grew to a full-blown schism. A splinter group of 500 congregants broke off and formed what the *Day Book* said was "the first Independent Orthodox Russian church ever established."

Holy Trinity was elevated to the Russian Holy Trinity Cathedral in 1923. The lofty status, of course, did not preclude the interesting personal stories that played out inside, some of them comical—at least to outsiders.

On January 20, 1935, Bruno Austin married Marie Brenko here. As he left the cathedral, he was arrested on a charge of robbery. The *Chicago Tribune* later reported, "The honeymoon was delayed by this unfortunate occurrence, but a jury acquitted Austin in late March."

The newlyweds resumed their plans for the honeymoon. "Then the United States government seized upon Austin and took him to St. Paul to stand trial on an indictment charging him with conspiring to kidnap Edward G. Bremer," wrote *The Tribune*. "Again he was acquitted and in late May returned to his bride."

Then, on July 4, the *Tribune* ran the headline, "Bride Of Bruno Is Alone Again; You Guess Why." The opening sentence of the article read, "Bruno Austin is in jail again," and went on to explain, "The action, the sergeant said, had to do with theft of an automobile."

A far less amusing story played out in August 1955. In 1931, Henry L. Obetz had purchased and donated to Holy Trinity two large icons. He bought them from a woman who said she had acquired them in Russia when her husband worked for the Bolsheviks, following the Revolution. The paintings, oil on gold leaf layered on wood, were about two feet by two and a half feet in size and weighed about 45 pounds each. Reverend Emilian Solanke, pastor of the cathedral, estimated that they dated from the 15th or early 16th century.

All Obetz knew about the history of the icons, valued at several thousand dollars, was that they had hung in a Russian church. The *Chicago Tribune* later reported, "He did not know whether they had been sold by the Communists, who pillaged the churches, or obtained from an individual Russian."

Following the evening services on August 20, 1955, the paintings, *The Coronation of the Blessed Virgin* and *The Nonburning Bush*, disappeared. It was Reverend Solanke's theory that the thief, or thieves, had hidden in the choir loft or the belfry during the 8:30 service. At about 9:30 that night, a man with a flashlight was seen leaving the rear of the church.

The rarity of the pieces and their easy identification made the unsolved crime puzzling. Obetz told police, "They are of a rare type and could be sold by the thieves only to a collector willing to hide them."

Holy Trinity Orthodox Cathedral continues to serve its community, although most services are now conducted in English. The architectural importance of their church is not lost on the members. The cathedral's website notes, "Being aware of a structure so magnificently designed…we live in constant awe and gratitude for this gift. We realize however, that it is not ours to keep to ourselves, but as good stewards, to maintain and preserve it for those who are yet to follow."

In 2002, a $2 million restoration was initiated with the goal of returning the cathedral to Louis Sullivan's original design. The magnificent relic is, perhaps, a bit out of place on a street of boxy houses and across from a modern hospital. It is nonetheless a rare and wonderful gem in Chicago's architectural jewel box.

OUR LADY OF SORROWS BASILICA
3121 WEST JACKSON BOULEVARD

Father Austin M. Morini brought a group of Servite Friars, also known as the Servants of Mary, with him to Chicago from Wisconsin in 1870. That same year, Bishop Thomas Foley granted the Servites "the strip of territory bounded by North Avenue, Western Avenue and Twelfth Street, and running west indefinitely," on which to establish their monastery and a mission church.

In 1874, Father Morini began construction of the Church of Our Lady of Sorrows. In December that year, the building was enclosed and the first regular services were held there. Then, on Sunday, September 19, 1875, the $12,000 building—deemed by the *Chicago Tribune* as a "neat, two-story brick"—was officially completed and formally dedicated.

Despite a storm and the still-remote location, the new church was crowded. The *Tribune* noted, "The attendance at the dedicatory exercises, notwithstanding the disagreeableness of the weather and the difficulty in reaching the edifice, was very large." A band was on hand for the event, and the newspaper made special note that "The church was prettily and appropriately decorated for the occasion."

The Church of Our Lady of Sorrows served an immigrant parish of mostly Irish and Italians. The neighborhood continued to grow until the little brick church was no longer adequate.

According to church records, ground was broken for a new structure in 1890. Rather confusingly, it was not until June 1899 that *Stone: An Illustrated Magazine* reported that architect John F. Pope had "completed plans for a $100,000 church, to be erected at Jackson Boulevard and Albany avenue, for the Servite Fathers."

Before long two other architects would be involved in the project—Henry Engelbert and William J. Brinkman. Pope's collaboration with the German-born Engelbert might be traced to Engelbert's earlier work for the Servites. In 1867, he had designed the Church of Our Lady of Sorrows in Manhattan. William J. Brinkman was best known for his work in designing several Chicago area churches.

The Church of Our Lady of Sorrows, as it was called before Pope Pius XII deemed it a basilica, served a large Irish and Italian immigrant congregation.

The architects created an imposing and stately Italian Renaissance structure of brick and rough-cut stone. Two angular English Baroque spires flanked the central Roman basilica-style front facade.

The *Record-Herald* got the style wrong when it described the new structure as "one of the most magnificent in the country. It is built of blue Bedford stone and the style of architecture is pure Romanesque. Almost severely plain outside, it is the beauty of the interior that is most impressive."

Indeed, the grand but reserved exterior gave little hint of the opulence inside. Here a complex, coffered, and barrel-vaulted ceiling, soaring fluted pilasters, and pedimented niches echoed Renaissance Rome. Balconies flanking the high altar were inspired by those in the Sistine Chapel.

The dedication of the new Church of Our Lady of Sorrows took place on Sunday, January 5, 1902. One newspaper confused the Servites with a different order, calling the church "the largest Jesuit edifice in the world." Another predicted the dedication would be "the occasion of the greatest gathering of dignitaries of the Roman Catholic Church ever held in Chicago."

The service, including a papal delegate, "many prelates," and Bishop Peter Muldoon, was impressive. What was not impressive, at least to *American Architect and Architecture*, was the structure. In a blunt critique, it blasted the use of stone for the front and brick for the sides. The corner lot made what the critic felt was cheating evident, and "using two different materials is more than the mind of the mortal man can perceive, especially in a church, where everything is supposed to stand for truth." He complained about the towers being stone only "up to a certain point," and that the entrance columns were not monolithic, but "badly discolored and cracked" cemented blocks.

Even the interior did not escape the magazine's brutal assessment. "The details are all Classic in character, but are often civic rather than ecclesiastical, as evinced by the fasces over some of the doors. This is unexpected in a

Catholic church, where symbolism is apt to be rampant."

Despite this, the lush decoration of the interior and the dignified exterior drew overall applause. The cavernous church served thousands of parishioners and weekend Masses would sometimes see lines of worshippers waiting to enter.

Evidently, however, not everyone viewed the Servites with the respect of their parishioners. On May 26, 1914, Father Boniface was in the church garden when a man named Murphy drove his automobile across the lawn. Unhappy with the vandalism, the priest "remonstrated with the man." Apparently not pleased with being corrected, the *Urbana Daily Courier* reported, "Murphy pulled a revolver

The magnificent altar is made entirely of Carrara marble.

from his pocket and fired six shots at the priest." Father Boniface was uninjured and Murphy got away.

Priestly counsel was not always so straightforward as hearing confessions and handing out penances. A few months earlier, another priest, Father John Mulhern, gave difficult advice to a 19-year-old orphaned parishioner, Dorothy Moore. Dorothy had recently come to Chicago and found a furnished room on West Harrison Street. She started work as a stenographer with a woman named Mrs. Campbell in the First National Bank Building.

Dorothy's comings and goings caught the eye of another tenant in the building, John P. Cummings, described by one newspaper as "a wealthy manufacturer." The married maker of liquid cleaning products owned a home on the upscale Sheridan Road. One day he dropped into Mrs. Campbell's office and asked if he could borrow the services of her stenographer. She agreed.

Dorothy worked for Cummings for several days and each day he took her out for lunch and tried to ply her with alcohol. When she refused a cocktail, Cummings urged her to eat the cherry, "just to show we're friends."

She did. Immediately she felt dizzy, began losing consciousness and was slightly aware of being lifted into a taxicab. When she awoke it was night and she was in a strange room in the New Albany Hotel on West

Fire, possibly caused by lightning, amputated one of the spires of the basilica, causing its asymmetrical face.

Randolph Street. Her clothing had been torn off. When she realized what had happened, she fainted.

Rape in 1914 was a matter of shame for the victim, making sex offenders like John P. Cummings confident in not being exposed. Dorothy went to confession at Our Lady of Sorrows, assuming it was she who had sinned. Father Mulhern was shocked and indignant. He urged Dorothy to summon up the courage to fight her attacker: "I'll give you advice, and it's just this. I want you to forget your own dread of publicity and think of the countless number of little girls who are in danger of similar attacks. And I want you to have this man arrested."

Dorothy Moore went to the authorities on March 1. The *Day Book* reported the following day, "A story as shocking as the Stanford White-Evelyn Nesbit story was told to Judge Scully's courtroom this morning when Dorothy Moore, nineteen years old, with the bloom of fresh girlhood on her face, appeared and swore out a warrant making serious charges against John P. Cummings." Cummings was arrested and held on a significant $5,000 bail—$125,000 now.

The wealthy manufacturer tried to bribe the judge to "fix the case" for $200. He lost not only his freedom and reputation, but his wife. Shortly after Dorothy's testimony on March 19, Mrs. Cummings applied for divorce.

On June 26, 1929, Father Ansel Keenan was celebrating the Eucharist when terror gripped the congregants. A *United Press* article reported, "Five hundred communicants at mass in a large west side Catholic church here were thrown into panic today when a drunk-crazed man invaded the sanctuary and fired five shots, wounding one parishioner kneeling at the altar rail."

The shooter was Charles O. Foster, who lived directly across the street from the church. When he quarreled with his wife, he decided to "get" Father Keenan. He entered the church from the side door. There were about a dozen parishioners kneeling at the communion rail when he started firing at the priest.

The *Urbana Daily Courier* reported, "The congregation took refuge behind pews and pillars, the women screaming and several men grappling with the intruder." Father Keenan "dodged behind the altar when the shooting started and was uninjured."

As congregants wrestled with the would-be assassin, he tried to commit suicide, but the bullet he fired toward his head merely scraped his scalp. The newspaper noted, "Three bottles of liquor were taken from his pockets while he lay at the foot of the altar bleeding from the scalp wound." When police arrived, Foster told them, "I've been drunk for a week."

As the Great Depression and Prohibition years progressed, the neighborhood around Our Lady of Sorrows was home to gangsters as well as law-abiding citizens. *Chicago Tribune* reporter Alfred "Jake" Lingle made it his objective to expose criminals and bring them to justice. It cost him his life on June 9, 1930, when he was the victim of a mob hit as he waited for a subway train.

The *Tribune* offered a $25,000 reward for information, saying, "An organized gang planned and executed the murder of Lingle." It added, "The murder of Lingle is the twelfth in Chicago in the last ten days which may be classed as 'gang' murders."

Jake Lingle's funeral was held at Our Lady of Sorrows on June 13, 1930. Respectable citizens of Chicago were incensed over the assassination, and 25,000 people crowded into the streets surrounding the church. The *Daily Illini* reported on the irony of the masses of people. "He had covered elaborate funerals of big gangsters but he, shot down by some gunman of the underworld, had a bigger funeral than any he had reported for the Tribune." Police Commissioner William Russell was among his pallbearers.

The Servites focused on the sorrow of the Virgin Mary; and in 1937 Father James Keane compiled a prayer booklet to be used for the Sorrowful Mother Novena. The novena spread to 2,300 other churches throughout the country.

Our Lady of Sorrows still drew immense numbers of worshippers. One estimate put 70,000 persons at the Friday night services throughout the year.

In May 1956, Pope Pius XII declared the Church of Our Lady of Sorrows a basilica. It triggered a long chain of events that climaxed January 8, 1957. On that afternoon, a pontifical High Mass preceded the inaugural rite. The *Chicago Tribune* reported, "Before the symbols—a canopeum, a bell, and a coat of arms and seal—were brought in, the pope's decree was proclaimed in Latin and in English by Msgr. E. M. Burke, chancellor of the archdiocese of Chicago." Then, with great pomp, the organ blasted a papal march and attendants wheeled the 14-foot-high canopeum (the canopy protecting the Blessed Sacrament) into the sanctuary. Made in Rome, it weighed 100 pounds.

In designating the church a basilica, the pope had said, "Wonderful are the graceful towers rising at each side of the church…an outstanding place of devotion in America." But shortly after midnight on August 20, 1984, fire broke out in one of those steeples. Residents from blocks around reported seeing the flames bursting through the roof. Although one theory was that lightning had struck the tower, Father Frank Falco felt it was caused by a discarded, smoldering cigarette. Whichever the case, the 200-foot tower was lost, and smoke and water resulted in the "blackening of the white marble altar [and] covering the ornate, coffered ceilings with soot," according to the *Tribune*.

By then the congregation was seriously depleted (down to about 300 families) so the $1 million cost of replacing the steeple was out of reach. It would be another two years before restoration was completed—all except for the lost steeple. The *Tribune* used the word "lopsided" and one parishioner, Ina Houston, told a reporter, "The two steeples were very, very important to me…Now it just don't look right." Decades later, however, Chicagoans have grown used to the missing spire.

And the "lopsided" exterior did not discourage location scouts, either. A year after the restoration of the interior, the church was the location of a scene in the motion picture *The Untouchables*, where actors Sean Connery and Kevin Costner used it as a private place to talk.

While the once-Irish-and-Italian neighborhood around Our Lady of Sorrows has greatly changed over the century, the stately church that took three architects to design survives—albeit one steeple short.

SAINT IGNATIUS COLLEGE PREP

1076 WEST ROOSEVELT ROAD

Arnold Damen was born in Holland on March 20, 1815. At the age of 22, he traveled with three other religiously inspired young men to America, in the company of well-known Jesuit missionary Reverend Father DeSmet. As the American wilderness was settled, religious groups were not far behind, establishing churches and schools in the pioneer communities.

After serving his novitiate in Missouri, Damen was ordained a Jesuit priest in 1844. When Bishop O'Regan ordered that a church and school be established in Chicago in 1857, Reverend Damen and Reverend J. R. Druyts were chosen for the mission. Land was acquired for the Holy Family Church on 12th Street, between May Street and Blue Island Avenue. Historian A. T. Andreas in his 1884 *History of Chicago* noted, "When Father Damen first organized the parish in 1857, almost all that portion of the city was unredeemed prairie."

While the parish already operated several elementary schools, there were no provisions for education beyond the 8th Grade. In 1869, Reverend Damen began construction on St. Ignatius, the first Jesuit college in Chicago. Canadian architect Toussaint Menard was hired to design the structure. He produced an up-to-the-minute French Second Empire pile of beige brick with limestone trim. The architectural style had erupted in Paris in the 1850s and reached the East Coast of America in the early 1860s.

Each of the stately arched openings was outlined in stone, and Menard gave the building dimension by projecting the two central sections slightly away from the main facade. A shallow slate-shingled mansard roof finished the design.

The Goodspeed Publishing Company's 1891 brochure, "Industrial Chicago: The Building Interests," remarked, "The St. Ignatius college building, on Twelfth street near Blue Island avenue, is a monument to the educational enterprise of the builders…One must admire the chaste outline of that large house, raised above the prairie almost twenty-five years ago, and ask himself whether the projectors and designer were not prophets in their own land and their own days."

Construction was completed in 1870 and classes began on September 5 that year, with five Jesuits teaching. The initial 37 students chose among classical, commercial, and preparatory courses of study. The following year enrollment had almost tripled, with 99 young men attending classes.

In the fall of 1871, Father Damen was in New York conducting a mission when the Great Chicago Fire broke out. He received a telegram on October 9, informing him that the fire was out of control and heading toward 12th Street. In the meantime, according to the *Chicago Tribune*, "Early in the morning terrified women and children rushed to the shrine of the Madonna. The fire was headed in the direction of their parish, and the church of the Holy Family was directly in its path."

Father Damen, according to the newspaper, prayed before the altar of St. Michael's Church in Brooklyn that his parish might be spared. He "vowed a sanctuary light would be kept forever burning before the image of Our Lady of Perpetual Help if his prayer was answered."

When Father Damen returned home, not a single house in the parish had been lost; and the church and St. Ignatius College were unharmed— miraculous survivors in a landscape of devastation. The parish women told him that they watched the flames approach within blocks, only to be turned back by a change in the winds.

College enrollment mirrored growing parish membership; and before long graduation exercises were elaborate ceremonies with a full orchestra and much pomp. A unique commencement ceremony took place on June 26, 1879, however. The *Chicago Tribune* reported the following day that "There were no graduates this year, owing to a change in the course of study." Nevertheless, several musical presentations—including an overture by the orchestra—were played; the mayor spoke, and awards for proficiency were handed out.

The high-school-aged young men studying Greek and Latin at St. Ignatius College were expected to display proper demeanor. In 1881, young J. A. Talbot was expelled for his "crankishness." It was a personality flaw that would reap nearly disastrous consequences later. Talbot, who also went by the name Anthony Funk, had landed a job in the City Public Library in 1884. He was arrested on January 23, 1885 for stealing books. When detectives entered his home, they found not only 3,000 stolen volumes but "two mysterious packages." One box contained a nickel-plated revolver, packed in glycerin-saturated sawdust. The other held 12 six-inch sticks of dynamite. Together, they formed a homemade bomb.

The *Prairie Farmer* newspaper reported, "The crank admitted these packages were dynamite, and that they were sufficient to blow up the whole court house block." His nefarious plans were never made clear.

In the still-developing Midwest of the 19th century handguns were ubiquitous. The most popular method of celebrating Independence Day for schoolboys, for instance,

In 1965, despite its pristine appearance, the building faced almost certain demolition.

was not with firecrackers, but with the firing of revolvers. And so (rather astonishingly to 21st-century minds) when six-year-old Sims McGuire asked to purchase a pistol in March 1892, the merchant readily complied. Tragically, the boy brought it to school.

For some reason—possibly overcrowding or repairs in the elementary school—on March 30 Sims McGuire's class was being held in St. Ignatius College. Just after class had been called to order, little Sims decided to show off his new pistol to five-year-old classmate John Keegan. The *True Republican* reported on the tragic event. "In some manner the weapon was discharged, the bullet penetrating young Keegan's heart, killing him."

St. Ignatius College was, of course, a religious-based institution, a fact reflected in its educational philosophies. Those philosophies sometimes spilled over into secular life as well. On February 14, 1907, a petition from the school was laid before the State House. It complained of the graphic reporting of criminal activities in the various Illinois newspapers.

"In reporting crimes and criminal trials the newspapers of our State often go into details that are shocking and disgusting to any but the most hardened. Is it right that under the name of news, newspapers should be allowed to spread throughout the land what cannot but work great havoc among the young and innocent? Cannot it be truthfully said that many innocent young persons have received their first lesson in crime in the news?"

The following year, on October 17, 1908, the college invited Dr. Godfrey Raupert to speak to the students about Spiritualism. The craze had spread across America, capturing the imaginations of men and women alike, who attended séances and paid egregious sums to mediums. The priests of St. Ignatius intended to educate its boys against the un-Christian fad.

Raupert, who was a professor of the Vatican's Propaganda College (known today as the Urban College), told his audience that the church recognized spiritualistic phenomena. But, he warned, "there are grave dangers to faith, to morals, and to health of mind and body connected with any attempt by the average man or woman to meddle in the matter." Offering no real evidence for his assertion, he insisted, "It is well known, although both spiritualists and scientific investigators are apt to attempt to hide this truth, that the greater number of mediums degenerate and eventually become insane."

In 1909, the Jesuits formed Loyola University at St. Ignatius College. In reporting on the newly founded institution, the Jesuit leaders announced, "Both Catholic and non-Catholic educators will sit on the faculty," and explained that St. Ignatius College had been used as an experiment in using non-Catholic instructors. Within a few years, Loyola University moved on to

St. Ignatius College Prep still serves as a prestigious high school.

other Chicago campuses, while the younger students remained in the original building, now St. Ignatius High School.

In October 1939, the old school building was the scene of a reunion of the Fathers' Club of St. Ignatius High School. Successful graduates headed back to Chicago to celebrate the 70th anniversary of the school. Included were seven who had risen to bishops within the church, and six who were now judges. James F. Hanley was a songwriter, whose "Back Home In Indiana" had sold two million copies. Almost as well known were his hit songs, "If You Knew Susie," "Rose of Washington Square," and "Just a Cottage Small."

By the second half of the century, the old building was falling into serious disrepair. In 1965, just five years short of the structure's century mark, the school announced its intentions to raze it. A new campus was planned on the 5.6-acre site adjacent to the school. On April 29, architect Champ R. Maxey promised that the church would be saved, but St. Ignatius "will eventually be razed."

Despite the plans, St. Ignatius survived, and in 1981 the school president, Jesuit Donald F. Rowe (an architectural historian) urged restoration. A $9 million project was initiated that brought the structure back to what the *Chicago Tribune* deemed "its 19th Century splendor, which included high ceilings, a library paneled in carved wood, a great hall and auditorium, and gas light fixtures throughout."

Restorers worked with a wealth of original elements: the Cuneo Chapel of the Jesuit Martyrs of North America was intact—including its Victorian stenciling; the heavily carved doors; and the old natural history museum, the Brunswick Room, with its butternut-wood staircase and oak-paneled walls.

The Brunswick Room was named after John Brunswick, who designed and installed the room in 1872. The restoration of this space cost $300,000 and was funded entirely by the Brunswick Corporation—a well-known manufacturer of outboard motors, bowling equipment, pool tables, and similar products—founded by John Brunswick. The ceiling fresco, which had been painted over, was revealed again. Because the room had housed the school's natural history collection, the wall carvings were of various plant species.

The completed restoration revived the structure's stately 1870 appearance. St. Ignatius, now known as St. Ignatius College Prep, continues as a vibrant educational center. And its remarkable building—a survivor not only of fire but of modernization—is a splendid example of handsome Victorian academic architecture.

SAINT JOHN CANTIUS CHURCH

825 NORTH CARPENTER STREET

Adolphus Druiding published his ponderously titled *Church Architecture: Containing Twenty-One Plates Showing Elevations, Perspective Views, Interior Views, or, Low and Moderate Priced Churches, Including Miscellaneous Church Details* in 1889. In its preface, the Bishop of St. Cloud, Minnesota, Otto Zardetti, said that the "first aim of truly Christian art and architecture [was] to make the 'stones cry.'"

By the time the book was published, Druiding had designed scores of churches—at least one in almost every city in the Midwest. Four years later he would be at work on another substantial structure, this one in Chicago.

Although Polish immigrants had begun arriving in America in the 18th century, the first great wave came in 1854 when they fled political insurrection. By the early 1880s, thousands of Polish immigrants were landing in New York and moving west, having been invited by relatives and friends already there. By 1893, in his *Wśród Polonii W Ameryce* (*Among the Poles in America*), author E. H. Dunikowski deemed Chicago the "capital of the American Poles" and estimated the membership of the parish of St. Stanislaus Kostka at 40,000.

In 1892, the parish had petitioned for an additional church to accommodate its swelling numbers. Father Vincent Barzynski was instrumental in acquiring lots—costing $75,000, or around $2 million now—on Carpenter Street, near Chicago Avenue, and Adolphus Druiding received the commission to design the structure.

Excavation and initial construction began in the spring of 1893, and by the end of August plans were made for the cornerstone laying. On September 3, 1893, the *Chicago Tribune* reported on the ceremonies taking place later that day, saying, "This will be an eventful day among the Polish people of Chicago. At 11 o'clock some 50,000 or more of them will come together on Carpenter street to participate in the sacred ceremonies of laying the corner-stone of a new church."

The newspaper said that this ceremony would be different from normal rituals: "In many respects it promises to be an event much more interesting and impressive than generally attends upon such affairs. It not only celebrates the construction of the largest church edifice in the city, but prepares the way for the formation and permanent establishment of an entirely new congregation."

Indeed, the Church of St. John Cantius promised to be an imposing structure. The Carpenter Street frontage was 120 feet and the site extended back 195 feet. The main auditorium would seat 2,000 worshippers and the basement schoolroom could hold 1,400 children. Druiding had included a massive bell tower at one corner, rising 240 feet and containing six large bells.

A sketch of the church accompanied a *Chicago Tribune* article about the cornerstone laying on September 3, 1893.

The architect had always been more interested in religious functionality than architectural purity. For St. John Cantius, he married Renaissance with Romanesque Revival and threw in a touch of the Polish homeland in the bell tower, loosely based on St. Mary's Basilica in Krakow.

The church was completed five years later, in 1898. The rusticated Bedford stone facade featured a stately Roman temple design, sitting upon a Romanesque base, with three massive arched entrances. A broad, sweeping stone staircase gave the structure a majestic appearance. The *Tribune* said, "Its architecture is of the Roman style modified according to Adolphus Druiding, the designer and contractor, to meet the requirements of Chicago's climate."

Druiding also considered the city's climate when he had a modern hot-water heating system installed. The *Tribune* noted that the new parish "insisted on having a church edifice fully in keeping with the conditions and progress of the times." That modernity was reflected in the cross atop the bell tower, which was wired so as to be illuminated at night, and in the statue of St. John above the small tower being "made of aluminum." The material, which had been used for the capstone of the Washington Monument a decade earlier, was highly expensive. One ounce cost about the equivalent of the daily wage of a laborer at the time.

Weddings among the Polish community were joyful affairs, followed by dancing and singing. But the wedding ceremony of Elizabeth Cwiak and John

Wriblaski, on October 15, 1913, ended in tragedy. The bride was extremely close to her 10-year-old sister Anna. The little girl could not find happiness in her sister's marriage; she only knew that Elizabeth would be leaving home. In her mind, she may never return at all.

As the bridal party proceeded down the aisle toward the altar of St. John Cantius that afternoon, Anna began crying. Following the ceremony, she was taken home, rather than to the reception, because of her emotional condition. Her uncontrolled weeping was such that a physician was called in.

At a hall at North May and Front streets, the wedding dance was in full swing when a friend of the family arrived and took the new bride aside. The *Chicago Tribune* reported the following day that the dance "was cut short when Mrs. Elizabeth Wriblaski, the bride, learned of the death of her sister." Little Anna Cwiak had sobbed so uncontrollably that doctors said she succumbed to physical exhaustion.

Within five years of this sorrowful event, St. John Cantius would reach its greatest membership at about 23,000 parishioners. It served its congregation for decades with weddings, confirmations, funerals, and first communions. But the service on the morning of June 10, 1934, was unique. As the pastor, Reverend Walter Bartylak, celebrated Mass, another priest, Father Theodore Wroblewski, prepared for the next service. He discovered a fire in the locker room near the choir loft and, with the assistant organist, Albert Kashuga, tried to put out the flames with a fire extinguisher. Kashuga ventured too far into the smoke-filled room and was overcome. The priest dragged him out, and then called the fire department. He whispered the situation to Reverend Bartylak, who went on with the service.

The fire department arrived a few minutes later, making sure to silence their gongs and sirens before reaching the church, so as not to interrupt the Mass. Several priests led the firefighters up a spiral staircase. The *Tribune* reported, "As they went up toward the fire they shut doors leading into the main part of the church in an attempt to keep smoke from the auditorium. A window was broken and a hose line pulled up 50 feet from the street below while another line was taken up the stairway."

While 1,000 people worshipped, a second alarm was sounded. "Several more fire companies" responded, all of them arriving silently. When the fire burned through the organ wiring, the instrument stopped working. Nevertheless, the 20-man choir, "perilously close to the flames," went on singing a cappella.

In keeping with the latest technology, the cross on the steeple of St. John Cantius was electrified in 1903 to light up at night.

Amazingly, no parishioners left their pews while the scores of firefighters fought the blaze for a full 30 minutes. The damage was estimated later to be about $2,000.

The neighborhood around St. John Cantius continued to be home to the Polish community. In 1943, when the Polish Roman Catholic Union of America celebrated its 70th anniversary, the observances began with a parade to the church. The *Tribune* estimated that "thousands of Chicago Poles" were expected to participate in the solemn High Mass.

The parish of St. John Cantius was devastated by the construction of the Northwest Expressway (later renamed the Kennedy Expressway) in the late 1950s. The project razed thousands of homes and buildings, forcing parishioners to relocate.

Among the families who stayed on were the Oprondeks. The parents of 10-year-old Richard Oprondek were panicked when he failed to return from Mass on Sunday, January 28, 1962. The *Chicago Tribune* reported, "While 50 policemen and a score of friends were searching the near northwest side yesterday for Richard Oprondek…he turned up in San Francisco trying

The ornate baroque interior features frescoes and a richly decorated groined ceiling.

to hitch a plane ride to Hawaii." Still carrying his prayer book and $4, he had stowed on an American Airlines flight by mingling with the boarding passengers. In California, he raised the suspicions of airline employees when he continually asked about flights to Hawaii. They found his identity written inside his prayer book and put him on a plane back to his parents in Chicago.

The parish, which had been threatened with closure in the 1960s and 1970s, was rescued by Father Frank Phillips, who became pastor in 1988. He initiated a fundraising effort and a program to attract new parishioners. The revitalization resulted in a restoration of the nearly century-old church. A new religious community of men, the Canons Regular of St. John Cantius, was formed under Father Phillips in 1998, and that group now staffs the parish.

The neighborhood, where once Polish was the predominant language, was also revitalized at the turn of the 21st century. Renamed River West, the streets are filled with trendy restaurants, and upscale residences have replaced the modest homes of the working Poles.

Through it all, St. John Cantius and its "crying stones" have survived. The church's website notes that the parish "has adopted a policy of historical preservation and restoration." That policy not only conserves Adolphus Druiding's important structure, but preserves the pre-Vatican II liturgies and traditional Gregorian chant and Renaissance music. And despite the changed neighborhood, the website adds, "The parish also maintains the customs and traditions which relate to its Polish heritage."

SETH P. WARNER HOUSE

631 NORTH CENTRAL AVENUE

Seth Warner was among Chicago's earliest settlers, arriving from Amherst, Massachusetts in 1837, and was active in the affairs of the burgeoning community. *A History of the First Presbyterian Church*, the oldest church in Chicago, noted, "Mr. Seth Porter Warner was received into the membership of the Church, September 13, 1838, and led the Choir for several years." His love of singing and music resulted in his co-founding the Choral Union in 1846, "composed of the best singers" of the city.

That same year he went into partnership with Charles M. Gray, manufacturing farm equipment. The following year, an inventor from Virginia, Cyrus McCormick, arrived in town, looking to expand the production of his "Virginia Reaper." For four years, his labor-saving harvesting device had been constructed in rural shops. Gray and Warner's operation offered a means to expand the manufacturing process. The partnership of the three men would eventually evolve into the International Harvester Company, one of Chicago's largest and most famous businesses.

Seth Warner continued to change the face of the young city. He was a co-organizer of the city's first fire company, a hook and ladder company with a firehouse near Lake and Dearborn Streets. In 1851, he erected Warner's Hall at 104 Randolph Street, at the corner of Clark. The auditorium was not only the scene of musical and minstrel shows, but of political and civic meetings.

During the Civil War, Warner was outspokenly pro-Union and the wartime meetings in the hall were reflective of his stance. On November 17, 1863, for instance, the *Chicago Tribune* reported on the "full turnout of the members of the League and of Union men at Warner's Hall last evening."

Speaking first was a Mr. Hagan, from Arkansas, who "gave a very entertaining narrative of his travels and trials from the time he was driven from that State, his escape from the rebels at sundry times and places, and an account of his journeying northward." Following Hagan on stage was the Honorable I. N. Arnold, whose speech was "The Days of Slavery Are Numbered."

Four years after the end of the war, things had returned to normal. Construction resumed and the city's population continued to grow. In 1869, a new suburb, the village of Austin, was being planned. According to the account of A. T. Andreas in his 1884 *History of Cook County*, Warner "was the first to erect a fine and costly residence" there.

The Warner House, located at 631 North Central Avenue, was in the latest of architectural styles. The Italianate villa was clad in light-brown brick with stone trim. Sitting well back from the street line, it featured a broad Italianate veranda, hip roof with a fashionable cupola, and a slightly projecting central pavilion.

Early 20th-century renovations removed the cupola, altered the porch, and added a pyramidal-roofed attic room to the "fine and costly residence" of one of Chicago's earliest pioneers.

The interiors were models of high-end domestic living spaces of the 1860s. Nearly a century later, historian John Drury would remark that each of the rooms was "notable for veined Italian marble fireplaces, doors of solid walnut, and old-fashioned chandeliers."

The Warners reared four children in the house: Orrin, Irene, Eva, and Porter. While still active in Chicago civic matters, Seth Warner was influential in the development of Austin as well. In 1871, he co-founded the Austin Presbyterian Church.

Warner died in the house of his daughter, Mrs. James Wallace, at 388 LaSalle Avenue on Sunday, June 12, 1892. The family retained possession of the Central Avenue house until 1899, the year after Austin was annexed to Chicago.

A series of owners resulted in several modernizations as the mid-19th-century villa fell behind architectural fashion. A porch in Arts and Crafts style porch replaced the original veranda after the turn of the century, the quaint cupola was removed, and an addition—a full-height attic room with grouped arched windows and a pyramidal cap—punched through the roofline. Those Edwardian changes were most likely the work of the Benson family, living here in the years just before the outbreak of World War I.

In the 1980s, sympathetic owners restored the Warner House nearly to its original mid-19th-century appearance.

In 1924, the Warner House was purchased by the Austin Academy of Fine Arts, called by one historian "one of the liveliest and most influential cultural centers on the city's West Side." The group painstakingly preserved the interiors and outfitted the house in period-appropriate furnishings. In his 1941 *Old Chicago Houses,* John Drury remarked, "Glimpsing its many high-ceiling rooms with their fine woodwork trim, one is taken back to the Victorian period—to the days of bustles, Prince Alberts [frock coats], and coaches-and-four."

The academy remained in the house until 1979. The new owners returned it to a single-family dwelling and instituted a near restoration. A replicated cupola was returned to the roof and the Edwardian attic room was removed and replaced by a triangular pediment, sympathetic with the style. Only the incongruous porch remains out of period. Nevertheless, the handsome mid-Victorian structure survives, thanks to the handful of owners and an institution that early on recognized its importance.

Oddly enough, although it was placed on the National Register of Historic Places on June 3, 1982, the Seth Warner House has never been designated a Chicago Landmark—the excuse often cited being that it is not threatened.

SOUTH

STARTLING MEMORIAL TO A FASCIST: BALBO MONUMENT

BURNHAM PARK, EAST OF SOLDIER FIELD AND MUSEUM CAMPUS DRIVE

On July 1, 1933, Italo Balbo took flight, leading a group of 24 "flying boats" from Italy to Chicago's Century of Progress International Exposition. The 37-year-old aviator had been a member of the National Fascist Party since 1921, and by now was Air Marshal of Italy, and considered by many to be second only to Benito Mussolini in Fascist power.

America was thrilled at the arrival of the Italian airplanes. On Saturday, July 15, 1933, the *Chicago Tribune* ran a banner headline, "BALBO HERE THIS AFTERNOON," and included a photograph of the general flanked by the American and Italian flags, captioned, "Air Heroes! Welcome!"

A crushing throng of 20,000 Chicagoans waited near Navy Pier on Lake Michigan, searching the skies for any sign of the two dozen planes. When General Balbo landed his twin-engine craft, a group of high-level officials was waiting to greet him. With grand bravado Balbo appeared in full dress uniform, standing on the wing of his plane while the other 23 seaplanes landed. The *Tribune* reported that Balbo "strolled out on the deck of his seaplane as if going to afternoon tea. He had on a gray-blue uniform decorated with eagle and crown, and orders of his war service. In his hand he carried a swagger stick."

Balbo and his 96 airmen were taken to Soldier Field stadium, where more than 60,000 people had been waiting for hours. The *Tribune* later reported, "Among every crowd greeting Balbo and his men were men in black shirts and ties who raised their arms in the Fascisti salute."

For three days, the Italians were feted with receptions, dinners, and balls. Although the general did not include politics in his agenda, he sent a cable to Mussolini telling him that Chicago's reception proved that reports of anti-Fascist sentiments among Americans were "mere myth."

Balbo managed to slip away from the obligations of diplomacy before heading home. Around 1:00 in the morning on July 18, while being entertained at a dance at the Casino Club, he confided to Major Reed Landis, chairman of the

Italo Balbo was a novice aviator when he was appointed Italy's Secretary of State for Air, but he led several successful transatlantic flights of seaplanes.

"armada reception" arrangements, that he would like to visit the exposition, "free from the crowds and attention that have followed his every move," according to the *Chicago Tribune*.

Landis gathered a small party, and provided the general with a dark business suit. "He pulled a slouch hat over his eyes, and then with his friends slipped away," the newspaper reported. "Thereupon Gen. Balbo became a playboy.... He was just another visitor. He grinned and his eyes sparkled in anticipated thrill. This was his big moment."

Eight days later, long after the squadron had left Chicago, Mayor Edward Kelly received a telegram from the Balbo airplane: "Never will be erased from our eyes the vision, nor removed from our hearts the remembrance of the great and hospitable metropolis of Chicago and the heartfelt demonstration of friendship which reached us on the arrival of the Italian Atlantic air squadron in the skies over the great World's Fair, which was our objective. Will you accept our heartfelt thanks, which go to all the citizens of Chicago while we are about to leave the skies of the United States."

Balbo's successful visit was of significance to Mussolini. Despite glaring differences of opinion regarding social and political issues (and Fascism in particular) between them, Balbo's charisma and popularity created a valuable propaganda tool, which Mussolini took every advantage of.

On August 12, 1933, Balbo's returning squadron reached Italy, landing at Lido di Ostia, where there were ancient Roman ruins dating from the time of Julius Caesar. Mussolini selected a Corinthian column composed of compressed stone known as breccia, once part of a temple, to be presented to the City of Chicago as a memorial to Balbo's transatlantic trip.

With symbolism typical of Mussolini, the column was dismantled and loaded on 24 hydroplanes—the same number as were in Balbo's squadron—and flown to the Italian Pavilion at the Century of Progress. Architects Capraro & Komar designed a fitting base for the column, incorporating fasces at each corner. Inscribed on the column's base was an inscription in Italian, translating as:

This column of twenty centuries ago, erected on the shore of Ostia, port of imperial Rome, to watch over the fortunes and victories of the Roman triremes, Fascist Italy, under the auspices of Benito Mussolini, presents to Chicago in laudation and as a symbolic remembrance of the Atlantic squadron led by Balbo, which with Roman boldness flew across the ocean in the eleventh year of the Fascist Era.

The unveiling took place on Italian Day, June 15 in 1934. The *New York Times* reported that "Thousands of Americans of Italian descent attended." There were around 150 Italian societies in the accompanying parade, as well as army and navy bands, and sailors from Camp Roosevelt. General Balbo spoke directly via radio to Mayor Kelly, who thanked him and Mussolini for the gift. Balbo responded, "Let this column stand as a symbol of increasing friendship between the people of Italy and the people of the United States."

Within months, the Century of Progress International Exposition was over and the Italian Pavilion was gone, but the column remained, if now isolated and out of place. A five-block roadway farther north, traversing Grant Park, between Lake Shore Drive and State Street, was renamed Balbo Avenue.

Within only four years many Chicagoans had forgotten how the relic had come to stand in Burnham Park. On August 27, 1938, the *Chicago Tribune* printed a short article reminding its readers of Balbo's exploit and Mussolini's gift. The newspaper described the column as "The oldest work of human hands in Chicago not under a museum's roof."

By now, however, the air force created by Italo Balbo had dropped bombs on unarmed Africans during Mussolini's unprovoked invasion of Ethiopia. As America entered World War II, Chicago's love affair with Balbo, and America's

After sitting unnoticed for decades, the 1st-century column became a focal point of controversy.

relationship with Fascist Italy in general, came to an abrupt halt. The City of Chicago was left with an embarrassing monument to a powerful Fascist and by 1946 a movement was under way to remove the aviator's name from Balbo Avenue. Mayor Kelly proposed in December that year to rename the street in honor of Lieutenant Commander John C. Waldron, the leader of Torpedo Squadron 8, who had died with 28 of his 29 men in the Battle of Midway.

Although 90 percent of the property owners along Balbo Avenue supported the proposition, some politicians were hesitant. The *Chicago Tribune* noted on December 30, 1946, "The city hall Democratic machine has by-passed the proposal because the machine fears the loss of Italian-American votes if the name of the street is changed." Among the Italian-American groups fighting the redesignation were the Sons of Italy and the Legione Garibaldi. On the other hand, the newspaper pointed out that the groups could expect a "fight by patriotic Chicagoans and property owners to remove the stigma that hovers over a major Chicago street."

In the end the street name as well as the commemorative column remained, but many Chicagoans held resentment against the monument and name for decades. With brutal candor, *Tribune* columnist Vernon Jarrett opined on June 8, 1983, "It is sickening to recall how Chicago bowed before one of the architects of European Fascism, which reached its climax in the mass carnage and destruction of World War II. But our city went further; it shamelessly named a street in memory of his 1933 visit."

Over the decades the cruel memories of war and atrocities faded. Few Americans remembered Italo Balbo at all and many Chicagoans confused the origin of the street name with Spanish explorer Vasco de Balboa. The remarkable 2,000-year-old Roman column sat rather forlorn and ignored in Burnham Park (a far cry from Italian Day 1934) until its ignominious rediscovery in 2017.

The tragic demonstrations over Confederate statues in Charlottesville, Virginia in August that year sparked a nationwide reevaluation of monuments. Protests were held at the Balbo Monument, demanding its removal. But, as was the case elsewhere, others insisted that history cannot be erased; and vocal Italian-American leaders saw the monument as evidence of their ethnic heritage in Chicago.

After months of difficult debate, by late spring 2018 the City Council seemed to have decided to keep the monument in place, pointing out that Balbo spoke out against Mussolini and was both pro-Jew and anti-Nazi. In May 2018, it was announced that a plaque explaining the history of the monument and Italo Balbo would be placed at the site, next to the column.

HENRY B. CLARKE HOUSE

1827 SOUTH INDIANA AVENUE

Charles Walker arrived in the tiny prairie town of Chicago early in 1835. There were only about 350 residents, yet Walker recognized the immense potential of the West. He set up a business selling guns, boots, and leather goods shipped from the East. He soon wrote to his brother-in-law, Henry Brown Clarke, about the financial promise to be had for a merchant in the pioneer town.

Leaving Utica, New York must have been a disquieting decision for Clarke. The town was booming. It had a population of nearly 20,000, and the recently completed Erie Canal had substantially increased commerce. Moving his wife and three children from their comfortable home and away from the extended family to a pioneer town of dusty dirt roads was a matter for serious consideration.

But the decision was made, and later that year Henry Clarke traveled to Chicago where he opened a hardware business with William Jones and Byram King. Jones, King & Company provided desperately needed building materials, trapping equipment, and farm implements.

In June, before his family's arrival, Clarke bought 20 acres along the shore of Lake Michigan. He chose the site for his home at what would become Michigan Avenue.

Once her husband was established, Caroline Palmer Clarke, 23 years old, arrived with the children and one maid, Betsey, in mid-October 1835. Three weeks later, on November 1, she wrote to her sister-in-law about Chicago. "The buildings are now mostly small, and look as though they have been put up as quickly as possible," she noted. "The houses are all small but they are well filled I should think, from the appearance of people I see in the streets, going and returning."

Caroline had noticed that the frontier town, populated mostly by men and married women, had little time for religion. "I am told there has been but very little attention paid to the Sabbath until lately." She was relieved that she had brought her housemaid with her. "Betsey is well and I think

Four members of the Clarke family are just visible, posing on the porch in 1902. Note that the floor-to-ceiling parlor windows can be opened as doors in the hot summer months.

will do very well for me. It is well I brought her for it is almost impossible to get girls at all here and what there are here, secure from two to four dollars a week. There is a girl here in the house where we are staying that I am sure you would not keep in your house at six shillings a week, that secures three dollars and a half."

She also mentioned the house her husband envisioned for her: "Our house is a [large] one to be sure, but it will be very comfortable, when we get settled in it. I think I shall feel as much at home as I ever could anywhere away from my Father and Mother. I cannot feel yet as though it would ever be quite home to me anywhere away from them."

In 1836, the elegant new home was nearly completed. Possibly in an attempt to help Caroline through twinges of homesickness for the cultured East, Henry Clarke provided her with a stately residence, fitting of a metropolis. Although constructed of wood, its Greek Revival design outshone any building in Chicago with the possible exception of the William B. Ogden house to the north. The house, built at a cost of $10,000, according to historian William H. Bushnell in 1876, featured a broad flight of steps leading to a columned Classical portico. Inside, the parlor level boasted 12-foot ceilings, cherry and pine woodwork, and marble mantels.

The Clarkes moved in before the interiors were completely finished, most likely at the prodding of Caroline. She had pointed out in her letter to Mary, "I feel as though I should be glad to have a home of my own once more—be it ever so homely. I am quite tired of living among a crowd of strangers."

By April 3, 1935, when Albert J. DeLong took this photograph, the porch had been removed and apartment buildings were inching nearer.

Unfortunately, the Clarkes were about to run into "financial reversals." The Financial Panic of 1837 nearly put Jones, King & Company into bankruptcy and the Illinois State Bank, of which Henry Clarke was a director, failed. Finally, on February 23, 1842, the District Court of the United States declared Henry B. Clarke bankrupt.

Without the funds to complete their home, the Clarkes took in boarders. Henry supplemented their income by farming and hunting. The wild fowl he bagged were cleaned and sold. One boarder, Alice Barnard, wrote that "half a dozen deer, hundreds of snipe, plover and quail, and dozens of prairie chickens and ducks" hung in the uncompleted parlors.

By 1849 things had improved. The economy had rebounded and, although three infants had died just after birth, there were now six children in the Clarke house. Caroline had earlier written home to Utica that "The lake water, which they use for almost every purpose, is as pure and good tasted as any I ever saw in my life." After flooding that year, however, the water supply was contaminated and a cholera epidemic swept the population. On July 23, 1849, Henry Clarke contracted the disease and died within 24 hours. He was 47 years old.

Caroline remained in the house until her death in 1860, and the house became popularly known as "Widow Clarke's House." According to Chicago historian John Drury in 1941, "During the 1850's the house was a favorite stopping-place for families taking buggy rides 'out in the country' on Sunday afternoons."

By the time of her death, the interiors of the mansion had been completed, and it was most likely Caroline who had added the stylish cupola to the roof. The eldest daughter, Mary, and her husband, Frank B. Williams, moved back into the family home to care for the children, the youngest of whom was only 12. A year after the Great Fire of 1871, the Clarke children sold the house to John Chrimes, a prominent Chicago tailor, and his wife, Lydia.

Chrimes's fear of another devastating fire—the house was, after all, constructed of wood—led him to move the house farther into the country, to Hyde Park. Unfortunately, to facilitate the major project, the front and back porticos were removed and replaced with simple porches when the house reached its destination 28 blocks to the south.

Just six years later, John Chrimes died. Following Lydia's death, the house became home to the Chrimes's daughter and son-in-law, Mr. and Mrs. William Walter. Walter was a well-known livestock commission merchant. The couple was proud of their historic home and carefully documented its history. William Walter died in 1933 and his wife in 1936. Their daughters Laura and Lydia, both public schoolteachers, remained in the house (now numbered 4625 South Wabash Avenue) until 1941.

The sisters urged the City of Chicago to purchase the house as an important piece of Chicago history. The city was not interested, and so when St. Paul Church of God in Christ offered to buy it, they accepted.

Eleven years later, on January 6, 1952, the *Chicago Tribune* updated its readers on the status of the Widow Clarke House. St. Paul's congregation had accumulated $5,000 for exterior repairs—replacement of rotted clapboards, for instance—and mortgaged the house for another $8,000. A further $5,000 was still necessary for interior upgrades like electrical and redecorating.

By 1977, when the church needed the real estate for other purposes, the City of Chicago had changed its mind concerning the historic house. It saved the Clarke House from demolition by relocating it to its current site at 1827 South Indiana Avenue.

The move was not without a near catastrophe. Chicago winters are notoriously brutal and the house was being moved in December. A tricky obstacle was the railroad tracks of the Englewood-Jackson Park line. The only way to get the house past the tracks was to lift it over. On a frigid night the operation began, and then, with the house in the air, the hydraulic equipment froze. It remained that way for two weeks before a thaw allowed it to inch its way along again.

The house, spruced up and back to its old self.

An exhaustive five-year restoration in the late 1970s brought the Clarke House back to its 1836 appearance with the reconstruction of the porticos. The interiors were restored and furnished with period-appropriate carpeting, furniture, and bric-a-brac. Opened in 1982, it is operated as a house museum, an unlikely and precious survivor from Chicago's earliest pioneer days.

"HE SHALL GO TO THE WAITING ROOM": FIRST CHURCH OF DELIVERANCE
4315 SOUTH WABASH AVENUE

In only four years since he founded the First Church of Deliverance in 1929, the Reverend Clarence H. "Preacher" Cobbs had grown his followers from a few women sitting on boxes in his mother's home to an entire congregation in a church set up in a former factory at 4315 South Wabash Avenue. Cobbs introduced the "Spiritual" denomination, a religious sect born in New Orleans, to Chicago. Under his pastorate, it grew to be the core of African-American religious culture during the Great Depression.

The charismatic Reverend Cobbs attracted congregants through practices and principles that strayed far from the religious mainstream. With shrewd understanding that by demonizing vices like gambling, card-playing, and dancing he would push away Bronzeville residents who needed reaching, he turned a blind eye.

Decades later, Martin Sevela of the *Chicago Tribune* explained, "He is not against drinking, high life or sex. He says that if God had not meant for us to have whisky or enjoy our bodies, He would not have created them…. The Rev. Mr. Cobbs welcomes ex-convicts, prostitutes and gamblers into the church. Yet this is not to say that he advocates indulgence in the vices…. He is likely to say during a sermon: 'When you see a drunk walking down the street I want you to look at him with respect. Hear me. Even in a drunk there's something you got to respect.'"

This perspective resulted, sometimes, in raised eyebrows. One fundraising effort, during the first year of the church on South Wabash, was far from conventional, for example. On October 23, 1934, the *Chicago Tribune* reported that "Alonso McNeal and George Walker, both Negroes, were electrocuted Oct. 12 for the murder of Policeman John Officer." Ten days later their bodies had still not been buried.

An informant told the coroner's office that admission was being charged to view the bodies at the undertaking shop of James M. Hall. When deputies arrived at the Church of Deliverance on the evening of October 22, the funerals were just starting. "Loud speakers were carrying the words of the Rev. C. H. Cobbs, Negro spiritualist, to throngs in the street, and Undertaker Hall and others were discovered taking 'collections' from those who desired to enter for a last look at the departed."

One of the church's most dramatic events was the mass baptism that took place on August 14, 1938. Reverend Cobbs led 41 members to the shore of Lake Michigan at 31st Street, while a throng of more than 10,000 lined the banks.

Despite the ongoing Depression, by 1939 the congregation had amassed enough money to renovate the old hat factory into a proper church. Walter T. Bailey, the first African-American architect registered in Illinois, was awarded the commission. The original structure was doubled in height by the addition of a second story, and doubled in width by an addition to the south.

Bailey turned away from the expected ecclesiastical architectural style— neo-Gothic—and embraced the contemporary. His terra-cotta-clad Art Moderne design was sleek and new. Horizontal green stripes provided the only ornamentation, giving the edifice a jazzy, up-to-the-minute look more expected in a grocery store or bus station. But like Reverend Cobbs and his congregation, the building refused to follow the norm.

The new structure included a radio broadcasting booth. Since 1934 the First Church of Deliverance had been broadcasting gospel music, still in its infancy, and is sometimes credited with popularizing it in the North. The Radio Choir of the First Church of Deliverance became so well known that their concerts were held in venues as large as Comiskey Park stadium. Over the years, artists like Louis Armstrong, Nat King Cole, Dinah Washington, and Earl "Fatha" Hines performed with the choir.

In December 1945, a fire caused substantial damage to the interior of the church. The architectural firm of Kocher, Buss & DeKlerk was hired to do the renovations. The completed interiors complemented the Art Moderne architecture of the exterior with curved corners and stainless steel trim.

Simultaneously the exterior was embellished with two towers that seamlessly matched the original design. Their glass-block windows were repeated in the main building. An entrance canopy sliced through the towers above the first floor.

The renovation included the installation of two murals by Chicago artist Fred Jones. In a style reminiscent of the Works Progress Administration's civic murals, the artist depicted *People Coming to Christ*, with the Chicago skyline in the distance in one; and the *Church's Relationship to God* in another.

Fred Jones was also responsible for carving the double entrance doors. The oak was taken from a century-old tree on the grounds of Reverend Cobbs's summer estate (Cobbs lived well).

Among the questionable activities that Reverend Cobbs overlooked were "policy" games—an illegal numbers racket that garnered fortunes for its operators and often preyed on the poor. The *Daily Illini* explained, "The policy game...flourishes mostly in the South side Negro belt. It is a form of lottery in which the player buys a number.... [Theodore] Roe estimated about 60 percent of Chicago's Negroes play the policy game."

Roe, a congregant, was investigated by the U.S. Senate Crime Investigating Committee in 1950. In return for leniency, he told all regarding the operation and his accomplices. He testified on December 19 that year that "his wheel takes in about $24,000 on two drawings a day—a total of $8,760,000 a year."

Testifying against organized crime figures was rarely a healthy decision. On August 6, 1952, the *Daily Illini* noted, "Roe, 53, a reputed millionaire, was shot to death Monday night as he walked from his South Side apartment toward his automobile. Investigators said two men opened fire with shotguns from behind a signboard in a vacant lot next to Roe's apartment building."

The funeral for Theodore Roe was held in the First Church of Deliverance on August 8. The *Daily Illini* reported that it "was attended by thousands in and around" the church. In his eulogy, Reverend Clarence Cobbs did not, of course, praise Roe's criminal career, but, as always, he was careful not to outright condemn it. "Roe didn't go to Heaven and he didn't go to hell," he told the mourners. "The spirit of Theodore Roe shall go to the waiting room."

All but one of the six pallbearers who carried the casket to the graveside were arrested shortly after the coffin was lowered into the grave. Homicide Bureau Lieutenant John Golden had sent agents to the funeral to bring the men back for questioning. He told reporters, "If they were that close to Roe they must know a lot about him."

Despite the sometimes off-center appearance of Cobbs's practices and of his congregation, he worked feverishly to help the impoverished people of the South Side. In 1952, he acquired a building next to the church for his $1-per-day nursery. Able to accommodate 300 children, the day nursery enabled mothers to work. Cobbs told *Jet Magazine* he was charging rates "the $35-a-week domestic can easily pay."

By 1972, the church, born in Reverend Cobbs's mother's living room, had 8,500 members. In an interview that year with the *Chicago Tribune*'s Martin

The unexpected-looking church is as singular as its founding minister, "Preacher" Cobbs.

Savela, Cobbs was asked who designed the church. "I did," he responded flatly. It was a rather surprising response for readers who knew the building's history. But, perhaps, the minister was referring to the Spiritual Church, and not its structure.

South Wabash Avenue had been thronged with mourners many times since the First Church of Deliverance opened its doors; but the funeral of Reverend Clarence H. Cobbs on July 2, 1979 outdid all other such services. One reporter declared that there were so many police needed to direct traffic at the service that crime went up in all other areas of Chicago because of the lack of police presence. It was, obviously, an exaggeration—but not by much. There were more than 100 cars in the funeral procession. Clarence Cobbs had been a confidant of the late Mayor Richard J. Daley, and when the current mayor, Jane Byrne, did not appear at the funeral, black Chicagoans remembered the slight for many years.

The colorful Reverend Cobbs had sternly prohibited the publishing of an obituary. He told those closest to him, "May the work I've done speak for me."

Nearly 90 years after the Reverend Clarence H. Cobbs founded the First Church of Deliverance, it forges on with his work and vision. The extraordinary Art Moderne building, now designated a Chicago Landmark, survives intact—a rare example of the sleek architectural style used for a religious structure.

HENRY HOBSON RICHARDSON'S FINAL WORK:
JOHN J. GLESSNER HOUSE
1800 SOUTH PRAIRIE AVENUE

Nearly forty years after his house was built, John Jacob Glessner wrote a detailed letter about it and its contents to his two children. He wanted to leave them with a first-hand understanding of the remarkable home in which they had grown up. Designed by Henry Hobson Richardson, arguably the preeminent American architect of the 1880s, it was also a repository of irreplaceable furniture, textiles, and artwork of the period. Glessner wrote in part, "Though I had heard much of Richardson, I didn't go to him first when seeking an architect, for Boston friends had told me that he would undertake only monumental buildings."

The fabulously wealthy Glessner was a founder of the International Harvester Company. In 1885, he and his wife, Frances, were laying plans to construct a new mansion on South Prairie Avenue, where other Chicago millionaires were relocating. (Glessner later explained that their growing children made more space essential.)

Glessner traveled to New York City to consult with McKim, Mead & White. He asked them to submit proposals, but warned that he might also seek plans from competing architects. Upon his return to Chicago, he sent a letter to Richardson in Massachusetts, mentioning his friends' cautionary advice. The architect replied, "I'll plan anything a man wants, from a cathedral to a chicken coop. That's the way I make my living."

Richardson visited Chicago and rode out one afternoon with Glessner to the vacant lot at 1800 South Prairie Avenue. He never stepped out of the carriage, but sat quietly studying the location. Finally, according to Glessner later, he asked, "Have you the courage to build the house without windows on the street front?"

Glessner quickly said, "Yes," admitting later that he knew he could tear up the plans if he did not like them. An excited Richardson lamented that he had

"How do you get into it?"
The house was unconventional
– and baffling to many of the
neighbors.

to dine with Marshall Field that evening, but promised to give Glassner the plan of his house "in the morning."

In April 1886, Frances and John Glessner were in Brookline, Massachusetts at the home of Henry Richardson, who was gravely ill. From his bed the 47-year-old architect presented the last of the detail work for the house— the locations of the lighting fixtures. Richardson commented, "My part is finished." Glessner's letter to his children four decades later said, "He did no more work of any kind, and in three weeks from that day he was no more."

Construction began on the house on June 1, 1886. Glessner sent word to Frances to bring the children and meet him at the site at noon. George MacBeth Glessner was 14 years old and his sister, Frances, was eight. The four Glessners broke ground for their new home.

The mansion was completed in November 1887 and the family moved in on December 1. Richardson had created for them a house like no other. His challenge to live in a house "without windows on the street front" resulted in the residence's turning its back to the public. The 18th Street elevation was a brooding Romanesque Revival pile of undressed granite.

While not technically "without windows," the openings at sidewalk level were caged in heavy stone mullions and the upper windows were small and joyless. The architect had told the Glessners that the windows of a city house "were not to look out of…You no sooner get them than you shroud them with two thicknesses of window shades, and then add double sets of curtains."

It was a mansion that ensured the utmost privacy to its owners. The actual "front" of the residence was in the ample courtyard behind. Glessner later relished that the critics did not realize that "Mr. Richardson had put generous

Light from the inner courtyard pours into the house.

windows that let in a flood of sunlight when the sun shines in Chicago." Here towers and turrets, contrasting stone, and entertaining angles and bays were the antithesis of the forbidding 18th Street front.

The Glessners had moved into a neighborhood of more expected Victorian mansions. Mansard roofs, iron-railed balconies and high stone stoops lined the block. In those houses lived moguls with names like Pullman, Armour, Kellogg, Otis, Field, and Spaulding. The Glessners' staid neighbors were not all pleased with the unorthodox design. The industrialist George Pullman, who lived directly across the street, reportedly grumbled, "I don't know what I have ever done to have that thing staring me in the face every time I go out of my door." Frances began to keep a diary of visitors' reactions. "You have astonished everyone with your strange house. How do you get into it?" was a typical comment.

The house consisted of 35 rooms, each one an Arts and Crafts tour de force. William Morris, a leader in the Arts and Crafts Movement in Britain, designed several of the rugs created especially for the house, as well as curtains and portieres. He personally hand-drew patterns on the silk for certain pieces, which were then embroidered by Frances Glessner herself. The parlor walls were painted burlap, executed by English artist William Prettyman; and the library was painted "blue over yellow after repeated experiments by John Leary, an artist from Davenport," according to Glessner. The "Davenport" to which he referred was almost certainly the A. H. Davenport Furniture Company in Boston, with which Richardson had a strong relationship.

In keeping with the beamed ceilings and wooden paneling, Richardson designed the main staircase with turned balusters in four patterns, copied from the 1759 Longfellow House in Cambridge, Massachusetts—one full set on each step. John Glessner vividly remembered that each baluster cost him $1.

The eclectic mix of furniture included new pieces designed for the house and heirlooms that the family brought with them, like Glessner's mother's horsehair-upholstered sofa, a mahogany worktable that his great-grandfather personally crafted, and a Steinway piano with a cabinet made by Francis H. Bacon.

Bacon had begun his career with the New York City decorating firm of Herter Brothers, whose clients were the likes of William H. Vanderbilt. By now he was the principal designer for A. H. Davenport Furniture. The suite of furniture in Frances's bedroom was also his design.

The Glessners filled the house with their vast art collection. Paintings included examples by Glessner's "personal friends," John La Farge, Albert Herter, Joseph Lindon Smith, Sir Hubert von Herkomer, and Francis Hopkinson Smith. There was a bronze of Abraham Lincoln's death mask and hands, executed by Leonard W. Volk, ancient marbles, and bronze statuettes by Frances Glessner's renowned cousin John Quincy Adams Ward.

In 1898, the house was the scene of daughter Frances's wedding. The ceremony was performed by Reverend Philip Mowry of Pennsylvania,

The interiors were a blend of Colonial Revival and Arts and Crafts styles. Each banister of the staircase cost Glessner $1, a figure he never forgot.

John Glessner's study.

who had married her parents 28 years earlier. The rugs and furniture were removed from the parlor to accommodate the event.

The Glessner mansion was the site of the elder Frances's Sunday open houses in the parlor and her "Monday Morning Reading Classes" in the library. The Reading Class had a membership of about 80. While one member read that week's passages, the other women were busy at needlework "and other womanly occupations," according to John Glessner. He added chauvinistically, "and when the reading stopped doubtless their tongues grew active in womanly conversation."

Frances Glessner was active in charitable causes. She opened the house on holidays to "waifs and strays, so-called, who so often find holidays depressing, young men and women without families or homes in the city." At the outbreak of World War I, she turned the focus of the Reading Classes to knitting sweaters and other items for the soldiers. So satisfying was the work that, after peace came, the women continued making blankets and garments for convalescents and infants at the Cook County Hospital.

Before that happened, Frances caused a new fashion to spread through the drawing rooms of Chicago society. The *Tribune* had earlier described the Reading Class membership as "smartly arranged women in glossy furs, becoming hats, and the latest importation in work bags over their arms." But by 1915 Edwardian millinery had grown to nearly absurd proportions. On February 20 that year, the newspaper reported that Mrs. Glessner's demand to her Reading Class had caused a "sensation." "It was the request that women

The pink granite of the fortresslike facade actually fronts structural walls of conventional bricks within.

remove their hats during the reading. The result is more elaborate coiffures among Prairie avenue women now."

The Glessner family was well acquainted with Theodore Thomas, the first celebrated American conductor. Before he founded the Chicago Symphony Orchestra, his Theodore Thomas Orchestra was in high demand across the nation. On several occasions, the group played for Glessner affairs in the mansion. However, Frances did not expect its appearance there on January 1, 1903, her birthday.

The orchestra sneaked into the 18th Street entrance and up the back stairs (Glessner once commented that Richardson had designed the house so servants could access all points in the house unseen). Guests were gathered for a reception for Frances, when suddenly, at around 4:00, the strains of a double quartet of horns wafted down from the upper hall, to her great surprise. In appreciation, the musicians were invited back to the mansion three weeks later as dinner guests.

On December 7, 1920, a third Frances Glessner was feted in the mansion. The coming-out reception for George's daughter was held on the 50th wedding anniversary of her grandparents. John and Frances kept the fact a secret from the guests so as not to detract attention from the debutante.

John and Frances Glessner lived on in the Prairie Street house together until October 1932, when Frances died. The *Chicago Sunday Tribune*'s society columnist, "Cousin Eve," reported on October 30 that the Chicago Symphony Orchestra had performed a concert in her memory. While the concert played, she said, "Lying in state was Mrs. Glessner at 1800 Prairie Avenue, in the house built long ago by the famous Richardson. It is of granite, looking like an old Scotch fortress, and the Glessners had lived there fifty years and seen many changes." Those changes included demolished mansions, vacant lots, and factories in the once-exclusive neighborhood.

John J. Glessner's widowed daughter-in-law moved into the Prairie Avenue house with him. Three years later, on January 25, 1935, the *Tribune* reported, Glessner "will celebrate his 92nd birthday quietly at home tomorrow." His daughter-in-law and his granddaughter and her husband would be in the mansion for the occasion. "Other members of his family are living hundreds of miles too far to come," said the newspaper.

Almost exactly one year later John Glessner was dead. In his obituary on January 21, 1936, the *Chicago Tribune* noted that the Glessner mansion had "been a landmark of the older south side residential district for more than 50 years. In 1924 Mr. Glessner announced the house would be given to the American Institute of Architects on his death."

In April 1936, Frances Glessner Lee and her sister-in-law sent out invitations to the old members of the Monday Morning Reading Class. It would be the last vestige of the elegant Glessner traditions in the mansion.

The American Institute of Architects found that it had inherited a white elephant. When in 1937 it realized that remodeling the mansion would cost about $25,000 (in the neighborhood of $415,000 today), it returned the gift to the Glessner family. The family donated the house again, this time to the Armour Institute of Technology for use as a research center. In 1958, the house suffered the indignity of being converted to a printing plant for the Graphic Arts Technical Foundation.

When that organization moved to Pittsburgh in 1965, it put the house on the market. At the time, all but three other examples of Henry Hobson Richardson architecture in Chicago had been demolished. The *Chicago Tribune* announced that the "uncertain destiny" of the Glessner House "has aroused the fears of several history-conscious Chicagoans."

However, in 1966 the house, "surrounded by industry and tenements," as the *Tribune* put it, was saved. A group of architects formed a foundation (which became the Chicago Architecture Foundation) to purchase and restore it. Vandals had destroyed many of the fixtures, but photographs and documents (including Glessner's detailed description) gave restorers a wealth of material for their replication. Today the mansion is operated as a house museum.

WILLIAM H. HOYT HOUSE

5704 SOUTH DORCHESTER AVENUE

William H. Hoyt and his wife, the former Mary Betteley, arrived in Chicago from New York City in 1854. He established himself in the real estate business, quickly amassing a sizable fortune in the rapidly developing city. His personal business would be put on hold when the war erupted between the North and the South in 1861.

Hoyt was put in charge of a civilian supply unit that traveled to the front lines. Organized by the Chicago Board of Trade, his team transported 500 woolen blankets to the 72nd Regiment in Memphis; and another 500 to the 113th Regiment at Vicksburg, Mississippi.

In the years just before the outbreak of the war, suburban communities began cropping up north and south of the city. Planned neighborhoods, they took advantage of the new railroad lines, which provided businessmen easy commutes into Chicago, but afforded families the fresh air and other amenities unavailable in the city.

One of these was Hyde Park, envisioned by Paul Cornell and boosted when he deeded 670 acres of his land to the Illinois Central Railroad in 1856. Cornell laid out large residential plots—just 18 per block—and open green spaces.

In 1869, William Hoyt purchased a building plot on Madison Avenue (later renamed Dorchester Avenue) from Cornell's uncle, Hassan Hopkins, in the neighborhood that would later become known as South Park. Hopkins, too, had been a pioneer in the development of Hyde Park. An early property owner, he constructed and operated a one-story grocery store that doubled as the post office.

Hoyt erected a genteel two-story Italianate villa—the height of domestic architectural style. The refined, 13-room, red-brick residence featured a hip roof, handsome paneled fascia board below the roofline, and a broad veranda. A small balcony no doubt served the centered second-floor opening. The flattened center of the roof suggests today that there was a cupola—a nearly obligatory element of the Italian Villa style.

In a 1941 photograph, a scar still attests to the missing veranda roof, although its base remains. The double-hung windows survive as well.

In 1874, Hoyt built a two-story wooden hotel at 51st Street and Cottage Grove Avenue, the South Park Hotel, which gave the suburb its name. He continued, nevertheless, his daily commute to his office in Chicago.

The Hoyts sold the house at 5704 Dorchester Avenue to sisters Mrs. Clarence Gordon Sholes and Mrs. William P. Campbell (the former Mary and Alice Ten Eyck). According to Chicago lore, their husbands were both out of town on business and they schemed to purchase the house as "a surprise package" for them when they returned. Whether the tale is true or not, it is charming. Not only did the two couples move into the house but the sisters brought along their aging parents, Major Tenedor Ten Eyck and his wife, Martha.

All three men had been active during the Civil War. Major Ten Eyck served in the war, and then survived the bloody battle against the Cheyenne, Arapaho, and Lakota tribes on December 21, 1866. Known as the Fetterman Massacre, or the Battle of the Hundred Slain, it was the worst military defeat suffered by the United States in combat with Native Americans until the Battle of the Little Bighorn.

Clarence Gordon Sholes was General Tecumseh Sherman's personal telegraph operator during the famed March to the Sea. And when the Railway Mail Service was organized at the outbreak of the conflict, William P. Campbell was among its first three clerks.

Another Civil War veteran frequently at the house was Brigadier General William Wallace Robinson, husband of the third sister, Minnie. Like Ten Eyck, following the war he joined the military campaign against the Indians.

At some point, the family attempted to modernize the house by removing the roof of the veranda and adding a late Victorian porch. It was probably at this time that the cupola was also removed.

Martha H. Ten Eyck, the matriarch of the family, was highly regarded in society. She was a member of the Daughters of the American Revolution; and as the Columbian Exposition neared, Bertha Palmer, the queen of Chicago society, appointed Martha to the Board of Lady Managers.

In 1899, the house was the scene of the wedding of Mary and Clarence Sholes's daughter Pauline to Dr. George Francis James, secretary of the Chicago Educational Commission. James had already written several educational papers. He would go on to be dean of education at the University of Nevada, and, during World War I, assistant director of the Army Educational Corps, and educational secretary for the Military Training Camps Association.

The fascinating string of extended-family members who frequented the house included Clarence Sholes's father, Christopher Latham Sholes, credited with inventing the typewriter, and poet Bertha Ten Eyck James, daughter of George and Pauline.

By 1921 Dr. and Mrs. James had returned from Nevada and were living in the Dorchester Avenue house. But the family was gone by 1926, when it was converted by Anne Douglas to the Gargoyle, a popular tearoom. The second floor became the restaurant's "sitting room," where classical string music was played. According to historian John Drury, the patrons consisted "largely of professors and their wives from the University of Chicago near by."

In describing the house in 1941, Drury noted, "Here may be seen the fine marble fireplaces, ornamented ceilings, and mahogany trim of the days when this house, shaded by elms and surrounded by flowering bushes, was a show place of old Hyde Park."

In 1951, the house was reconverted to a single-family residence by new owner Lenore Wood, a physical education instructor at Herzl Junior College, who preserved the interior detailing while updating the house with gas heat and modern necessities. She also removed the remnants of the Italianate veranda, leaving just the Victorian porch. She dubbed the house "Woodhaven," and gave each of the 13 rooms its own name.

The unmarried teacher already had a large collection of Victorian furniture (inherited from her grandparents), Asian carpets and chests, and what she deemed "whimsical keepsakes" from around the world. A corner shelf in one sitting room contained her teapot collection; in the kitchen were English

The exterior of the building.

horse brasses (at least 50); and she claimed to have "the finest collection extant of honey amber thousand-eye glassware, made 80 to 90 years ago."

Her lovely mid-Victorian furniture had a Great Chicago Fire story of its own. Anne Douglas of the *Chicago Tribune* (almost certainly not the same Anne Douglas as the Gargoyle tearoom's proprietor) related in November 1951 that as the fire neared Lenore's grandparents' Clark Street house, they removed all the costly furniture to the back yard, where they buried it. "Months later, when they had a house to put it in, it was dug up, refinished and reupholstered, and was as good as new."

In September 1953, Lenore's thousand-eye amber glass collection was displayed at the Chicago Public Library for a month. In reporting on the loan, the *Tribune* noted, "Miss Wood, a schoolteacher who collects glassware and china as a hobby, uses her thousand-eye glass to accompany table settings of the old tea leaf pattern china."

Lenore Wood was gone by the early 1960s, when the residence was home to the Getzels family. The dramatic social changes since 1869 when the Hoyts built the house were evidenced in Mrs. J. W. Getzels' work with the Hyde Park Neighborhood Club. In May 1963, the group sponsored a Pop Art Ball in the mall of 55th Street and Lake Park Avenue shopping center.

"The club has invited dancers to come in costumes carrying out the theme of the dance. 'Pop art' is a new art form, named either for pop bottle art or for popular art," advised the *Chicago Tribune* on May 26. The newspaper assumed that the women's auxiliary "won't be surprised if guests appear dressed as cans of tomato soup."

Despite the missing cupola, an ill-advised coat of paint over the brick, and the lost veranda, the Hoyt House retains its graceful appearance. It survives as a charming relic of the earliest days of this Chicago suburb.

FREDERICK C. ROBIE HOUSE

5757 SOUTH WOODLAWN AVENUE

George T. Robie arrived from New York State around 1873, as Chicago rebuilt upon the ashes of the Great Fire. Around 1876, after working as a sewing machine salesman for a few years, he established the Excelsior Supply Company, manufacturing sewing-machine parts.

At the time inventors had been tinkering with the bicycle—still an expensive contraption with limited practicality. Change came in 1885 when the "safety bicycle" was produced. With its wheels of identical size, a steerable front wheel, and a chain drive, it sparked a nationwide craze. The bicycle rapidly became a popular means of transportation and sport. "Wheel clubs" were formed, women's bikes provided equality between the sexes, and parks and drives became crowded with bicycling couples and groups on weekends.

Over two decades later, writing in the 1912 *Chicago: Its History and Its Builders*, Josiah Seymour Currey said of Robie, "In his business when success was achieved in one direction he branched out into other fields." Robie recognized that a manufacturer who got in on the ground floor was almost certain to make a fortune. He turned the focus of his firm to the design and manufacture of bicycles.

Robie and his wife, the former Anna Snook, had one son, Frederick (known familiarly as Fred). When he enrolled in a mechanical engineering course at Purdue University in September 1895 at the age of 16, he was already selling bicycles. Fred later explained that he found experience more valuable than education, and he left Purdue with no degree in 1899 to enter the family business.

Three years later, on June 25, 1902, Fred's engagement to Springfield, Illinois debutante Lora Hieronymus was announced. The daughter of B. R. Hieronymus, a founder of the Illinois National Bank, she was cultured and well educated, a graduate of the University of Chicago. In announcing the engagement, the *St. Louis Republic* noted, "She is well known in social circles." Their June wedding took place in the Hieronymus home.

Constantly aware of new developments and trends, Fred Robie branched out, manufacturing motorcycles (the "Excelsior Auto-Cycle") and then automobiles.

The deeply overhanging eaves and long bands of glass were made possible by structural steel.

In 1906, he designed and built a streamlined, experimental motorcar. His father wanted nothing to do with that part of the business, and provided only financial assistance.

After Fred and Lora's first son, Frederick Jr., was born on February 19, 1907, the couple began looking for a site for their first real home. Lora, according to her son years later, was still active in the academic and social life of the University of Chicago. That no doubt had much to do with Fred's purchase of the nearby long, narrow lot on the northeast corner of 58th Street and Woodlawn Avenue. He paid $13,500 for the site on May 19, 1908—in the neighborhood of $371,000 today.

The interest that Robie exhibited in his business life—his focus on the new and innovative rather than the tried and traditional—was now reflected in his ideas for his future home. He told Fred Jr. decades later that he knew what he wanted—he just could not explain his concepts clearly. He sketched out his thoughts on scraps of paper. They included light-filled spaces, and few interior walls. Today we might call his vision an "open floor plan."

The reaction of architects, he told his son, was almost always the same: "Oh, I know what you want—one of those damn—one of those Wright houses." And, indeed, that is exactly what he was describing.

Robie met with Frank Lloyd Wright, who immediately understood his 28-year-old client's vision. The men worked together harmoniously, finally agreeing on a plan in the spring of 1909. Construction began that April and was completed exactly one year later. The total cost (including land, construction, and furnishings) would equal $1.5 million now, but this is a deceptive figure—the house could never be built for that amount today.

Frank Lloyd Wright used tall chair backs to create "space within a space."

Wright had designed what even he would deem an architectural masterpiece. An outstanding example of the Prairie Style, the three-story home featured projecting, cantilevered eaves and long bands of art-glass windows. With the generous budget Robie gave him, he was able to incorporate steel in the structure: this allowed for long, horizontal lines without columns or other distractions.

Inside, sunlight washed through leaded glass into vast open spaces. Wright, of course, designed the furnishings, light fixtures, and textiles as well. (He commented, "It is quite impossible to consider the building one thing and its furnishings another.") Twenty-nine different abstract geometric designs made up the 174 art glass windows and door panels.

The first floor contained the billiards room and the children's playroom (Lorraine was born on December 2, 1909). Robie's interest in automobiles resulted in an attached garage. The living room and dining room were on the second floor, with the kitchen. The master bedroom was on the third floor, termed by Wright "the belvedere." It included a dressing room, bathroom, and balcony. Two additional bedrooms were on that level.

Three months after construction had commenced, George T. Robie died, following an appendicitis operation. His death was the beginning of a string of troubles for Fred. The family moved into 5757 Woodlawn Avenue in May 1910, but it would not prove to be a happy home.

Eleven months later, Lora packed her things and took the children to Springfield, where she filed for divorce, claiming infidelity on Fred's part. In December 1911, he sold his beloved house to advertising executive David Lee Taylor and his wife, Ellen West Taylor.

Taylor, who was the president of the Taylor-Critchfield Company, was nationally known in advertising circles. Seven months before purchasing the house, he was honored at a dinner at Chicago's Blackstone Hotel for his 45th birthday. Newspapers nationwide covered the event. The Salem, Oregon *Daily Capital Journal* reported on May 4, "Advertising men from all sections of the country united in declaring David Lee Taylor…the ideal type of advertising man." The article noted that Robert H. Davis of *Munsey's Magazine* called him the "kingpin of Chicago advertising men" and the "best fellow ever met."

But, like the Robies, the Taylors would not be in the house long. On October 23, 1912, the Illinois newspaper *Rock Island Argus* ran a one-line article: "David Lee Taylor, a leading advertising man, is dead." Within the month, Ellen Taylor sold the residence to Marshall D. Wilber. The Chicago *Examiner* reported on November 26, "A consideration of $1 appears in the deed, but it is understood that the actual price is around $45,000."

Wilber was a partner with his brother, Mark D. Wilber, in Wilber Mercantile Agency. Born in Poughkeepsie, New York in 1864, he was married to the former Isadora Ludlow Runyon. The couple had two daughters, Marcia Dodge and Jeannette Runyon. An avid sportsman, Marshall was commodore of the Chicago Yacht Club in 1904 and 1905, treasurer of the Adventurers Club of Chicago, and a member of the Chicago Athletic Club. The *Bulletin of the Commercial Law League of America* called him "a big game hunter and a very ardent fisherman."

Unlike the two families before them, the Wilbers stayed on for 14 years. Then, in June 1926, the house and its contents were sold to the Chicago Theological Seminary. Although the school used it as a dormitory and dining hall, the underlying purpose in purchasing the property was always for future expansion. And the time for that came in 1941.

By luck, a graduate student at the Illinois Institute of Technology learned that the seminary had slated the Robie House for demolition. He sounded the alarm to his instructors, one of whom was the architect Ludwig Mies van der Rohe. A furious backlash followed, including the voice of Frank Lloyd Wright himself. The plans stalled, but it would appear that it was not the protests so much as America's involvement in World War II that postponed action.

In March 1957, the seminary once again announced its intentions to raze the Robie House. Groups nationwide joined the efforts to stop it. Once again, Wright joined the chorus of protests. On April 5, the California newspaper *Desert Sun* reported, "Famed architect Frank Lloyd Wright, on learning the Chicago Theological Seminary plans to tear down Robie House, one of his favorite creations [said]: 'A religious organization has no sense of beauty. You can't expect much from them.'"

Wright returned to the house and remarked on its innovations. The *Daily Illini* wrote, "He pointed out the various merits of the building. It was the first split-level house in the world, he said. It was the first to have a complete wiring system, the first to have an attached garage, the first to have indirect lighting, and the first to have multiple baths and vaulted ceilings." Wright placed it among his three greatest works, the other two being Unity Temple in Oak Park, and the Imperial Hotel in Tokyo.

On April 20 that year, the *Vassar Chronicle* announced, "a group of students at Yale have organized a fund raising committee" to save the house. The article explained, "The Chicago Theological Seminary plans to destroy Robie House in order to make room for a new student dormitory," and quoted the Yale committee's description of the house as a "great masterpiece of modern architecture which embodies the American soul in the forms and images of poetry."

It was Wright's friend, New York real estate developer William Zeckendorf, who rescued the Robie House. Acting on Wright's urging, he acquired the property in August 1958. Following the formation of the Robie House Preservation Committee, Zeckendorf donated it to the University of Chicago in February 1963. The architectural significance of the Robie House was not lost on the school. On September 22, 1965, the *Daily Illini* reported, "In an effort to save one of the greatest works of one of the world's greatest architects, a small group of University students are spearheading a drive to raise $5,000." The money was to go toward the Robie House Preservation Committee's $250,000 target to restore the building. Hermann Pundt, assistant professor of architecture, had alerted his students to its poor condition. The article said, "The house now stands vacant and bare, with a badly deteriorating interior and exterior."

The students put together a Frank Lloyd Wright exhibition that included original Robie House pieces. "Fortunately," said the article, "the group was able to contact owners of much of the original equipment of the Robie House." Included in the exhibition was the Robie House dining-room set, which had been sorely abused during the seminary's time in the residence.

The set of table and eight chairs was an especially important example of Wright's designing of furniture as an element of architecture. It was one of his first "space within a space" works. By adding high backs to the chairs, he created what he termed a "room" within the dining room. Sadly, according to the *Daily Illini*, "The top is now chipped and scarred. Generations of hot pots and greasy platters have left their calling cards on the table's fine finish."

Following the successful restoration, the house became home to the university's Adlai Stevenson Institute of Foreign Affairs. It was inaugurated by West Germany's foreign minister, Willy Brandt, on February 16, 1967. The institute was formed in the "hope to attract people who are active in the solving of problems," said director William R. Polk.

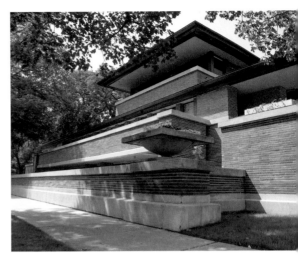

Long iron-spot Roman bricks accentuate the horizontal emphasis of the design.

To that end the house was the scene of lectures and discussions, like the two-day conference in November 1968 titled "No More Vietnams?" The discussion included issues like, "Where does the Vietnam experience leave us in our relations with the U.S.S.R. and China?"

At least one student had an unsettling approach to "the solving of problems." Eqbal Ahmad, one of the Harrisburg Seven, was described on February 10, 1971, as a "Pakistani student at the University of Chicago's Adlai Stevenson Institute of International Affairs," after he was charged with (but never convicted of) plotting "to kidnap President Nixon's foreign affairs adviser, Henry A. Kissinger, and bomb heating tunnels between government buildings in Washington." Certainly less disturbing was the institute's hiring of former UN Secretary-General U Thant the following year.

On September 15, 1971, the Commission on Chicago Landmarks gave the Robie House Chicago Landmark status. The university moved its offices out in January 1997 and turned its operation over to the Frank Lloyd Wright Preservation Trust. With its survival assured, the Robie House is counted among Chicago's architectural jewels, along with the Charnley-Persky House (1892) by Louis Sullivan and Frank Lloyd Wright, Egerton Swartwout's Elks National Memorial (1926), and Mies van der Rohe's Crown Hall (1956).

VICTORY MONUMENT

3500 SOUTH DR. MARTIN LUTHER KING JR. DRIVE

On December 8, 1918, General Vindendon, commanding officer of the French 59th Division, wrote a letter to the officers and soldiers of the 370th US Infantry, which began: "You are leaving us. The impossibility at this time that the German Army can recover from its defeat—the necessity which is imposed on the people of the Entente of taking up again a normal life—leads the United States to diminish its effectives in France. You are chosen to be among the first to return to America. In the name of your comrades of the 59th Division, I say unto you: Au Revoir, in the name of France, thank you."

The general added, "The blood of your comrades who fell on the soil of France, mixed with the blood of our soldiers, renders indissoluble the bonds of affection that unite us. We have, besides, the price of having worked together at a magnificent task, and the pride of bearing on our foreheads the ray of a common grandeur."

The 370th Infantry was known as the 8th Illinois National Guard Regiment before the war and the "Fighting Eighth" during it. They were also called the "Black Devils" by the Germans because of their ferocious bravery, and the "Partridges" by the French because of their proud bearing. The unit was made up entirely of African-Americans.

These soldiers came from Chicago's "Black Belt," an area that got its name as much from its geographic shape as from the racism that formed it. That same discrimination prevented the patriotic men from entering white regiments.

In fact, according to special adjutant to the secretary of war, Emmitt J. Scott, in his 1919 *The American Negro in the World War,* "There was some question in military circles as to whether or not this regiment should be sent overseas, to meet the Huns with its colored Colonel and a full complement of colored officers; but the splendid way in which Colonel Denison had handled his men and maintained discipline at Camp Logan, and at Camp Stuart (Newport News, Virginia), proved to the War Department that he was every inch a man, that he was an intelligent and experienced soldier, and a competent officer who knew how to command and to guard the interests of his regiment."

Under Colonel Franklin A. Denison, the Fighting Eighth trained and fought with the French army, part of the regiment that finally drove the German forces from the Aisne-Marne region of France just prior to the armistice. They were awarded 71 medals and special citations for valor and merit from the Allies, and 21 Distinguished Service Crosses from the United States Army.

Returning home, the men found that little had changed for them there.

On March 1, 1919, the *Broad Ax* printed a letter to the editor exposing the shameful treatment of the heroic soldiers. "The Homecoming of the Old 8th Regiment, now the 370th Infantry, was a glorious event, but the women who [toiled] so faithfully on that bleak and blustery Monday a few weeks ago to raise funds to entertain all of our returning soldiers, want to know why a better dinner was not served to the gallant heroes, who covered themselves with glory on the fields of France."

The writer complained that out of the "large sum of money turned over to the committee," something more deserving could have been served than "mis-called roast beef, yellow turnips, undrinkable coffee, et cetera.... Those brave boys deserved the best that money could buy, for were they not willing to give their lives to make the world a decent place in which to live, while the slacker sought every conceivable excuse to remain at home in safety.... Who is to blame? Where is the shame to rest?"

Over the next years, memorials to valiant army units rose throughout the country. On May 20, 1925, the *Chicago Tribune* reported that "The question whether a $25,000 monument to honor the 370th Infantry, a Negro regiment, will be built at Thirty-fifth street and Grand avenue, Chicago, is up to Gov. Small."

The State Senate had already passed a House appropriation bill to pay for it; and yet the debate dragged on. Nearly a year later, the South Parks board ruled that a monument to the heroes would not be erected "on the grounds it would create a traffic problem." It was the last straw for the frustrated neighborhood.

On St. Patrick's Day, a delegation of black community leaders protested the decision. They convinced three Irish board members—including the future Mayor Ed Kelly—to change their votes and the movement to erect the monument forged ahead.

Two years later, on March 7, 1928, the memorial neared completion. The *True Republican* announced that the base of the monument, executed by Charles G. Blake & Company, would be laid within the month. Designed by the Swedish-born architect John A. Nyden, the granite Neoclassical shaft would contain three bronze panels in deep relief by Leonard Crunelle.

Crunelle was born to a family of coal miners in northern France. Coming to Illinois with his family at the age of 10, he worked with his father in the Decatur coal mines and sketched pictures in his spare time. In an astonishing American Dream story, his pictures were shown to Chicago sculptor Lorado Taft, who mentored him. By the time he received the commission for the Victory Monument, his career had flourished.

Each of his panels was 10 feet high and 4½ feet wide. The deepest relief was 19 inches and it was claimed that the figures "will be the largest of their kind ever used in Chicago."

"The bronze figures are to represent Miss Columbia, a doughboy, and a colored maiden," reported the newspaper. "The names of the 137 members who died in France will be on a bronze tablet."

When the memorial was unveiled that summer, the crowning figure, a doughboy, had been cast but was not in place, giving the classical column a rather stubby look. Crunelle's monumental panels depicted Victory, an African-American woman holding a branch; Columbia, a classically clothed female holding a tablet with the names of the battles in which the 370th Infantry had fought; and the Soldier, which depicted a bare-chested black man in the garb of a Roman soldier, with an eagle at his feet.

It would be another eight years before the doughboy statue was installed on top of the shaft.

When world war again erupted, the 8th Infantry was again called to action. On August 31, 1940, the *Chicago Tribune* reported, "It was confirmed from Washington today that the 8th, with a record of 45 years of distinguished service, will be reorganized and armed with 155mm. howitzers." Inevitably the regiment was deployed, arriving in Naples, Italy on August 1, 1944. The soldiers saw battle throughout Italy until the end of the war.

During the war, a $1,694 contract to illuminate the monument with automatically controlled floodlights was announced. The floodlights, perhaps, only highlighted its neglected condition.

On June 8, 1942, *Chicago Tribune* reader Marshall Beymer fired off a letter to the editor complaining, "It does seem as if it should occur to the park board that it would help war morale if they would let the WPA scrub that fine victory monument at 35th Street and South Park Way. Won't somebody wash this monument or tear it down? It's a disgrace."

It was an issue that was raised again two decades later by Alderman William H. Harvey, who filed a resolution with the recreation committee to

Depictions of a realistic doughboy and an idealized, bare-breasted black soldier share the Victory Monument.

renovate the monument. In his resolution Harvey said he "was amazed at the monument's poor condition."

In 1996 the King Drive Gateway Project was established to rejuvenate the neighborhood, now known as Bronzeville. Among its far-reaching projects was the restoration of public artwork, including the Victory Monument. Having regained its dignity, it once again honors a group of valiant men who had to struggle for the respect they had earned in battle.

IDA B. WELLS-BARNETT HOUSE

3624 SOUTH DR. MARTIN LUTHER KING JR. DRIVE

Martin Meyer arrived in America in 1859 from Hamburg. While many German immigrants went no farther than New York City's Lower East Side, Meyer moved west to Chicago. In 1865, he opened a men's hat store on Lake Street, "which at that time was the Broadway of Chicago," the *Clothier and Furnisher* would recall decades later.

He and other new German residents carried on many of their native traditions, and Meyer became a lifelong member of the singing club, the Germania Maennerchor. He was among that group as it sat by the bier of Abraham Lincoln, when it lay in state in the old Chicago Court House on May 2, 1865.

Things were going well for Meyer in 1870, the year he married, but the following year his store and stock were wiped out in the Great Fire. Unwilling to be beaten, he started over. In 1895, the *Clothier and Furnisher* wrote, "Before the ashes of that famous fire were cool he had made arrangements to open for business on the southwest corner of Clark and Monroe streets."

Meyer's business was an overwhelming success. In 1889, he moved his main store to 82 Adams Street and opened two branch stores, one on 22nd Street and the other on Indiana Avenue. And he laid plans for a sumptuous new home that would reflect his financial and social status.

On October 19, 1889, the *Sanitary News* reported that architect Joseph A. Thain had filed plans for Martin Meyer's new residence on Grand Boulevard near 37th Street. The house, it noted, was to cost $15,000—about $400,000 now.

Thain's own business was thriving at the time. On June 8 alone the previous year, he had filed plans for H. C. Walker's $25,000 mansion on Michigan Avenue and 43rd Street, and for three houses for developer G. H. Fox on Prairie Avenue at 32nd Street.

Thain turned to the highly popular Romanesque Revival style for the Meyers. Faced in rough-cut stone blocks, its asymmetry and whimsical details showed a Queen Anne influence as well. A broad stone stoop led to the gaping maw that sheltered the entrance. The romantic character of the design was enhanced by paired arched openings in the oversized dormer, stubby medieval columns, and a fanciful turret that clung to the corner and pierced through the steep pitched roof.

Meyer and his wife moved into the home with their two sons and four daughters. There were 14 rooms and four baths. The ballroom was tucked into the high-ceilinged third floor.

By 1895 the hat business had prospered to the point where, on April 13, Meyer "opened his palatial quarters at 169 Dearborn street, in the old Stock Exchange Building," as reported by the *Clothier and Furnisher*. "This store is one of the finest of its kind in America," it added.

Later that year, on Sunday, June 9, 1895, the Grand Boulevard house was filled with family and friends as the Meyers celebrated their silver anniversary. A newspaper noted that the house "was beautifully decorated with American Beauty roses, palms, ferns, etc. Music by a mandolin orchestra enlivened the evening hours."

The building was variously a hatter's residence, a boarding house, and a brothel before Ida B. Wells and her husband, Ferdinand Barnett, called it home.

On July 22, 1913, Martin Meyer died in the house at the age of 75; his funeral was held in the parlor on the morning of July 24 at 9:30.

The house saw two relatively quick turnovers in ownership. It was purchased by Floyd P. Brushhart, who operated it as a boarding house. He resold it to actress Gray G. Wick in July 1917. It would seem that Brushhart's "boarding house" was being managed by a Mrs. Violet Phipps. Gray Wick was no doubt humiliated when "morals inspectors" raided the house days after the sale and arrested Mrs. Phipps for running a disorderly house—an early-20th-century term for a brothel.

The young Ida B. Wells-Barnett.

At her trial, the vice officers testified that they had taken a room in the building next door and "viewed the proceedings in her domicile by peering across a ten foot areaway." Violet was found guilty by a jury on July 18 and fined $200.

At the time of the messy incident, Grand Boulevard was seeing change. Four months earlier, actor Richard B. Harrison purchased 3624 Grand Boulevard. His was the first black family to move into the neighborhood.

The next year, Ferdinand Lee Barnett and his wife, Ida Bell Wells, a journalist and activist, purchased the Martin Meyer house for $8,000. The "liberal" North was by no means immune to racial hatred and that same year, after two bombings of their home in May, the Harrison family left Grand Boulevard in June 1919.

Ferdinand and Ida were well acquainted with racial injustice. On May 4, 1884, more than 70 years before Rosa Parks refused to give up her seat on a Montgomery Alabama bus, Ida, a daughter of slaves, sat in the ladies' first-class car on the Memphis & Charleston Railroad. When she refused to move, she was dragged off the train.

In 1893, Wells had come to Chicago specifically to protest the exclusion of Blacks from the Chicago international exhibition. She circulated a booklet, titled "The Reason Why the Colored American Is Not in the World Columbian Exposition," she had written, including contributions from Frederick Douglass and attorney-journalist Ferdinand Barnett. She married Barnett two years later. Typical of her independent-mindedness, Ida became one of the first American women to keep her maiden name, joined with a hyphen to her husband's.

The couple had four children by the time they moved into the Grand Boulevard house. The ballroom, according to daughter Alfreda years later, was used as an apartment for their son Herman and his wife.

A fighter as fervent for the rights of women as for Blacks, Ida Wells-Barnett headed a group of black suffragists joining a march in Washington, D.C. in 1913. When the placard-carrying protesters were being organized, the black women were instructed to march in the rear. As she had done on the southern railroad car, Ida balked. She quietly took her place marching alongside two white women among the Illinois contingent.

The Harrisons were not alone in being bombed. Earlier that year, on January 28, 1919, a bomb exploded in the home of the African-American Head family at 3365 Indiana Avenue, killing their little child. On Wednesday, June 4, Ida gathered Emma Head, Kathryn Rutherford, and Colonel Richard E. Parker as a committee of four to call upon Mayor William Hale Thompson. Their goal, according to the *Broad Ax*, was "to implore him to at least say or do something to save the Lives of Law abiding citizens and attempt to protect their property from being destroyed by the honorable gentlemen who seem to have the right of way to enjoy themselves to their hearts content in throwing bombs into the homes of decent and highly respectable citizens."

The mayor refused to see Wells-Barnett and her committee. He sent word out, according to the *Broad Ax*, "to inform Mrs. Barnett and the others, to go and tell their troubles to Chief of Police, John J. Garrity, that he had no time to waste on them."

Three weeks later, Wells-Barnett's attentions were drawn to problems of race riots and the beatings of black workers. Although police had promised to protect the black workers if they returned to work, severe beatings continued and the homes of black residents were raided and searched for weapons.

On July 31, she complained to the press, "An eyewitness told us that policemen with the three colored men who were beaten senseless in the stockyards yesterday morning stepped aside as a mob of Polaks attacked them and didn't raise a club. This after colored workers had been promised protection if they returned to work—and urged to return." And regarding the searches of houses she said, "It is an unjust discrimination. Homes of white people are not searched but the constitutional right of citizens to bear arms is violated without compunction in the case of colored people."

Wells-Barnett was hospitalized on December 15, 1920, for a gallbladder operation. Complications set in and it was not until Christmas Day that the family was allowed to see her. She did not return home until January 1921, and not until late March did the *Broad Ax* happily report, "she is now able to be up and around in her lovely home at 3624 Grand Boulevard." In her autobiography she would recall that during the year's convalescence she concluded that she "had nothing to show for all those years of toil and labor."

Injustice and racial discrimination were not always so blatant as bombings and beatings. High-end retailers and restaurants discovered that simply by ignoring black patrons, they could induce them to shop elsewhere. The ploy did not work against Ida B. Wells-Barnett. Her daughter related a story to Miriam DeCosta-Willis, who was compiling *The Memphis Diary of Ida B. Wells*: "After discrimination intensified, Mother went to Marshall Fields department store. She waited and waited, but no clerk would help her. Finally, she took a pair of men's underpants, put them over her arm, and walked toward the door. Immediately, a floorwalker stopped her, and so she was able to buy them."

The Barnett family left the Grand Boulevard house in 1929, two years before Ida's death. The woman who felt she "had nothing to show for all those years of toil and labor" was remembered as a force in both women's and racial equal rights. She had helped integrate the Women's Suffrage Movement and found the NAACP, organized the Negro Fellowship League for black men and the first black kindergarten, and had documented and exposed lynching in the South.

Appropriately, Grand Boulevard was renamed Dr. Martin Luther King Jr. Drive in 1968. Although somewhat abused today, the house where the indomitable civil rights activist lived and worked has not suffered gross exterior alteration. It was designated a Chicago Landmark in 1995.

THE YALE APARTMENTS

6565 SOUTH YALE AVENUE

Apartment buildings in the first years following the Civil War were viewed with disdain by the upper and middle classes. Multifamily dwellings, or tenements, were designed for lower-class working families—most often immigrants who survived in squalid, unhealthful conditions. By the last quarter of the 19th century, however, the concept of high-class apartments had spread westward to Chicago. Sometimes known as French flats, to distinguish them from tenement buildings, they were designed and outfitted as private homes, with servants' rooms, libraries, parlors, and even picture galleries.

In 1892, as the city assembled the Chicago Columbian Exposition, architect John T. Long designed the ambitious Yale Apartments at 6565 South Yale Avenue. Completed a year later, just in time for the exposition, Long's seven-story take on Romanesque Revival was gentler than most of the chunky, fortresslike stone structures of the same style that were rising throughout the city.

Six stories of beige brick rose above a rough-cut stone base. In keeping with the Romanesque Revival style, the architect embellished the arched entrance with medieval carvings, and placed engaged turrets that sprouted from carved stone bowls at the corners. Yet he unexpectedly turned away from the medieval motif by adorning the upper two floors with delicate Neoclassical festoons and garlands alien to the architectural style.

At a time when fresh air and sunshine were believed to prevent or cure a multitude of diseases, such as tuberculosis, Long designed the apartments around an innovative interior light court. Ornate cast-iron railings and stairways girded the central atrium, which rose to a 25-by-80-foot glass skylight. The court not only allowed for circulation of air, but brought light into the otherwise gloomy interior.

Despite their own social standing, the residents of the Yale Apartments found themselves at times dealing with a less elevated class. On December 17, 1898, the *Chicago Tribune* noted that a group of the Yale residents had complained to the Englewood police about "annoying" boys. "It is said that twenty-five of them meet nightly and insult women," the article disclosed. "Citizens who try to remonstrate with them are abused and sometimes roughly treated." Particularly worrisome was the gang's leader, Charles Judd, who reportedly assaulted the Yale's engineer (the maintenance person charged with keeping the boilers, furnace, and other equipment working) with a brick. The police promised that warrants would be issued and "efforts used to break up the gang."

Among the Yale Apartments' most respected residents in the first years of the 20th century was Mary Deneen, the mother of Illinois Governor Charles S. Deneen. She was born in 1836, the daughter of pioneers and, a rarity in pre-Civil War years, had attended the Illinois Women's College in Jacksonville, and graduated from Wesleyan College in Cincinnati in 1855.

Mary Deneen's grandfather had been one of the founders of McKendree College in Lebanon, Illinois, where her husband, Samuel H. Deneen, who died in 1895, was professor of Latin and ancient and medieval history. She often assisted the governor and his wife in social events, like the annual protocol-driven New Year's Day receptions in the executive mansion.

At the other end of the social scale, Louis Bour lived in the basement of the Yale Apartments. He was one of the building's engineers at the time; but it was discovered in 1909 that he made extra money on the side. Two Chicago officials, L. J. Griffin, secretary of the Board of Examining Engineers, and John Jenkins, journeyman engineer and member of the board, were accepting bribes to issue engineering licenses. In order to keep the graft discreet, they hired Bour as their go-between man.

He placed advertisements in several foreign-language newspapers that indicated he could make getting a license easy. Responders were told that for $92 (in the neighborhood of $1,500 now) Bour would arrange it so they could bypass the examination. The lucrative scheme unraveled when Joseph Hornyanski, an undercover investigator, paid his $92 and received his engineer's license. Louis Bour was arrested and indicted on April 30, 1909. When promised immunity, he "is said to have betrayed his alleged confederates," according to the *Chicago Tribune*. Indeed, Bour appeared before the grand jury and laid out all the facts. Griffin and Jenkins were arrested and charged with "obtaining money by false pretenses."

Some politicians were outraged that Louis Bour was set free, but the *Chicago Eagle* later explained that "Bour was freed on the ground that the purchaser of a license was not mulcted under false pretenses, since he knew the license thus obtained was not valid."

The comfortable apartments were originally built for visitors to Chicago's 1893 World's Fair.

Bour would not be the only occupant to bring unflattering publicity to the Yale Apartments. On September 22, 1914, tenant John R. Walters was arrested on charges filed by Lillian Shrimplen, who lived at 915 West 63rd Street. She accused him of being "a masher"—the common term for an aggressive male who made unwelcomed advances.

Also in 1914, two days after her 78th birthday, Mary Ashley Deneen died of what newspapers deemed a "stroke of paralysis" in her apartment here. Her death was mourned throughout the state.

On July 19, 1919, W. A. Stambach, another resident of the Yale Apartments, drove to the Jackson Park golf course and, according to the *Chicago Tribune*, was "paying too much attention to his putts…to notice the movements of two men who hopped into his highly polished roadster and drove it away."

The massive doorway leads to light and air from an atrium and galleries inside.

Even when he realized that his automobile was gone, Stambach could not have imagined the criminal adventure it would take the crooks on. The *Tribune* reported, "Before they had completed their jaunt around the city the thieves had relieved twelve unsuspecting citizens of several hundred dollars in currency and jewelry." When the thugs saw a likely victim, they stopped the car and threatened him. If they encountered resistance, the victim was beaten or shot.

Their first target was Norman Mitchell. "Being a well built engineer, Norman gave battle, but after taking three shots in the leg yielded," said the newspaper. Another was Thorn Nelson, who "was halted, and parted with $21. They gave him a black eye for remembrance."

By the late 1920s, the neighborhood around the Yale Apartments had changed, as had the social station of the residents. In 1927, 19-year-old John Sabot lived here, making his living as a telephone repairman. The teen entered a gas-filled sewer to rescue a co-worker, Peter Fannon, but his heroic actions nearly turned fatal when he re-entered the manhole to retrieve his tools, and was himself overcome by the fumes. He managed to crawl to the manhole entrance, where he was pulled out by a passing motorman.

Sabot was one of the last people to live in the aging building. After sitting empty for years, it was purchased by a developer who gutted the interiors and converted the building to modern apartments.

Among the residents in the renovated Yale Apartments in 1955 was Ann Connelly, a teacher at Brownell School on Perry Avenue. When teachers protested the appointment of W. Gloria Williams as principal that year, the students sided with Williams. At around 11:00 on the morning of June 24, about 200 pupils gathered in front of the school, jeering and daring the teachers to leave. When the teachers ran to their cars, they were pelted with rocks. A mob of 50 students followed Ann Connelly to the Yale Apartments, where, according to witnesses, some brandished knives at the terrified 40-year-old. It took police to dispel the group and restore peace.

An even more disturbing incident occurred in 1957. On October 17, police found resident J. Bryan Beck unconscious in his vehicle. He had run a hose from the exhaust into the car in an attempted suicide. Upon further investigation, they found Beck's wife dead in the apartment.

The 61-year-old railroad ticket agent had married 39-year-old Ellen only six weeks earlier. Much younger than her husband, she apparently had second thoughts because, he told police, "she repulsed his advances and threatened to leave him," according to the *Chicago Tribune*. In a fit of rage, he strangled her with a necktie and then bludgeoned her with a bottle. After realizing what he had done, he tried to kill himself. Beck was tried in March 1958 and sentenced to one to four years in prison.

Paul W. Watkins worked as a bartender in a bar on West 79th Street in 1964 while living at the Yale Apartments. On Christmas night that year, he tried to break up an altercation between Charles W. Jackson, his brother Clyde and the bar owner, William Slay. Charles Jackson did not appreciate the interference and drew a gun, shooting Watkins and, accidentally, his brother.

Clyde Jackson was removed to St. George's Hospital, just half a block away, for treatment. Charles was in the emergency room waiting area when he saw Watkins being wheeled in. "Police said that Jackson became enraged in the lobby when he saw Watkins being brought in for treatment," explained the *Chicago Tribune*. Armed with two pistols, he began spraying the area with bullets. When the commotion was over, Paul Watkins recovered, and Charles Jackson was charged with attempted murder.

As had happened in the 1930s, the Yale Apartments became vacant and neglected. Faced with demolition, the historic building's fate seemed clear. But in 1999 developer John Luce began accumulating $9.5 million in public and private funds to restore the structure and preserve it. The masonry was repaired, the atrium restored, and the enormous skylight brought back. The project, completed in 2003, resulted in 68 one-bedroom apartments for seniors. The commendable effort in recycling a vintage structure won the Yale Apartments Landmark designation and an award for preservation excellence.

John T. Long's unique version of Romanesque Revival is an important example of the early period of grand apartment buildings, and its skylighted atrium is a rare survivor in Chicago.

INDEX

Page numbers in **bold** refer to illustrations or captions.

ACKNOWLEDGMENTS

The author wishes to thank Penelope Miller for her thoughtful and knowledgeable editing and Becky Clarke for her clever design. They are astonishing and nothing would have happened without them.

Note: All photographs *not* appearing in the following list are by the author. "LC" marks photographs from the collection of the Library of Congress. "HABS" marks photographs from the Historic American Buildings Survey Vintage postcards from the author's collection appear on pages 9, 25, 45, 64, 85 (by J.L. Le Beau), 88, 95, 120, 135, 144, 186 and 198.

Page 17: J. W. Taylor, LC
Page 19: J. W. Taylor, LC
Page 27: Ron Cogswell
Page 35: LC
Page 37: LC
Page 43: Carol M.
Highsmith, LC
Page 52: S. A. Maxwell
advertisement 1887,
copyright expired
Page 54: Bill Dinsmor
Page 56: Gerry Miller
Page 58: Gerry Miller
Page 60: (left) *The Real
Estate Record & Builders'
Guide*, October 8, 1892,
copyright expired;
(right) Ken Lund
Page 65: Gerry Miller
Page 69: Gerry Miller
Page 75: *The Architectural
Record*, 1912, copyright
expired
Page 80: Rand McNally's
*Pictorial Chicago and
Illustrated World's
Columbian Exposition*,

1893, copyright expired
Page 86: Runner1928
Page 94: *The Continent*,
September 26, 1912,
copyright expired
Page 106: Harold Allen,
June 12, 1964, HABS,
LC
Page 107: (left and right)
Harold Allen, June 12,
1964, HABS, LC
Page 119: *The Clay-Worker*,
April 1922, copyright
expired
Page 127: Nineteenth-
century cabinet
photograph, original
source unknown,
copyright expired
Page 128: Gerry Miller
Page 129: (left and right)
Gerry Miller
Page 131: *Old Chicago
Houses*, John Drury,
1941
Page 136: Tony The Tiger
Page 146: Gerry Miller

Page 148: Original source
unknown
Page 154: (left and right)
Chicago Commerce
magazine, June 12,
1914, copyright expired
Page 156: Gerry Miller
Page 158: *The Music Trades*
magazine, November
18, 1922, copyright
expired
Page 162: LC
Page 167: Jason Hernandez
Page 168: Buster7
Page 180: (left and right)
Harold Allen, HABS,
LC
Page 181: (left) JeremyA;
(right) Harold Allen,
HABS, LC
Page 187: *Illustrated
Souvenir of the Archdiocese
of Chicago*, 1916,
copyright expired
Page 193: Harold Allen,
HABS, LC

Page 197: *Chicago Tribune*,
September 3, 1893,
copyright expired
Page 200: Sjcantius
Page 202: *Old Chicago
Houses*, John Drury,
1941
Page 207: LC
Page 209: J. Crocker
Page 212: *Harper's Weekly*,
1902, LC
Page 213: HABS, LC
Page 220: HABS, LC
Page 222: HABS, LC
Page 223: (left and right)
HABS, LC
Page 224: HABS, LC
Page 227: *Old Chicago
Houses* by John Drury,
1941.
Page 233: Cervin
Robinson, HABS, LC
Page 234: HABS, LC
Page 237: David Arpi
Page 243: Mary Garrity,
c.1893; restored by
Adam Cuerden